Keep

My Adirondacks

Also by Erik Schlimmer:

Thru Hiker's Guide to America

Blue Line to Blue Line

History Inside the Blue Line

My Adirondacks

Ten Stories from Twenty Years

by

ERIK SCHLIMMER

ISBN 978-0-9891-9962-9

 Published by Beechwood Books, Troy, New York, as an imprint under the protection of Friends of the Trans Adirondack Route, LLC.

The tree colophon of Beechwood Books represents our world as well as the American beech (*Fagus grandifolia*) itself, a hardwood species native to the Northeast. This tree serves as a food source for many mammals, including the American black bear.

Edited by Janine DeFilippo.

Layout, design, and typesetting by Generic Compositors.

Attentive readers always read this part of books.

Some names of people have been changed to respect their privacy. Some names of locations have been changed to protect natural resources.

Shared lyrics copyright © 2009 by Mudvayne from "Scream with Me" within the album *Mudvayne*, Epic Records, Sony Music Entertainment.

Shared synergism definition courtesy Landau, S. (Ed.). *Reader's Digest Great Encyclopedic Dictionary*. Pleasantville, NY: The Readers Digest Association, 1968. Print.

The typeface primarily used throughout this book is Melior (*melior* being Latin for "better"), invented in Frankfurt, Germany, in 1952 by Hermann Zapf. A master calligrapher and type designer, Zapf is credited with the design of more than thirty typefaces. Melior is known for its elegant yet straightforward design, which can be easily read in a variety of point sizes and applications, particularly in newspapers.

Chapter titles are in Sabon typeface. Sabon was invented by the German Jan Tschichold and was released in 1967, seven years before his death. Tschichold is credited with creation of the Transit, Saskia, and Zeus typefaces as well. Sabon is named for the Frenchman Jacques Sabon, former student of the sixteenth century French publisher Claude Garamond, who the Garamond typeface is named for. The Sabon typeface is regarded as graceful yet highly readable.

For all the underdogs

CONTENTS

ACKNOWLEDGMENTS

Special thanks to those who shared their passion and professionalism during this writing project. Janine DeFilippo reconnected with me and led us back into each other's lives. She's also one heck of an editor. Generic Compositors designed and typeset the manuscript, and, like during composition of my other titles, they were a pleasure to work with. Special thanks to Terry Bradshaw. Proofreaders Ed and Maureen Gardner and Yolanda Sun picked all the bits of lint from the manuscript with great attention to detail. My favorite authors have influenced how I write and how I see the world: Ed Abbey, Ted Kaczynski, David McCullough, Hunter S. Thompson, and Guy and Laura Waterman.

There is a saying in the North Country: "There's only one thing more difficult than making friends in the Adirondacks: losing them." Mike Hagadorn, New York State forest ranger since deceased, is the man who handed me a compass and taught me how to use it, circa 1987. His passion for the out-of-doors latched onto me and eventually brought me to remote, beautiful, wild places; places he protected for a living. Ranger Hagadorn started it all for me.

North Country Community College professor Jack Drury harnessed my passion for exploring wilderness and showed me how to lead others; teaching me there is hiking, and then there is leading. New York State forest ranger Jim Waters supported me more than he likely realizes when I worked as a seasonal backcountry ranger in the Western High Peaks. Jim's a great man, loving his job while serving the public faithfully. Mike Kudish, Ph.D., author of my prior book's foreword, stands out as a man, like me, who was born a century or two too late. His knowledge of Adirondack Mountain ecological history is surpassed by no one. Guy and Laura Waterman had me fall in love with the mountains of the Northeast and propelled me to find the meaning of wildness. Partners featured in my stories were good sports and some worked alongside me during manuscript production. Many of them are still good friends. All are good people.

To produce something of consequence—a publication that effectively communicates passion, intelligence, and thoughtfulness—an author needs a support network he can rely on once he shuts his laptop down. I am indebted to Dr. Stan, Erin, Jamie, and Judith of the Department of Veterans Affairs' behavioral health team. Each day these selfless professionals strive to help veterans "get themselves back." I am very fortunate to have had my path cross with these care providers— thank you.

Without the men who went into the Adirondack Mountains before me, I wouldn't know much about these mountains at all, and this range may not be protected today. Due to these forefathers' efforts, we have valleys covered in trees, not pockmarked with condominiums; lakes as still as glass, not stirred by motorboat wakes; summits entangled in forests and drooping branches, not technological towers and tentacles of bright wires. State land within the Adirondack Park is marred only by rambling trails, a few footbridges and lean-tos, and a handful of fire towers. The Adirondacks are wild because of the selfless efforts of visionary preservationists. The men who had me enter an "Adirondack state of mind"—to fall in love with this range—have all gone to the Happy Hunting Grounds, and their efforts were never in vain. Now it's our turn to carry the torch.

Appreciation

"Hey, Air!" was the greeting I always received from my grandmother when I walked into her and my grandfather's home, a simple brick house at the end of a quiet dead-end street in Poughkeepsie, New York. "Air" (no one knows for sure how this nickname of mine was spelled, but it was pronounced that way) was short for Erik. My grandparents had nicknames for each of their four grandchildren: My sister, Kerri, was "Care-Care"; my cousin, Krista, was "Kay-Kay"; and my other cousin, Ian, was "Eee-Eee." In turn, the grandsons and granddaughters gave their grandparents nicknames: Grandma Nancy J. Ward became "Grams" while Grandpa Richard C. Ward became "Gramps." These nicknames were usually joined like the couple themselves: "Grams and Gramps," later shortened to "G and G."

My grandmother died at the age of 87 during August 2014, three weeks after the first hard copy manuscript of *My Adirondacks* was printed. During most of her days at home she would sit on a couch in the family room, an addition off the back of the house that overlooked the backyard that was home to a half-acre lawn, a shed, a few bushes, and an enormous red maple. Next to her couch were copies of my first three books, *Thru Hiker's Guide to America*, *Blue Line to Blue Line*, and *History Inside the Blue Line*. She was always proud of my writing. Each book I sent as a surprise, catching my grandparents unawares. I'd include brief, modest notes inside each new title sent: "Look what I've been up to," "See, I told you I've been busy," and "I hear this is a good book. Enjoy." Grandparents have a propensity to be proud of their grandkids. Grams must have been beaming when she opened each package to see my latest release. It is with great sadness that this title will not arrive at their home unannounced.

Accompanying my grandmother's death is history lost to the grave. She was born in Poughkeepsie during the summer of 1927 when Calvin Coolidge was President, Babe Ruth was the highest paid baseball player, the Ford Motor Company made the last Model T, and *Time Magazine* named Charles Lindbergh their Person of the Year. 1927 was twelve years before the start of World War II, 43 years before a Boeing 747 took flight, and 82 years before Barack Obama assumed office. Few children of The Roaring Twenties survive.

Tom Brokaw calls people who share similar dates of birth with my grandparents as "The Greatest Generation." Indeed. My grandmother lived in Poughkeepsie "from cradle to grave," and my grandfather, now 89 years old, will do the same. They lived in an era before the Mid-Hudson Bridge connecting

Poughkeepsie with Highland was built; these days it's difficult to even imagine that span not being there. My grandmother grew up in the second oldest house in Poughkeepsie. My grandfather survived the Great Depression, at one time selling his beloved guitar so his family had food to eat on Thanksgiving. He then served in World War II, surviving the Battle of the Bulge where 19,000 Americans were killed and 800 U.S. tanks were blown into scrap. The Greatest Generation worked hard, bought things with cash, minded their own business, and loved their neighbors and families.

Poughkeepsie is the town I was born in, so my grandparents' unique view of this city never ceased to interest me. They would tell me stories about residents not even thinking of locking their doors. When it was too hot to sleep inside during those steamy Hudson Valley nights, families would go to local parks or down to the shore of the Hudson with their blankets and pillows to sleep in the cool, open air. Beyond the napping public, the Poughkeepsie port was consistently busy, yet safe. Goods, especially beer, were shipped south to New York City and beyond. Freight and passenger trains flowed in and out of the city like lines of army ants.

Things are different today. The changing of Poughkeepsie's identity hurt my grandmother and still hurts my grandfather. If you leave your doors unlocked, you may come home to notice things missing. If you sleep in a park or down by the river, you may not wake again, and homicide detectives will never locate your wallet. Even the air seems worse. Heavier, dirtier, hotter. The Poughkeepsie port is quiet, not safe. Commuters are the bulk of rail goods shipped these days. When they stagger out of the cars at the end of the day they look gray, tired, and depressed. In a 2013 *Slate* article, Michelle Nijhuis called her hometown of Poughkeepsie "a particularly awful little place." As a kid she found it hideous: "boring and ugly, with its gray skies, low hills, and flat, gray river." I wonder if my grandmother saw Poughkeepsie this way during her final years.

No matter how her town changed, she did not. If there is such a thing as a cool grandmother, she was it. My grandmother was brightly humorous, making quips here and there, and if you weren't paying close attention you didn't get all of her jokes or the meanings that stood behind them. My grandfather, though returning from World War II without even a bruise, is extremely prone to accidents. Working as a road engineer for the State of New York during the 1970s, he was run over by a massive motor grader. In the 1980s he lost a leg to a steamroller. Seriously. And after he retired from the State of New York, the snow blower gnawed off two of his fingers. My grandmother empathized with his losses and then warned him with a tsk-tsk tone, "Dick, if you keep this up they're going to bury you in a shoebox." That's humor.

Grams showed particular interest in my wilderness lifestyle. While other family members wrung their hands about me being an on-again, off-again student and on-again, off-again functioning member of society during my youth, my grandmother didn't fret over my nomadic way of life. She "got" why I wouldn't be caught dead spending more than four months of the year alongside juvenile college students, and she realized why I loved disappearing off the face of the Earth for months at a time, bushwhacking in New England, hiking across Florida, mountain biking across the United States, or couch surfing and guzzling canned beer. She got *me*.

During my nomad life of the 1990s and early 2000s I occasionally needed a base of operations, somewhere to replenish my supplies, clean my car, scrub my gear, do laundry, and sleep in an honest to goodness bed. I went to my grandparents' house. I'd drift in like a cloud, drink all their orange juice, eat all their English muffins, and put their washing machine through a workout, its agitator scrubbing hiking pants, mountain biking jerseys, and running shorts caked in pine pitch, sweat, and mud. With each visit they created an impromptu to-do list for me. I mowed the lawn, cleaned the shed, trimmed the bushes, chopped up the big branches that fell off the red maple, and did the little things that they didn't feel safe doing—like getting on a stepladder and changing a light bulb.

As I returned to their house after each adventure, my grandmother would insist on a slide show of where I had been, what I had seen. She loved seeing areas she had never set foot in and probably never would have like the Chihuahuan Desert, Rocky Mountains, Great Plains, Everglades, Sierra Nevada, Southern Appalachians, and, of course, the Adirondacks. She loved my stories of sleeping in a yurt in Utah, snowshoeing through frozen New England forests, eating a half-gallon of ice cream in one sitting in Arizona, and stumbling upon bull moose in Maine. My photos and stories, those virtual tours of my adventures, gave her respite from the city that had changed so much but that she still loved.

My grandparents were always kind to me, always good to me, and never abandoned me. Many times they were more like parents to me than grandparents, and that's why her death is one of the hardest things I have had to face. With death, as they say, comes life. Raised under the wing of Grandma Nancy J. Ward, her four grandkids (and four great-grandkids) now roam the world, taking on life pursuits ranging from operating a turkey farm, to teaching reading, to waiting tables, to writing books.

I'm the grandkid who writes books. So, Grams, this one's for you.

STORIES

Adventures near Friends Lake

Beginner campers are easy to pick out. They carry an awful lot of stuff. So my buddy, Joey, and I must have looked like total neophytes. I can't remember everything Joey was carrying with him, but I remember what I carried. Strapped to the outside of my blue external frame pack, my first pack, which I had purchased used for $7, I had my sleeping arrangement, which was an L.L. Bean mummy sleeping bag, an L.L. Bean two-person dome tent, and an L.L. Bean wool blanket, which I would use for a sleeping pad. I liked L.L. Bean. Also hanging off my backpack was a gallon jug of water. For clothing I had a mound of fabrics, some warmer than others, stuffed into the main compartment. This included long underwear, a wool shirt, an extra pair of jeans, three extra pairs of cotton socks, a winter hat, a baseball hat, a windbreaker, a pair of gloves, a pair of mittens, and snow pants.

Then I had my kitchen. This included a Peak One cook set, which consisted of a medium-sized cooking pot, a small cooking pot, a small fry pan, a small metal mixing bowl, and two lids, all neatly contained in a small, red stuff sac. The cooking pots and fry pan, one at a time of course, would rest on my stovetop, which was a one burner Peak One multi-fuel backpacking stove.

Add to this growing packing list an enormous MagLite flashlight, a hunting knife almost as big as the flashlight, a metal canteen full of water, newspaper to help start a campfire, fork, spoon, mug, and can opener. The can opener would bite open cans of pork and beans, Chef Boyardee ravioli, Campbell's chicken noodle soup, and Dinty Moore beef stew. I also brought a container of powdered cocoa. Being unique teenagers, we brought no beer. I wore a cotton flannel shirt, jeans, and a clunky pair of Dunham work boots one size too big, which hid two pairs of cotton socks inside. I wore a wristwatch.

Joey brought a similar mountain of gear, and he chose similar food for dinner: seven or eight cans of something. He also brought what any mountain man worth his weight in beef jerky brings into the woods: a hatchet. We planned on having a campfire keep us warm through the cold November evening.

It was 1989, and I was 16 years old. Joey was 18. In 1989 I never used the word "backpacking" because I had never heard it myself. If you slept in the woods and walked to get there you were camping. Still, I knew very little about camping. I grew up in Poughkeepsie. Being from Long Island, Joey knew even less. What I thought campers did was only understood from looking at photos of campers in my family's L.L. Bean and Cabela's catalogs. In these photos the campers looked like rugged individuals. All of them wore river driver-style shirts or flannel shirts, some made of chamois, some of cotton, some of wool. They wore jeans and earth-toned boots. I presumed these people had to have known what they were doing. They were in a catalog, and not just anyone gets into an outdoor catalog. You have to know what you're doing. When I was 16 it had not yet occurred to me that these people were models. It all looked so real. In the L.L. Bean catalogs I also thought the people were from Maine. They looked so convincing—so Maine-ish—I couldn't think otherwise.

Joey and I first met at work. We were employed at The Balsam House, a French inn on the south shore of Friends Lake, a few miles from where each of us lived. The building was old, built sometime during the late 1800s or early 1900s. It was white with green trim. Ancient Eastern white pines stood in front of The Balsam House, shading a shuttle board yard and rows of Adirondack chairs. Most guests, the owners of the inn, and those who built the inn probably mistakenly thought the rows of pines were balsams. No matter. "The Balsam House" sounds better than "The Pine House."

In 1988 I applied to work at the inn in a position that best represented my life experience, ability, and ambition: dishwasher. I was hired on the spot. By the time Joey and I met I had been working at The Balsam House for nearly two years. He was hired to join me in "the dish pit."

Serving as a dishwasher—which, to boost my self-esteem, I called a "ceramics decontamination engineer"—was the second job I ever had. Two years before, when I was 14 years old, I was a landscaper. I use this title liberally. Someone who knew someone in my town, Chestertown, heard that little Erik Schlimmer wanted to make some money. My mother, the facilitator of my employment search, gave me a ride into town where I met my new employer, Richard, an overweight old man who chain smoked and was probably the smartest man in the room if everyone else in the room was 14 years old. He was a landscaper (a *real* landscaper) at Green Mansions Golf

Course, which was only three miles from my family's house. When my mother introduced me to Richard in front of our town's diner on the first day of my first job he had one four-word question for me: "You ready to rake?"

I said goodbye to my mother and got into Richard's red two-wheel-drive Ford pick-up truck. It was very early—perhaps 8:00 A.M.—and I was sleepy. We drove out into the country in silence. I had no idea where Richard was taking me, and he looked at me out of the corner of his eye. Upon reaching the golf course that October morning, he turned onto a dirt road that led way, way back to the far corner of the nine-hole course. Upon reaching that far corner of Green Mansions Golf Course, the grass covered in light frost, he turned the engine off, and we got out.

Richard pointed to the areas I was to rake. He spoke to me like I was a dunce, even demonstrating how to rake, like there was a wrong way to rake. He said he'd be back around lunch-time to see if I was "still alive." He handed me a rake, and I started raking the moment he turned back towards his truck. The moment Richard and his truck were out of sight, I put the rake down and took in the work ahead of me. There were an awful lot of leaves out there. Any idea I had of finishing work quickly and then goofing off for the rest of the day were zapped. I picked up the rake and started methodically filing leaves into a big pile, raking neat row by neat row.

After fifteen minutes it was affirmed that raking leaves is incredibly boring. And being 14 years old, it was hard for me to concentrate on anything that was going to take more than fifteen minutes to complete. I raked and raked and raked. And then I raked more. And then more. Then a little bit more. Then I raked again. Eventually 1:00 P.M. arrived and so did Richard. He pulled up, shut off his truck, and assessed my five hours of work with two words: "Not bad." He then went back to his truck, opened the passenger door, and produced a can of Pepsi. "Here you go," he said as he handed me the cold soda. "This is for you." I thanked him, surprised by this act of kindness. Or maybe he feared I was going to fall asleep after lunch. The Pepsi would keep me up. He walked back to his truck, got in, and started it. Out the window he yelled over the grumbling engine, "Take thirty minutes for lunch! I'll see you at 4:30!"

I would have kicked a nun to have been in that truck leaving that godforsaken golf course. Three and a half more hours out here! It was going to feel like a century. I drank my can of Pepsi while I ate the bologna and cheese sandwich my mother had made me. I also had chocolate chip cookies and a tiny bag of chips. I felt like a little kid in a cafeteria and rolled my eyes at myself. Lunch was good, but I was so lonely out in that corner of the golf course. I wondered what other people in the world were doing with their Saturday.

To pass the time between lunch and quitting time, after making sure no one was around to see me, I threw the rake on the ground, sat on the grass, and watched the robins hop across the field. Other unknown birds flitted from branch to branch in the pines and birches. But then I'd hear a vehicle driving down the road towards the golf course entrance. It could have been Richard. I'd sprint back to my rake and start raking feverishly. The car would drive by. The rake would hit the ground.

As slow as death, 4:30 came not a moment too soon. Right on time, Richard pulled up. He stopped near me and didn't even bother to shut off the engine. He rolled down the window. "Hop in," he said. I grabbed the trash from my lunch, threw the rake in the bed, and hopped in the passenger's seat. He didn't ask how I was. I hoped he had a good day, too. Richard slowly drove around, assessing the area I had raked like he was looking for something tiny that he had dropped.

I sat on the bench seat as we drove round and round at four miles per hour. Get me off this golf course. I thought to myself, "Even if he finds a spot I didn't rake well, it doesn't matter. The day is over." But then I thought, "Wait. If he finds a spot I didn't rake good enough, I don't think he's going to pay me. Or he'll make me get out and rake more." Richard seemed that type of man.

A codger uncomfortable with multiple-syllable words, Richard said, "Looks good. Let's head back." We drove back across the course, out the entrance, down Green Mansions Road, and down Route 9 back into town.

Richard pulled up in front of the diner I had last seen more than eight hours ago. I got out of the truck, and there was my mother standing on the sidewalk. "So, how'd it go, Bud?" It was my first job. She was glowing.

"Fine."

Richard came over to my mother, and he told her that I did a good job out there, and he thanked her for letting him "borrow" me. Then it was time to get paid, every man's favorite part of the job. Richard did the math out loud. "Let's see. You worked from 8:00 to 4:30, took a half-hour for lunch, and . . . so . . . that's . . ." I could almost see smoke coming out of the man's ears. "That's $24."

$24?

My God, that didn't sound like much. And you know one thing: If $24 didn't sound like much to a 14-year-old kid in 1987, it was not much.

At The Balsam House I got $3.35 an hour. After working a forty-hour week, I took home about $100. $400 a month! Now that was a lot of money. During busy times through the summer, like when our staff hosted weddings, for example, I could get ten hours of overtime in one pay period. Ten hours at $5.03 an hour. I thought, "This is how Vanderbilt must have felt." I had heard you could get an entire apartment for $400 a month. "Wow," I thought, "I could get my own place," completely ignorant of the additional costs of living on my own. I stopped dreaming about owning a car when I found out how much they cost.

After working at The Balsam House for two years the chef brought on another dishwa– excuse me, ceramics decontamination engineer: Joey. Joey had drifted from his moorings in

Massapequa, Long Island, and somehow washed up on the shores of Chestertown. He had no relatives in the area; his parents remained on Long Island. It was a complete mystery concerning how and why he showed up. No matter how he got there or why he was there, Joey and I hit it off.

Joey was older than me by two years. He was 18 but was one of those kids who looked 25. The scruffy, patchy beard on his face helped people misjudge his age, which enabled him to purchase beer for his peers. Joey was a high school dropout with no goals on his horizon. He may not have even had a horizon. All he had was one thing on his mind and that was to make enough money to not be homeless. He was living in a small apartment in Chestertown. It cost less than $400 a month.

Eventually we learned that we shared a common love: the woods. Joey was a hunter and fisherman. I liked to downhill ski, mountain bike, and hike. After working with Joey for a few months I proposed, "Hey, Joey. Dude, we should go camping."

If you are the type of person that believes in past lives, after talking to Joey for a few minutes you would have deduced that he used to be a puppy that went berserk when you asked, "Wanna go for a ride?" Upon offering my camping suggestion, Joey enthusiastically replied, "Dude! That would be fucking awesome!" His affinity for camping was somewhat of a surprise for me. It was the Long Island accent that threw me off. Phonetically his response was, "Dude! That would be fucking oowe-sum!" I had never connected Long Islanders with camping. I associated them with hanging out at the beach.

But where to go? The Adirondack Park is home to more than 1,300 named lakes and 1,000 named mountains. Thousands more rest in the forest anonymous, unnamed. What helped us narrow our search was that neither of us owned a vehicle. We rode our bicycles to work. But still, there was a great selection of lakes we could visit within a ten-mile radius of Friends Lake. We had already been to Palmer Pond fishing, so that was out. We'd run into other people there anyway. We wanted to go somewhere where we wouldn't be disturbed. Friends Lake, Brant Lake, and Loon Lake all had shoreline homes and motorboat access. There were other, modest bodies of water like Antler Pond, Dipper Pond, Sullivan Pond, and Alligator Pond, but those were small. Plus they were surrounded by private land.

We set our sights on mountains. There were lots of little peaks in our township: McGann Mountain, McCarthy Mountain, Tripp Mountain, and Kipp Mountain to name a few. Those didn't interest us, likely because they were privately owned. Though Chestertown is a tight-knit, community (my high school graduating class totaled 32), neither Joey nor I knew who owned these mountains. My parents didn't know either. Who knew that finding a place to camp in the largest park and forest preserve in the Lower Forty-Eight would be so difficult?

We had nearly given up on our camping expedition. Or, more accurately, we had nearly decided to camp in familiar territory. My parents lived on forty acres of woodlands that spread across what was locally known at "Atateka Mountain," a north-south running ridgeline that topped out at 1,200 feet. We could have gone camping behind my parents' house up on top of that hill. But what teenager wants to camp near his parents?

As fortune would have it, one day, as Joey and I were sitting on my parents' deck, which provided a panorama to the southeast, Joey pointed and asked, "What's that mountain?" I didn't know. I went inside and asked my parents. I came back out to the deck and reported that they didn't know either. But Joey and I knew where this mountain was, which was just off Stock Farm Road and two miles from the deck where we were sitting.

I went back inside and asked my father, "Dad, do we have any topographic maps of the woods around Stock Farm Road?" My father went into a closet in my parents' bedroom and hauled down from the shelves a cardboard box with a bunch of junk in it: old photo albums, receipts, insurance forms, and, the only thing I cared about, a couple of topographic maps. He came back to the living room with a few rolls of United States Geological Survey maps of the Friends Lake area.

I brought the maps out to Joey who was staring off at the mysterious hill like a mountaineer assessing an unclimbed Himalayan peak. "Hey, check it out," I said, carrying the rolls of maps. "I bet that mountain is on one of these." One by one we unrolled the maps, searching for Stock Farm Road or any part of Friends Lake, two features that would be easy to find on a map. We unrolled the map titled "Chestertown" from 1968. There was Friends Lake. And there was Stock Farm Road. I traced my finger down the road to the bottom of the map where a hill on the east side of Stock Farm Road seemed to rise just off the map. Where the base of this hill began there was a label: "Remington Mountain."

We found the map that lined up with the bottom of the Chestertown map: the "The Glen" map, which was also from 1968. At the top of this map was a summit labeled "Remington Mountain." We folded the bottom border of the Chestertown map and the top border of The Glen map and joined the two together. There was the mountain. Our mountain. Remington Mountain.

1,370-foot Remington Mountain, to us, looked more like a hill than a mountain. With my parents' deck standing at 1,100 feet, our mountain rose a bit more than two hundred vertical feet above us. But there was something about the shape of the mountain that attracted us. Its west side, the right side as we were looking at it, dropped 250 feet almost straight down. Honing in on this steep face, our modest mountain suddenly seemed like a soaring palisade to two teenagers.

Remington Mountain was within biking distance. And though the peak was not on state land, it was likely on land owned by my former middle school science teacher, Mr. Boggia (pronounced "boe-jhuh"). If he caught us up on his mountain, he wouldn't kick us off; he'd ask if we needed anything.

Two young men had found their mountain. To further display our manliness, we decided right then and there that we, during the approaching month of November, would camp on top of Remington Mountain like true mountaineers would.

A few weeks after identifying Remington Mountain, it was time to climb it. The morning of November 4, a Saturday, Joey arrived at my parents' house. He rode his ten-speed bicycle four miles from town wearing his enormous external frame pack. As Joey pulled up to the front of our house around 11:00 A.M., he was winded from our driveway. It climbed 200 vertical feet during its half-mile journey from Friends Lake Road. But Joey was in good shape from riding his bike to The Balsam House from his apartment in town. He did this ride at least four times a week, each round trip being nine miles.

The weather was splendid. The night before the thermometer had dipped to below freezing, but such cold, clear nights are preambles to cool, clear days. As Joey parked his bicycle, the sky overhead was crystal clear. The sun shone down on the dying red, yellow, orange, and brown leaves still on our maples, beeches, and aspens. Eastern hemlocks sprinkled their gloomy dark green and murky brown silhouettes among the remaining fall foliage.

Joey hauled his pack inside and plopped it down in our living room. With a big smile he said he was ready. I was ready, too. We had all the gear, all the clothing, all the food, and all the gumption. What we didn't have were second thoughts, despite the forecast that predicted the first snowfall of the season that night. But first things first. We ate lunch.

After lunch my parents came into the living room to examine the hardy mountaineers and their gear before both disappeared into the wilderness. But then my mother spoke up and suggested we not be as tough as we had planned. "You're going to ride your bikes up there?" she asked. "What if it snows? Then your bikes will be all covered with snow. They'll rust."

My father chimed in. "Where are you going to even put your bikes? Just leave them in the woods on the side of Stock Farm Road? That doesn't sound like a good idea."

They were embarrassing me. Hello? Didn't they know we had our trip planned already? Put on our packs, get on our bikes, fly down the driveway, left onto Friends Lake Road, right onto Atateka Road, left onto Stock Farm Road. Ditch bikes. Hike. Camp. My parents were throwing a wrench into the works and, as far as I was concerned, insinuating that we were getting in over our heads with the biking.

Before I could speak up, Joey did. "I'll take a ride!"

I couldn't believe it! Here was Joey wussing out already. I let out a sigh. I couldn't stand it when my friends sided with my parents. "That's not the plan," I said looking at him. "You're missing the point. Here to the hike on our bikes."

There appeared to be a stalemate. Then my mother, the brains of my family, spoke up, much like a mediator. "Well, why don't you guys let us give you a ride up Stock Farm Road, you go on your camping trip, and then you walk home when you're done?"

I thought it over, analyzing if accepting her suggestion would make me look like a wuss. Joey and I had planned on biking two miles to the base of the mountain and then, of course, biking two miles back when we were done camping. Now we could get a ride for two miles and then walk two miles back. Since walking is about twice as hard as biking, it seemed that whether we biked-and-biked or rode-and-walked didn't matter. I wouldn't look like a wuss. A ride up Stock Farm Road it was.

Joey, my father, and I left the house. We put Joey's bike in the woodshed to keep it out of the snow that was predicted. Our packs went in the back of my parents' black and silver Chevy Blazer. I hopped in the front seat, my father got behind the wheel, and Joey jumped in the back. My father started the engine and then paused, looking at me and then Joey, asking, "You guys got everything?"

I replied, "Yeah, we got everything."

Joey could hardly contain himself. "Let's do this!"

We descended the driveway, turned left on Friends Lake Road, right on Atateka Road, and left on Stock Farm Road. The only residence on Stock Farm Road for the first two miles was Mr. Boggia's home and horse farm. As we drove by his house, my father asked, as a sort of legal afterthought, "Who exactly owns this mountain?"

I didn't know for sure. A guess was good enough. I casually replied, "I'm pretty sure Mr. Boggia owns it."

The big SUV dropped down a gear as it motored up the long, gentle climb of Stock Farm Road. We passed the old, tiny cemetery on the left, and then the road crested and leveled. We knew, from studying the topographic maps, that we needed to leave Stock Farm Road at its highest point and dive left—east—into the woods. As originally planned, that's where we were going to ditch our bikes. I advised my father, "Slow down, slow down. We should get off the road around here."

The vehicle slowed to a crawl as the three of us peered into the hemlock forest on the left-hand side of the road. All the trees looked the same. Nondescript and dense, the forest seemed to run away forever. "Okay," I said. "Can you drop us off here, Dad?"

We pulled over to the right side of the road. My father threw the Blazer in park, shut off the engine, and the three of us climbed out. My father swung down the back tailgate. Our packs looked heavy. We grabbed them. They were heavy. We wrestled our packs onto our shoulders, the main compartments bursting at the seams. The stuff that didn't fit in the main compartments—jugs of water, sleeping bags, blankets, and the tent—hung off like enormous ornaments. "You guys all set?" my father inquired with suspicion.

I assured him we were. Joey, wide eyed, clutching his hands into tight fists, and hopping up and down a little, ordered, "Let's do this!"

We disappeared into the forest. We had no map and no compass with us, but we had the map memorized. All we had to do was hike due east, straight away from Stock Farm Road. After one-third of a mile we should encounter the base of the mountain. At that point we would have to decide whether to climb straight up the west face of the peak or go left or right, still climbing but not as steeply. From the base of the mountain to the summit was less than a half-mile with nearly 300 vertical feet of climbing.

We walked a hundred feet from the road so no one would see us. After all, I was (and still am) only pretty sure Mr. Boggia owned Remington Mountain. We heard my father execute a three-point turn and drive away. We were on our own. Failure was not an option.

It was already 2:00 P.M., and the sun was due to set before 5:00. I looked at Joey. "You ready?"

He was a firecracker. "I'm fucking ready!"

For my reply I couldn't help but steal what had already become Joey's trademark line for the expedition: "Let's do this!"

I led the way towards the base of the mountain, taking the straightest line I could maintain. Afraid of getting lost, and having no map or compass (we only kind of knew how to use either of them and likely could not use both in conjunction), I plowed straight through the hemlock woods, never taking my eye off the horizon ahead of me. We dropped in elevation smoothly, which we were expecting from examining the maps of Remington Mountain. Soon the firm Adirondack ground turned soft. Then moist. Then spongy. Then soupy. Then straight-up wet. We were sinking into a small wetland that was not on the topographic maps we had consulted. My confidence wavered. I didn't know what to do. I looked back at Joey, who was right behind me, and asked, "What should we do?" I peered ahead to see if any dry ground rose in front of me.

Joey began his advice with "Fuck!" Then he suggested, "Let's just go through the fucking thing!"

His persuasive reasoning was intelligent enough for a 16-year-old. I continued our course straight through the swamp, the cold November water seeping through the seams of my work boots. I could tell Joey's feet were faring no better. He plodded behind me, sloshing through a jiggling mess of ferns, muck, mud, and ice water. He summed his experience as only a Long Islander could: "Fuck, that water's cold!"

Once on the other side of the swamp—and on dry ground, thank God—we entered better-drained soils that supported an American beech and sugar maple forest. I said, "When we get on top, we're gonna have to build a fire quick. My feet are freezing." As leaves crunched underfoot, water squished out the seams of our boots. A few hundred feet from the swamp we encountered the ramparts of Remington Mountain. With our feet partly numb and our packs feeling heavier than they had felt on Stock Farm Road fifteen minutes earlier, we decided to head left around the west face of the mountain.

The climbing felt good. It warmed us up. Except for our feet. Not yet a mountain climber at that point in my life, I was delighted to feel nearly every muscle, joint, and tendon in my body working to propel me upward. I was using muscles I didn't even know I had. We scaled a northwest spur of the mountain and headed north, then northeast, then east, and finally southeast up Remington Mountain's summit ridgeline. I said to myself, "Now this is a *mountain*."

Joey and I loved it. Two young men in the mountains. Mountain men! No work, no parents, no siblings, no school, no chores. No girls to muck it up. Though we had some work ahead of us, life seemed simple. That is what has brought me back to the mountains time and time again from this trip in 1989 to nowadays. It's the simplicity of woods life. The few things that Joey and I needed to do on Remington Mountain are still the same few things I am required to do in the mountains. I need to stay warm when it's cold, drink water, eat food, find a comfy place to sleep. Twenty-five years ago Joey and I were getting away from it all, that "all" being work, parents, siblings, school, chores, and girls (we didn't talk about girls once during our trip). Today I explore the Adirondack wilderness, usually solo, to get away from colleagues, bills, phone calls, the Internet, pop culture, pollution, and the overall daily grind. Sometimes I go to the mountains to get away from girls. The mountains are my castle, the forests my moat.

Joey and I trudged up the ridgeline breathing heavily, our breath visible in the chill of late afternoon. We could see the skyline dead-ahead of us, which meant we were getting close to the top. Contrary to what happens on bigger mountains, the first flat area we reached was in fact the summit. It had taken thirty minutes to get to the top.

There was no view from the apex of Remington Mountain. We didn't care. For us, a great view was never the goal. If we wanted a great view we would have had my parents drive us up Prospect Mountain above Lake George. All we wanted was the top of Remington Mountain. The effort to get to the top, to be successful, to be up there. That was enough.

There was no time for philosophical discussion about the intrinsic values of climbing mountains though. I couldn't feel my feet. I looked over at Joey and asked, "Are your feet frozen?" He looked back at me only with a pout that communicated, to paraphrase Joey's usual communication style, "They're fucking frozen!" I said, "Mine too."

We dumped our packs where we stood. We needed to get two things done, and quick. One, set up the tent. Two, get a fire started. We did the tent first, reasoning that if it began to snow at least we could keep all our stuff, sleeping bags especially, dry in the tent. After fifteen minutes the tent was up. It looked good. I was proud, and I bet Joey was proud, too. We threw all our stuff in, creating a giant mound of blankets, sleeping bags, and clothing in the middle of our two-man tent.

Hobbling around on frozen feet, we were dying to get a fire started. Without even communicating our intentions to each other, we both started searching the immediate area for rocks to make a fire ring. Every camper in the L.L. Bean catalogs seemed to be gathered around a fire ring. We followed their lead. I'd see a little point of rock jutting out of the ground and go over to grab it, but I'd pull it out all too easily and see it was the size of my fist. Too small. I'd look somewhere else and find another rock poking its head up for air. I'd grab it, but it felt like it went straight through the Earth to China. Too big. I felt like Goldilocks looking for something just right.

Joey and I gathered a dozen rocks each about the size of bowling balls. We were thoroughly warmed from digging them out of the cold ground with our bare hands and then carrying them to the middle of our campsite. Every part of our bodies was warm except our feet. We arranged the rocks in a circle like we were about to begin a Wiccan ceremony. We dashed back into the surrounding forest in search of anything that would burn. We grabbed armloads of dead sticks and logs ranging from the diameter of pencils to the thickness of our arms. Then we followed an old woodsman adage: When you think you have enough firewood for the night, double it. We went back out for a second wood run.

We made sure to pile all our firewood right next to the fire ring for two reasons. One, if any of the wood was wet it could dry by the fire. Two, it would be easy to grab this firewood when it got dark. We also took time to break all the sticks into lengths of about eighteen inches. This was so we wouldn't have to break long branches into smaller pieces when it was dark. As I broke branches into manageable lengths, Joey whaled away with his hatchet, smashing and slicing our logs. An hour after beginning our firewood-collecting, we finished, stacking enough fuel to fill a bathtub. I knew what time it was time, and Joey affirmed this: "Let's get 'dis muthah-fuckah staaah-did!"

A fire needs three ingredients: ignition (such as a spark or the flame of a match), fuel (from smallest to largest: tinder, kindling, and fuel wood), and oxygen. We had all three. I dug out the newspapers from my backpack while Joey found the tiniest sticks in our pile of fuel.

I asked Joey, "What do you think? Teepee or log cabin?"

Without hesitation he replied, "Log cabin!"

"Log cabin?" I asked. "The log cabin sucks. It's all about the teepee."

Joey thoughtfully reasoned, "Fuck the teepee! What are you—an amateur?" Joey then bent over and started assembling his log cabin fire.

Two young men equally passionate about campfire design had reached an impasse. The log cabin (which is inferior, trust me) consists of building a four-sided structure of small- to medium-sized sticks about one foot tall and one foot square. It looks like a log cabin. The logic behind this design is that the center acts as a kind of furnace, funneling oxygen upward from its center, thus bringing in fresh air, which every campfire needs. Ever see a real log cabin burn to the ground? If so, you have seen the effectiveness of this design.

The teepee (which is superior, I assure you) consists of lying small- to medium-sized sticks at high angles against each other, usually with the smallest sticks on the inside and bigger sticks on the outside. It looks like a teepee. The logic behind this design is that inner, smaller sticks burn quickly and the flames from these reach the outer, bigger sticks. The beauty of the teepee is that heat from the center radiates out and dries the bigger sticks on the outside. A teepee fire is ideal when you need to throw damp wood on a fire. There is also a furnace effect with this design, just like with the log cabin.

To be honest, both the log cabin and teepee designs are effective—it's that I feel the teepee should be used when initially building a fire. As a bed of coals accumulates, I then switch to the log cabin as the teepee collapses. As I used to tell my outdoor education students during fire-building instruction, "Fire-building should represent Manifest Destiny. The teepees were there first, but they got replaced by log cabins."

My feet were still frozen on top of Remington Mountain. I didn't have time to give Joey the above tutorial on fire-building. I kept conversation brief. "Amateur? Look who's calling *me* amateur. Dude, I was building campfires when you were in middle school on Long Island" (this wasn't true). "Let's get this thing started. Build a teepee!"

Joey had a mini meltdown. "Arrrrrggghhhhhrrrrr! Fuck! Just let me build the fucking log cabin!"

As a friendly reminder I told Joey, "But I want my feet thawed *tonight*, not tomorrow night."

"Fine! Fuck!" Joey said as he bent over and started taking apart his log cabin inside the fire pit. "We'll do a fucking teepee!"

I felt bad. Here I was squabbling with my friend in the middle of the woods, those beautiful woods, on top of a mountain, that beautiful mountain. I said to myself, "Shame on you" and quickly repaired the damage. "Joey. Let's do a log cabin. But can we put a teepee in the middle of it?" My feet felt like blocks of wood.

Joey stood erect and looked at me wide-eyed like a wild man. He said only three words: "Let's do this!"

It was the best of both worlds inside that fire pit. The furnace effect funneling oxygen upward from its center, the smaller sticks on the inside burning quickly and drying the outer wood. I saw it as Native Americans and European explorers having their homes engulfed in flames simultaneously. It really was Manifest Destiny but with a blurred timeline.

The newspaper caught, the tinder caught, the kindling caught, and the fuel wood caught. We had a roaring fire. A bed of red-hot coals grew. The heat was intense. We looked around our little campsite perched 1,370 feet above the sea (which was pretty cool—our hometowns of Massapequa and Poughkeepsie being 30 and 170 feet above sea level, respectively). We were proud of what we had accomplished. We had left Stock Farm Road undetected, made it through the hemlock swamp, navigated up the mountain, set up camp, and got a fire going. Neither of us were amateurs.

Joey realized we couldn't stand around our fire all evening. "We need something to sit on!" He grabbed his hatchet and revisited a log he had found while collecting firewood. "Dunk! Dunk! Dunk!" went his hatchet into that beast of a log, chips from the half-dead trunk flying over his shoulders. Within a few minutes Joey's last swing flew through the log. With two more cuts following (one to chop off a seat for me and another to chop off his seat), our seating was done. "Rustic" described our furniture best. But we were mountain men. Who needed right angles and cushions?

We shouldered the two log seats and dropped them by the fire, both of them landing at the same time with a solid "thump." We sat down and put our feet up on the rocks of the fire ring, the bottoms of our boots facing the fire. Joey loved it. "This is fucking awesome!" I was all smiles. It was the first time I had ever been cold in the woods and then built a fire to get warm. I found it psychologically satisfying, though I wouldn't have described the feeling this way back then. At the time it felt just plain good.

But there was something wrong. Despite having our boots nearly in the fire, our feet were still painfully cold. "I'm taking my boots off," I said.

"It ain't workin'!" Joey said. "I'm taking mine off, too!"

We sat our boots on the rocks, draped our soaking wet socks over the woodpile, and put our naked feet close to the fire but not too close. We were smart enough to know that we could burn our feet without knowing it since our feet were numb. Slowly the radiant glow of the fire penetrated our outer skin, then the inner layers, and finally seeped right into our bones. Steam rolled off our socks, our boots, our bare feet, and the half-frozen bottoms of our pant legs. The heat was intoxicating. After working hard to get up the mountain and then freezing our butts off, the heat made me drowsy, like when I laid in front of my parents' woodstove. We quietly sat in front of the fire and stared into it.

There is something about a campfire. It draws your eyes into it, clears your mind, and makes you feel safe. The way the flames wave and curl in their own thermal drafts reaching for the sky never to reach it. The different colors and how they lap against each other, turning yellow, orange, red, or blue. The way the colors sweep across a bed of searing coals. These visuals are special, unique, and tap into a kind of caveman contentness. Some outdoor educators I've worked with have called a campfire "caveman TV," and their facetious label is not far off the mark. A fire's colors and movements, familiar earthy smell, and beaming heat on your face cannot—and will never—be duplicated by any technological advancements. There is nothing like a campfire.

The fire could warm us, make us feel safe, entertain us, give us light, and dry our wet socks. Yet it couldn't fill our bellies. Dusk crept through the forest. Joey looked up and asked, "Are you hungry? I'm hungry!"

"Me, too. Are you gonna eat?" I asked.

"Sure!" Then Joey laughed. "What the fuck else are we gonna do?"

I laughed, too. With Joey's question, I noticed that once we got camp set up and our fire going, we hadn't done anything but stare into the fire. But then again, there's no such thing as boredom in the woods. Boredom is an invention of civilized man.

I got up from my rustic seat and walked over to the tent. I unzipped the big door, sweeping the zipper in a great arc. I stood my pack up in the tent as I kneeled inside, scrunched down so my head wasn't crammed against the ceiling. I dug out my stove and brought it back to the fire.

"You got a stove?" Joey asked.

"Yeah. I wanna try it out" I said. It was still brand new. "I want to see if it works in the cold."

"Dude!" Joey exploded. "We gotta cook on the fire!"

"You're gonna cook on the fire?" I asked.

"Fuck yeah!"

I wondered if by the end of the trip if I would be swearing as much as Joey.

"Well . . ." I paused. I wanted to try out my new stove. I had ordered it from L.L. Bean of course. But cooking over our fire seemed like a great idea. To me, it made the expedition complete and appropriately used our fire to its fullest potential. We had already used it for warmth, safety, entertainment, and light. We used it as a dryer. Now it was going to cook our food. I thought to myself, "What else can this thing do?"

I couldn't help impersonate Joey again. "Let's do this!"

I threw the stove back in the tent, and then reached in my pack and pulled out my cook set and hefty bag of food. My cook set was new, too. I was looking forward to testing it out, especially since I wouldn't be testing my stove. As I backed out of the tent and went to zip the door shut, Joey was right behind me wanting to get in. He needed his cook set and food, too.

I sat on my log and opened my food bag. As I peered inside I was immeasurably happy that I had brought a selection of foods. They all looked so good that it was hard to pick what to eat. During my youth I was partial to Chef Boyardee. Ravioli was on the menu.

Joey came back and sat on his log.

"Joey—what is that?"

"What?" he asked.

"Is that a pot from your kitchen?" I asked.

"Yeah!"

Since Joey didn't have a camping cook set like I did, he grabbed a three-quart pot from his kitchen. It looked out of place in the woods with its long, black handle and copper bottom. He forgot the lid. After selecting our dinners (Joey chose beef stew), we poured the contents into our pots and put them on the red-hot coals. After two minutes we gave our respective meals a stir with our spoons and were flabbergasted to find the contents cold. I couldn't believe how long it took to bring a pot of food to a boil. Sometimes the fire was so hot we had to move our seats back, but here were two pots on red-hot coals, and nothing was happening.

After five or ten minutes the food started to boil. We could hardly wait to dine. Though a fire warms you on the outside, especially your side that's facing the fire, our guts had been cold since the sun dipped behind the Town of Johnsburg to the west. Once the light was gone, it got cold fast.

I lifted my pot out of the fire with a stick since the bailing handle on top was scorching hot. Joey grabbed the long, black handle of his pot with his bare hand and drew it away in a flash. He jogged to the tent and came back with his hand inside a pair of socks, which served as his makeshift oven mitt. Since Joey forgot his lid and I had not bothered to put mine on, each of our dinners had abundant ashes mixed into them. At first we were hesitant to eat the ashes with our food, but we both found they only added flavor. We kidded how we should bring ashes back with us so we could put them on our food in civilization.

Joey has asked a good question before dinner: "What the fuck else are we gonna do?" To be honest, I do not remember the bulk of what we did between dinner and sunrise, a stretch of nearly fourteen hours. I remember bits and pieces, like a dream. I remember laughing a lot around the campfire. I remember eating a lot. I remember it snowing. Hard. (We only got two inches of snow, but it really came down.) I remember my feet freezing. I remember Joey putting his booted foot so close to the fire that the bottom melted. The inside of his boot became very hot very fast, he tore it off, and then stamped his bare foot in the snow to douse the heat that clung to it. That made me laugh a lot more. I remember the heat from the fire beaming onto my face. I remember a long, cold night in that tent.

My most vivid memory is of Joey, my friend. I can see his face lit by the fire, and I can hear his accent. I remember a great feeling on Remington Mountain. It was a feeling of being on top of the world with someone I trusted. I couldn't have done that trip on my own. It would have been too dark, too lonely, and too cold for me. I would have survived, but I wouldn't have had fun. Sometimes all you need in the mountains is another mountain man.

After a fitful night's rest in temperatures down to 25 degrees, sunrise did not come too soon for two half-frozen teenagers.

We put on nearly every stitch of clothing, doubled up our socks, put our frozen boots on, and crawled out of the tent. The wind had lashed our tent during the wee hours of the night, adding to our miserable housing situation. Snow was plastered to tree trunks. The snow looked beautiful, so white. It dangled from the remaining foliage, perched on the branches, and covered our fire pit. The ashes were dead cold. We stood around the campsite stamping our feet with our hands deep in our pockets. There was nothing to do but leave. Yet we didn't want to go. Remington Mountain had become home.

We took down the tent after managing to shake most of the snow and ice off it, packed our gear, shouldered our packs, and looked around to make sure we left nothing behind. The campsite looked so different than when we had arrived. It was cool to see how a little snow transformed the forest into another world. We looked at each other with big smiles. It had been quite the adventure.

We descended Remington Mountain by roughly the same route we took up, not daring to descend the steep west side. At the base of the mountain we curved our route northwest—not going west towards Stock Farm Road—to avoid the hemlock swamp. Our feet were cold enough. Within twenty minutes of leaving the summit we hit the pavement.

It was a gentle stroll down the smooth decline of Stock Farm Road. Mr. Boggia's house was off in the distance to our right, light blue smoke rising out of his chimney. He had his woodstove going, probably the first time that fall. If he looked out the window he would have seen two unkempt kids with enormous packs bumping down his road. I wonder what he would have thought we were up to. We were too far away for him to recognize me. We made it back to my parents' house on Atateka Mountain, the final climb up the steep driveway warming us up, making us unzip our jackets and remove our winter hats.

We walked up to the front door. My parents were excited to see us. They came outside on the front porch despite the cold. Joey and I stood there with our immense packs on, half covered in snow. We stopped stamping our feet out of pride now that we had an audience. Our jeans were muddy, the bottoms covered in layers of brown ice. We must have looked bushed. My mother said she had worried about us when it started snowing; that she had expected us to come back last night because it got so cold. Joey and I looked at each other with subtle grins, like my mother was innocently naïve. "But, Mom," I said, "of course we spent the night. We're mountain men."

Bear Patrol

It was the closest I had ever been to a bear. The clouds at 2:00
A.M. that night in August 2001 shut out the moon's white light
and all the little pin-pricks of stars. I could hear the bear
breathing, like he was out of breath, winded. His breath
smelled like that of a wild animal that had eaten a basket of
pine cones, a sweat-soaked t-shirt, and a small dog. It was
thick and muggy, like the breath of a fat man who had speed
walked a mile. I could see where this breath was coming
from. It was a mouth with big, white, menacing teeth—maybe

a broken one here or there from gnawing a signpost or crunching a stone along with his prey. His mouth was much like that of a dog's but bigger, stronger, and hotter.

I had met this bear twelve hours earlier when he tried to steal a backpacker's food bag. I was at work in the Adirondack Park's Western High Peaks. During 2001 I was employed from May to October as a Department of Environmental Conservation (DEC) assistant forest ranger. Out of the thirty or so assistant ranger positions throughout the state, the Western High Peaks was perhaps the best location to be stationed. Being the western half of 193,000-acre High Peaks Wilderness Area, the Western High Peaks are home to 4,000-foot summits, meandering rivers, dozens of bodies of water, and thousands of acres that no one has set foot in since the early 1900s during the great Adirondack logging era.

The assistant forest ranger faction was the "boots on the ground" according to the DEC. While the permanent, year-round law enforcement rangers with their trucks, guns, bullet-resistant vests, and handcuffs completed frontcountry patrols (that is, within a half-mile of their trucks in case they had to respond to an accident or crime), the temporary, seasonal rangers were deep in the backcountry for up to five days at a time. They carried only their camping gear and a communications radio that sometimes could not find reception.

Unlike law enforcement rangers, assistants had no enforcement powers, which was a godsend or a curse, depending on who the assistant was. For me, it was a godsend. Though the DEC wanted assistants to skirt around the issue, when talking to the public, of if assistant forest rangers possessed legitimate enforcement powers or not, I made it clear to hikers I interacted with that I had no such powers. I politely asked day hikers and backpackers to not burn down outhouses, cut down live trees, pollute water sources, or feed wildlife. I communicated that not doing these things was a noble pursuit, not only out of respect for the environment and other visitors but out of respect for me busting my butt, hiking up to twenty miles a day across the wilderness trying to educate people on how to keep the woods tidy. My approach was preventative education, not reactionary punishment.

Most assistants used this friendly approach. All hikers seemed receptive. It was good commonsense policy. If I walked up on a group of young men sitting in a lean-to smoking pot and drinking alcohol (which happened more than once), I didn't want them to think I was there to bust them. Why not? Because there are six of them, I have a radio that may not have reception, I have no weapons, no one knows precisely where I am, and they're probably high. I threw confrontation aside and replaced it with surprise and an eccentric sense of humor. I built a reputation for being everywhere at once and showing up unannounced anytime between dawn and dusk. After secretly surveying a group for five or ten minutes, I'd burst from the forest.

"Hi! I'm the backcountry ranger."

"Where the hell did you come from?"

"I'm *everywhere*. I've been watching you guys for a while. Don't forget to pick up your beer cans when you leave. Have fun!" Then I disappeared into the forest as quickly as I had appeared, leaving the partiers looking at each other, confused as to where I came from, where I went, and where I may spring again. I was a state-approved rampant goblin of the woods, hiking everywhere, watching everyone.

For other assistants, the absence of enforcement powers was a curse, and they brought this curse upon themselves. Young males were especially prone to regarding the assistant ranger job not as an educational position but as a law enforcement internship. This rubbed colleagues the wrong way. The law enforcement rangers felt insulted when a twenty-year-old kid with no law enforcement credentials thought he was going to bust someone for fishing out of season, parking in a handicapped space, or picking a few wildflowers. They were downright annoying, talking about the next State Police academy or how they were thinking about being a cop in their hometown.

They stressed me out. The public wasn't receptive to interactions with these types of assistant forest rangers because hikers, like all people, have the ability to tell who is an idiot and who is not.

My schedule was five days on, two days off. A common itinerary began with a ride down Long Lake, which Long Lake Village, my base of operations, was located on. After getting a nine-mile shuttle to the north end of the lake with the law enforcement ranger in his state motorboat, I hopped in my DEC one-man canoe. I floated down the Raquette River for a mile, then turned up the fourteen-mile-long Cold River, which poured in from my right. I paddled up the Cold River as far as I could, until my arms gave out or until the water became too shallow. I usually made it to Pine Point, two miles upstream.

At Pine Point I'd hide my canoe, PFD, and paddle, throw on my pack, and start hiking towards the interior via old, overgrown Pine Point Trail. Once in the interior, I went where I pleased, swam when I wanted, and explored the expanses of trailless terrain when I felt the urge to find solitude. I was a free man, educating backpackers, responding to emergencies, and completing trail work. And since the DEC admitted my radio wouldn't always get reception because I was patrolling in deep valleys, if my radio bumped a branch and got turned off on a sunny afternoon . . . I guess I had to live with that.

On day two of my first five-day patrol of August I approached Duck Hole after camping my first night near Shattuck Clearing, the former site of a DEC interior outpost and, before that, an old-time logging camp. Duck Hole, the source of the Cold River, was named in the mid-1800s for the ducks that could be found there. Prior to 1915 Duck Hole was a meadow and wetland. In 1915 it became a pond due to the Santa Clara Lumber Company building a ten-foot-tall wooden dam for logging operations (back then logs were floated down rivers, logging trucks not becoming commonplace until decades later). In 1936 the Civilian Conservation Corps rebuilt the dam, raising the water level another six feet. When I walked upon Duck Hole that Saturday afternoon in 2001, this remote, very pretty body of water was 61 acres in size. It was small by Adirondack standards but big enough to attract back-packers.

Walking under a cobalt sky, it was a fine day to be getting paid to hike. I rounded a bend in the trail and Duck Hole came into view, its surface shimmering in the afternoon light. With my radio strapped to the top of my pack and crackling a stat-icy, garbled "594 this is 591; 594 this is 591 on Blue" and other random, coded communications, a girl standing at a trail intersection above Duck Hole heard my radio before she saw me. As I came into view, she recognized my uniform as one of a ranger. That is, dark green pants and a tan long-sleeved shirt with a DEC patch on one shoulder, assistant forest ranger patch on the other. "I thought you might be a ranger. No one else out here has a radio." She was cute.

"You just missed it," she said. "I walked over here to let my food bag down to get something to eat, I look up, and there's this giant bear clutching the side of the tree. And he's got one paw on my food bag!" She looked up towards her food bag, thankful it was still there. I saw her large, bright red food bag hanging from a plump branch.

To keep human food from bears, backpackers hang their food from trees. You attach something weighty, such as a fist-sized rock or a heavy but small branch, to the end of fifty feet of rope. Then you fling your object, and thus your rope, over a branch high in a tree. Your weighty object, and thus your rope, comes sliding down the other side of the branch. Now you have your rope over your branch. When nightfall comes (or anytime you don't feel like keeping an eye on your food), you tie your food bag to one end of the rope, grab the other end, and pull. Then you sleep soundly knowing your breakfast will be waiting for you when the sun rises.

Doing a "bear hang" is a trivial challenge for veteran back-packers and a test of patience for beginners. I can complete a bear hang in a few minutes, having hung scores of them. I have seen other campers take upwards of hours picking the wrong tree, getting the rope stuck, then moving on only to pick another inappropriate tree. Then the rock comes untied each time they try to throw their rope over the branch. And so on. Establishing a quick bear hang comes down to two things. One is picking a tree with a solid branch that sticks way the hell out, perpendicular to the ground. Two is having played baseball so you know how to throw.

When this girl hung her food bag she had only one of three dimensions correct: at least ten feet from the ground. She failed at ensuring her foodstuffs extended at least four feet from the trunk and hung at least four feet below the branch. Without these two dimensions taken into consideration, a bear scoots up the trunk, and, if your food is resting against the trunk, he grabs it. If the food is away from the trunk but raised all the way up to the branch, he walks out on the branch and seizes his dinner this way. If he can't actually pull the food bag down due to carabiners or knots holding it fast to the rope, with a few quick swipes he turns your food bag into confetti, and the contents go tumbling to the ground. The bear likely feels like a kid who whacks a piñata at a party and all those goodies fall from the sky.

Once the bear gets your food, he often hides it in the woods and goes back on patrol. Not gluttons, bears are hoarders more than anything. Why spend your time stuffing yourself on the contents of just one food bag when you can strike while the iron is hot, accumulate a mountain of stolen food from different bags, and eat at will for the following days?

As I looked up at the girl's food bag pathetically resting against the trunk of the birch, she pointed something out to me, as if she needed to convince me that a bear had nearly stolen her food. "See? You see those? Just below the bag." The birch was gently scarred from the bear's powerful grip as he shimmied up when no one was looking and flew down when she approached the tree to grab an afternoon snack, catching the bear unawares.

I had only one question for her: "Where is he?"

She pointed to a thicket of young red spruce trees on the other side of the trail, beyond a small clearing where an interior outpost used to stand. The tangle of trees was so dense I could barely see a few feet into them. "He's in there."

"Well, let's see what he's doing."

"You're going over there?" she asked.

I had to play it cool. I casually replied, "Yeah, I want to see what he's up to."

I nonchalantly took off my pack, unzipped the top pocket, and took out my canister of pepper spray, which some of my colleagues called "mace," which is incorrect. Mace is a chemical, pepper spray is heat. A lot of heat. The eight-inch-tall black canister had labeling encircling it and nearly all of the print communicated that, whatever you do, do not get pepper spray on your skin and, for God's sake, don't get it in your eyes.

I told her my plan, which I was making up as things progressed. "If he's in there, I'll just spray him in the face, and I doubt he'll come back."

She looked at me. "What should I do?"

"If you see me get dragged into that thicket and I start screaming, pick up my radio, press the button on the side, and tell them I died doing what I loved."

With a hesitant look that said, "I don't think I'm up to this job," she asked, "Are you serious?"

"No. I'm just kidding." Nodding towards my radio I said, "Tell them whatever you want."

My radio may not have worked in some valleys of the Western High Peaks, but what does work, anywhere, is pepper spray. I learned the power of pepper spray through a completely innocent accident. After purchasing my canister (the DEC wouldn't supply me with one), I decided to test fire it. You don't want to be carrying around a canister of pepper spray unsure if it works, much like you don't want to storm a beachhead, pull the trigger of your rifle and hear "click" instead of "bang."

While on patrol earlier that summer I left the trail I was hiking on and walked a dozen paces into the forest. Then I made sure there was nothing living within sight. No birds, no humans, no animals. If there were black flies and mosquitoes where I was about to spray, so be it. The fewer of them, the better.

Before test firing the canister, I reviewed the directions.

1. Place forefinger through loop in handle with thumb on curl of safety clip.
2. With thumb, pull safety clip up and straight back.
3. Depress trigger lever with thumb, releasing a one second burst of spray.

The directions continued, explaining how it should specifically be used on a bear.

1. Canister should be sprayed as the attacking bear is charging toward you and is about forty feet away (two to three seconds from reaching you).
2. Be aware that wind or rain can greatly affect the accuracy of the initial burst of spray. In some cases you may have to wait until the bear is quite close before spraying.
3. If the bear makes it through the initial burst of spray, continue spraying, aiming for the face. Shield your eyes and face if you must face the wind.

The directions took up a tiny corner of the label. The bulk of the text was warnings. "Danger." "Strong irritant to eyes, nose and skin." "Individuals who suffer from asthma or emphysema may have a more severe reaction." "May cause irreversible eye damage if sprayed in the eyes." At the bottom of the label was an image of a man with a terrible head wound, a big flap of his scalp peeled back and blood running down his face. The caption read: "Produced by a grizzly attack survivor!"

I released the safety clip on top of the canister, made was upwind of where I was going to spray, and then pr̲ ̲ ̲ ̲ ̲ ̲ the trigger for less than a second. The results were amazing. An enormous cloud of pepper spray, dyed blaze orange, blasted out of the canister. The irritant came out so powerfully that the canister actually kicked back at me. I watched the cloud engulf a twenty-foot by twenty-foot section of woods and then dissipate to gently reach the ground. No trace of the cloud remained. Satisfied my canister would deter any North American mammal, I replaced the safety clip and made my way back to the trail.

Suddenly, something didn't feel right. I couldn't breathe. Or more accurately, I didn't want to breathe. When I took a breath in, it felt like I was inhaling tiny fragments of glass. I immediately recognized what had happened. My cloud of pepper spray, which I watched slowly dissipate, was not through. Apparently I saw most of the dye dissipate, but the potent, nearly invisible cloud of pepper drifted through the woods and stealthily descended upon me. I hightailed it down the trail and tried to take in as much fresh air as I could, but the irritant seemed stuck in my lungs. I coughed and wheezed down the trail. My throat burned for the rest of the day. I sheepishly realized why the DEC hadn't given me one of these things.

A much worse pepper spray incident happened in the Eastern High Peaks with Paul, another assistant forest ranger. He found a bear raiding a dumpster near the Adirondack Loj, a frontcountry bed and breakfast surrounded by state land. Knowing that the bear in the dumpster was the same bear that had been invading lean-tos and campsites in the High Peaks, searching for food, Paul seized the opportunity to flush him out. He casually strolled towards the bear like he was going to walk right past it, but then Paul quickly turned towards the bear and blasted it in the face with his pepper spray. The bear flew out of the dumpster and ran away, crashing headlong into the surrounding woods half blind.

Paul, proud of things going so well (it was witnessed by at least a dozen hikers, who were impressed with his casual effectiveness), calmly replaced the safety clip and strolled into the nearby parking lot where onlookers gathered. A husband and wife were standing there with their son, who was about ten years old. The mother went to speak, attempting to communicate something to the effect of "That was so brave of you," but the child interrupted, reporting, "Mommy, I don't feel good." Just as he finished that short announcement the kid barfed everywhere. "Blluuuhhhhh!" Then he started crying, rubbing his eyeballs. Then the dozen hikers who were so impressed with Paul a moment earlier had trouble breathing, much like I did when I test fired my pepper spray. People throughout the parking lot started placing their hands over their mouths and noses, rubbing their eyes, choking, and displaying expressions of extreme discomfort.

The same thing that happened to me happened to Paul and his fans. The blaze orange dye dissipated, but the pepper power had not. After fumigating two dozen people (and, to be fair, one bear) at the Adirondack Loj, Paul earned a nickname for the rest of his season: Dr. Pepper.

With the cute girl standing next to my pack I confidently strode across the small meadow towards the spruce thicket knowing that my canister functioned properly and that it could take care of any bear. I felt like a knight heading off to slay a dragon for my maiden. As I approached the wood line I let the bear know I was there. "Hey, Mr. Bear. It's just me," I warned. "I heard you've been trying to steal lunches. Now that's not very nice." Then I stopped and listened. Nothing. I moved closer to the thicket and asked in a kind tone, "Are you in there, Mr. Bear?"

The hidden bear snapped his mouth shut, then opened it, then snapped it shut again, and repeated this a few times. It's a scary sound that communicates a bear is pissed off because you have invaded his space. After snapping his powerful jaws he "huffed" at me, exhaling forcefully out his nose and mouth.

"Hrrruuufffff!" "Hrrruuufffff!" It sounded like a dog that half "woofs" when a car pulls into his master's driveway. Of course the bear's huff was much louder and much more sinister.

I couldn't blindly spray into the thicket. It would have done no good. There was no way I was going to poke my head inside that wall of spruce. But I didn't want to come back to my maiden without the head of the dragon. I swallowed my pride, did an about-face, and walked back to the girl.

"Is he in there?" she asked.

"Yeah, he's in there. And he's pissed off."

"How do you know he's pissed off?" she followed, also, like me, looking towards the thicket.

"He was snapping his teeth and huffing at me." I looked at her and asked, "You didn't hear that?"

"No."

With the bear out of our hair at least for the time being, I worked with her to fix her bear hang. First we took down the rope, deciding to start from scratch. After tying a rock to the end of the rope, I flung it over a high, stout branch on the first try. "Wow, you're good at this." I was beaming. Count vanity among the faults of assistant forest rangers. We hauled her enormous food bag up and were satisfied looking at it hanging in space, far from the trunk and well out of reach of any bear.

"That's a lot of food. How long you out for?" I asked.

"Oh, that's not all my food," she said. "I'm with a group of friends. They went for a hike to Wanika Falls, but they'll be back soon."

"Oh, okay. Well, when they get back," I warned, "just make sure you tell them not to leave any food lying around. The bear's gonna get it if they do, and then he's never gonna go away."

"Okay."

While she went back to the lean-to next to the Duck Hole dam, I had to find my own campsite. I never stayed in lean-tos or designated campsites while working because I presumed campers didn't want to camp with the ranger. If they wanted to smoke weed, piss next to the lean-to, or stay up late—all of which I had no problem with—they may have felt awkward, or may not have done any of these at all, if I was hanging around. I gave them space.

I went to the lean-to and told the girl I was going off to find a campsite if she needed me. I disappeared into the softwood forest behind the lean-to, hiking parallel with the Cold River on my left. After covering 300 feet, I plopped my pack down and started setting up my modest camp among a stand of young spruce trees, each about the diameter of a can of Coke. Sleeping pad, sleeping bag, eight-foot by six-foot tarp, ground sheet, extra clothes, first aid kit, cooking pot and stove, rain jacket, journal, camera, radio, and extra radio batteries. I brought a book to read on this trip, too: H.G. Wells's *The Island of Doctor Moreau*.

I also had my food bag. I usually don't hang my food. Most people think I'm crazy because I lay my food bag right next to me at night. No animal in its right mind would get so close to a human for food, even a bear. But I'm talking about "normal" bears; the truly wild ones that are scared of people. I respected Duck Hole's big, black marauder, which I had already begun to think was not normal at all. I decided to hang my food, finding a suitable paper birch twenty feet from my hasty campsite. I would have rather had my bear hang not so close to where I slept. It would do.

Digging out fifty feet of parachute cord, I tossed the cord over a high branch of the birch. I stood there looking up at the branch with my cord draped across it. Was it high enough? Would the food be far enough from the trunk? And far enough below the branch? There were few good trees near me. I thought this one would suffice. For the time being, at least before dark, my food bag would be in my campsite with me or in my pack on my back, never out of sight.

Back in my campsite I set up my tarp in a low A-frame design. I took off my boots and socks. I powdered my feet. Instantly making my feet dry and fresh, my Gold Bond powder cooled and cleaned them, making it feel like I had hiked two miles, not ten. I draped my stinky wool socks over a branch to air. I lay on top of my sleeping bag, which was on my sleeping pad, which was on my ground sheet. I balled up my fleece jacket and placed it under my head as a makeshift pillow. In Wells's book I read about giant insects—wasps the size of couches, for example—trying to kill and devour humans. It made the bear appear not so scary.

I put my book down. I was having second thoughts about my bear hang. I put on a pair of clean socks, put my boots back on, and visited my bear hang. I attached the food bag to a strong bowline knot tied at the end of the rope. I clipped the bag to the loop with a small carabiner, and hauled it up. My yellow food bag was well-placed in the air, yet one thing nagged me. If that bear gets my food, and that girl and her friends find out, I will look like an amateur, and no man likes to look like an amateur.

Satisfied a bear wouldn't be able to get my food, I let the food bag down, headed back to my campsite, and packed up my radio, first aid kit, rain jacket, pepper spray, headlamp, fleece jacket, and food. I walked back to the lean-to and there was the girl. And there were her friends: four guys and another girl.

My conversation with them was like most I had with the public. That is, relaxed and cordial. They asked the same questions I always got, and I gave the same answers I always gave: "May to October." "Yes, I sleep out every night." "Yes, even when it's raining." "Yes, by myself." "Five days at a time." "Macaroni and cheese. Sometimes Ramen." But then one answer was unique to this conversation: "Yes, I think you'll see the bear." I left them to their privacy. I had to go bear hunting.

I didn't have to walk far, just a few hundred feet up the trail that led away from Duck Hole. My bear was standing in the middle of the trail near the groups' food bag. He was on all fours with his big head pointed upwards, sniffing the air. It looked like he was concentrating. Then he slowly pointed his head down and gazed towards me. He didn't look surprised.

He was beautiful, like all black bears are. His jet-black fur shimmered in the fading afternoon sunlight, and he looked especially dark upon a background of powdery white paper birches and aspens. His brown snout looked like that of a teddy bear. His ears were tiny. I imagined running up to him and jumping on him, like a little kid does with a big family dog. But the cuteness wafted away with the August breeze when he let out a "Hrrruuufffff!" like he had at the spruce thicket.

I felt insulted. Here I was admiring him, and all he had to say in return was "I don't like you. In fact, you're an asshole!"

I dropped my pack, unzipped the top lid, and drew out my pepper spray. I reached in the main pocket and turned off my radio. It was *de hombre a hombre*. Man to man. I put my pack back on and walked towards the bear in my most serious stride. I was frowning. As I strode with determined steps towards him, I let him know who was in charge of the Western High Peaks. "Oh! You wanna be like that? Huh! Okay, well how about I come over there and spray this in your *face*! What do you think about *that*?!"

He sniffed the air no more. He looked surprised, if a bear can look surprised. I think he thought I was crazy, which is what I was going for. If I was loud enough, crazy enough, and confrontational enough, I was confident he would be driven from Duck Hole by sundown. As the mighty bear hunter I would drive him from the Snickers bars, Ramen, and hard candies and back into the trackless forests and the blueberries and beechnuts he was supposed to be eating.

The bear ran. So I ran after him. As I sprinted down the trail I screamed, "That's right! That's right! These are *my* woods! You'll see what's gonna happen! You'll *seeeeeeee*!"

The group of six campers ran up the trail towards me. Two of them were holding cameras. When they caught up with me girl #2 asked, "What happened?"

In a deadpan voice I said, "Oh, I was yelling at the bear."

"To scare it away?"

"Yes, that's right. I'm gonna chase him all day. Maybe he'll go away." Then I paused. We were all looking down the trail where the bear was a moment ago. I realized that my screaming may have upset them. They didn't hike ten miles to Duck Hole to hear a man yell. "I'm sorry about the yelling. I didn't mean to disturb you."

Nearly in unison they replied they didn't mind and that I was doing my job. In a sense they were right. The DEC hates marauding bears and harasses them at any chance. The harassment is not limited to pepper spray. Law enforcement rangers have used paintball guns and fired rubber slugs out of twelve gauge shotguns. Avoiding all euphemism, they are labeled "problem bears" by backcountry managers, and problem bears have been a headache in the Adirondacks for as long as people have been visiting the Adirondacks. Problem bears tear open backpacks, break into cabins, fling lids off garbage cans, and generally run amok in search of anything that smells good because anything that smells good might taste good. From blocks of cheese, to bird food, to boxes of wine, black bears have devoured it all. The problem is, like us humans, the more they have the more they want.

The rest of the afternoon I stalked the Duck Hole bear, springing upon him unexpectedly like I sprang upon people who drank beer in lean-tos.

There he was, wading across the Cold River. "Hey! Yeah, I'm talkin' to you!" Up the opposite bank he scrambled.

And over there, sniffing the bottom of the dam and then clawing at it like a cat claws a couch. "Hey! You're not allowed here! Scram, you rodent!" He bounded away into the forest.

Now back up in the woods, lurking off the side of the trail, assessing opportunities for stealing a picnic basket. "Hey! Yogi! This ain't no cartoon!" Gone.

There he was, walking along the western shore of Duck Hole, several hundred feet from the dam and the lean-to. I ran up the shoreline, slaloming between balsam firs and hurdling downed trees. As I approached I slowed and caught my breath. He sensed me and ran. I ran after him, belting out threats and prejudice judgments. "You better run! No manners! I'm gonna tell your momma! Then you'll see what trouble is!" I headed back to the lean-to. My voice was hoarse and my throat hurt. But God was I having fun. There I was, getting paid to run through the woods threatening a bear.

Dusk settled upon Duck Hole. When the group of six realized that my camp was hidden out behind the lean-to in a rocky, damp, tight spot, they insisted I at least cook with them. It was a kind invitation, one of few I ever received from the public. I set up my stove next to theirs. The hum of the burning gas jets was gentle. They talked among themselves. I was content not joining their conversation. I looked across Duck Hole. Its surface was like glass, not a wave or even a ripple. The clouds moved in, and the forests lining the shores were black, already asleep under a dark purple sky.

After dinner I disassembled my stove, rinsed my cooking pot, and brushed and flossed while the group went off to hang their food. I went back to my camp and hung mine. Due to the nearby rushing Cold River, at my campsite it was difficult to hear anything that may have been in the woods around me. The bear could have been anywhere. Before turning in for the night, I decided to do one last bear patrol.

By now the woods were inky black and the group of six backpackers was asleep. The lean-to's floor was uneven and knotty, with a couple of holes worn though it (it was built in 1960). They chose to throw their sleeping pads and bags on a grassy, flat area twenty feet in front of the shelter. They were in a deep sleep, their tired legs, sore backs, and tight shoulders letting gravity have its way. No one snored. Their sleeping bags were neatly arranged in a row, one next to the other. They looked like a platter of different colored burritos.

Though I gave my eyes time to adjust to the night by not using my headlamp for nearly a half hour, relying on the cones in my eyes to grab specks of light, I couldn't see a thing. Instead of walking down the trails blindly and perhaps literally walking into the bear, I donned my headlamp and turned it on. The batteries were low. It shined a mere twenty feet before night swallowed its blue-white beam.

I walked the trails surrounding Duck Hole for a half hour before I found the bear. He was just off the trail back near the clearing where we first met at 2:00 P.M. It was now 10:00 P.M. We had put in a long day. I turned off my headlamp and spoke softly, "Mr. Bear, I'm not going to yell at you anymore. I'll let you sleep if you let me sleep. So go to bed, and I will do the same." Then I closed my proposal with a respectful "Goodnight." I turned, clicked my headlamp back on, and left him to think about my offer.

Despite being tired, it was too nice of a night to go to bed yet. I walked back to the lean-to. The campers were sleeping so soundly they looked dead. I tiptoed past them and walked up to the dam. An old, rickety footbridge spanned the structure. I walked out to the middle of the bridge. To my left, below me, were the glassy waters of Duck Hole while to the right was the head of the Cold River, tumbling and surging over boulders. The white noise was consistent, soothing, the same tone and cadence I had heard a dozen other nights at Duck Hole. I leaned on the footbridge railing and looked across the body of water. My eye lids got heavy, and my pack sagged down my back.

I heard a faint noise over the foaming river. "Snap." A small tree breaking. "Snap." Again. Louder. Then again. I turned around and looked to where I thought the noise was coming from. It came from a spot about 300 feet behind the lean-to. I muttered in half surprise, half disappointment, "You're kidding me."

I left the dam and hurriedly walked back to the lean-to. The campers were still sound asleep. I don't know how they didn't hear what I had heard over the noise of the foaming river. I walked to the back of the lean-to and heard the bear huffing in the darkness and pacing around my campsite. I told the bear, "If you're in my campsite, you are going to have to vacate." Eerily the noise ceased. "Okay." I wasn't sure what to say next . . . "I'm coming in."

With my headlamp limply throwing its light, I walked due south, straight towards my campsite and the bear. I spoke firmly. "Here I come, Mr. Bear. I'm coming back to my camp, and you are going to leave." I spoke to the bear mainly out of fear that he would charge me. I simply didn't have the nerve to harass a 300-pound nocturnal creature who was already pissed off at me. Chasing a bear during daylight is completely different than chasing a bear at night.

Within fifty feet of my campsite, the bear jogged south, paralleling the river downstream. I stepped into the area where my campsite was located, but I could not find it. I was confused. 300 feet behind the lean-to. Due south. How could I not find my campsite? Then, from underneath the top of a spruce tree that had fallen to the ground, I spotted a corner of my light green tarp. The top of the spruce tree mashed most of my shelter into the ground. I looked up to focus my light towards the top of the broken tree. In the canopy surrounding my campsite were a half-dozen other broken treetops.

Trying to make sense of what happened, I remembered: my food bag! I quickly looked back up and scanned my weak light into the darkness, panning back and forth. Relief. There was my yellow food bag, still hanging from that stout paper birch. I deduced what had happened. The bear found my bear hang to be too good. I outsmarted him there. What I had not noted when I hung my food was that the bag was touching the top of a baby spruce tree, and other baby spruces were close to the bag. The bear had tried to climb up each spruce, but as he neared their tops each one could not support the burden. They bent, bent, bent, down, down, down, until the full weight of the bear, making its slow descent back to Earth, snapped the saplings one after the other.

Knowing my food was still safe, I assessed by campsite. The bear had trashed it. Over there, a thermal top. On that branch, a sock. Way over there, another sock. The only thing noticeably damaged was my copy of *The Island of Doctor Moreau*. Pages were torn from the binding, and a few holes from the bear's incisors punctured the book through front cover to back cover. A corner was shredded and sticky.

The broken trees, collapsed shelter, and gear that looked like it was scattered by a leaf blower were enough to have me decide not to sleep in my campsite. I presumed the hanging food would draw the bear back for another try. I grabbed my fleece jacket, sleeping pad, and sleeping bag, and headed for the lean-to.

I set up my sleeping arrangement and fell asleep, my boots, canister of pepper spray, and headlamp placed near my head. My pack hung on a peg on the back wall of the shelter. I slept for twenty minutes when I suddenly had the urge to sit up. I had heard something. I scanned the clearing in front of the lean-to, and all looked expectedly black except for a spot to the left of the campers. It looked blacker than the rest of the black. Mr. Bear. He stood twenty feet from the campers. I could barely make out that he was again sniffing the air, like a ravenous animal trying to pinpoint a cookout. Perhaps he too thought the campers looked like burritos.

I grabbed my pepper spray and was about to remove the safety clip. But then I remembered Paul's nickname and how he got it. No way could I blast this bear without some of the irritant covering the campers. They would have been very unhappy. I also didn't want to wake them. So I started yelling at the bear in a whisper-scream. "Hey, you! Fatso!" The bear walked away.

Varied collections of this sequence were repeated a half-dozen times. I fell asleep. The bear approached the campers. I had a sudden urge to sit up. The bear was there. I couldn't spray him. I whisper-screamed. He walked away. I fell back asleep.

This game of cat and mouse wore on me. By 2:00 A.M. Sunday morning I was exhausted. I had tasted only nibbles of sleep during the past twenty hours, having woken at 6:00 A.M. on Saturday morning, hiked ten miles, and spent most of Saturday chasing this bear. My nerves were on edge. Sleeping campers or not, I promised myself that the next time this bear approached I was going to scare the hell out of him, spray him, or both. There was no sense in getting another fifteen minutes of fitful rest. Instead, I put my fleece jacket on, put my boots on, donned my headlamp, held onto my canister of pepper spray, and sat in the lean-to with my back against a side wall. Then I waited. And waited. And when I got done with that I waited some more. And then, I heard a noise.

From behind the lean-to I detected the bear slowly making his way towards the shelter. All through the night he had approached the shelter from the front, but seeing I was looking out the front each time he was caught, he abandoned that approach. He approached along this alternative route, his big, soft paws gently smushing the ground under him. The muffled snap of a small twig or the scuff of a paw was all that gave him away. Besides his heavy breathing.

Though bears are reputed to be intensely aware of their surroundings at most times—as this bear had shown—I have no doubt that he, for some reason, had no idea I was in the lean-to. I don't know if he forgot, assumed I was out on patrol, or by approaching the lean-to from a different prospective had something not click inside. No matter the reason, I was convinced he did not know I was there, right on the other side of the shelter's wall, waiting for him.

He walked along the outer wall until he was directly behind my back. And then, he paused. Little by little I silently turned my neck and shoulders to look behind me. Then I put my eye up to a tiny gap between the rows of logs that made up part of the shelter wall. As I peered through this slit, there was the bear's side just six inches—the thickness of the wall—from my eye. He was so close I could smell him, a scent that mirrored his home, the Adirondack woods. He smelled like pine cones and fall leaves, swamp water and pine pitch, rotting stumps and soil.

He continued to cautiously move towards the front of the lean-to, and his body brushed along the side of the shelter producing a smooth sweeping sound. He moved forward methodically, inch by inch, until his head eased forward of the front of the shelter. Slowly, delicately, I, too, inched forward until my head approached the open front. Once I moved far enough forward to see him, but not to be seen, I slowly turned to the right and looked into the back corner of the bear's eye.

I could feel his deep exhales fill the space around us, that muggy, hot air reminding me of dog breath. In the darkness I could make out his chunky incisors and imagined them crushing the bones of tiny prey, cracking open beechnuts, or systematically ripping up wildflowers and grass. I treasured the closeness and was as still as a fencepost, my heart beating. He did not notice me. Food was what was on his mind.

In that tight space, all my frustrations with the bear evaporated. Trying to grab the girl's food bag, loitering around the shelter and dam, trying to get my food bag, wrecking my campsite, and snapping trees didn't matter anymore. To me, he was just an animal trying to find a meal to eat. This bear wasn't a "problem bear" anymore. He was just a bear.

I had an obligation to the campers. No bear should be that close to them, and no bear should be trying to eat human food. When bears do that they get more dependent on us, less afraid. Sooner than later that bear will walk up to a human and either the bear or the human will prevail. The bear will swipe at someone or someone will shoot the bear dead.

He had to go.

I took a last look. He was nothing less than a big, black, beautiful bear, all bear and then some. This was likely the first and last close-up I would ever have of a bear.

I took a deep breath in and let out the scream of a banshee. "*Daaaaaahhhh!*"

Three hundred pounds of bear bounded into the air, completed a 180-degree turn midflight, and sprinted away—due south, away from the lean-to, parallel to the Cold River, straight towards my campsite, straight back the way he came. He took no turns, dodged no saplings. He went *through* everything. A "snap" followed by a "thud" followed by a "slam" followed by a "crash" as he sprinted from that mean assistant forest ranger who had scared the shit out of him. He bulldozed through the woods, the sounds of destruction interrupted by a short period of splashing as he crossed the Cold River.

When all was silent I remembered: the campers! I looked over at them and could not believe what I saw. There they were, still sound asleep. Perhaps they thought the screaming was all a dream. Maybe they *were* dead. I tossed the pepper spray canister into a back corner of the lean-to. I stayed in the shelter and slept, not waking for a moment and recalling no dreams. It was the sleep of an assistant forest ranger who had a long day.

In the morning I related the story to the campers, and when I got to the part about letting out my scream I asked, "You guys didn't hear that?"

"No."

The campers packed up their gear. They were going to another shelter in another part of the wilderness. I trudged back to my campsite behind the lean-to, dragged the spruce tops out of the way, picked up all my gear, and packed it in my pack. I looked south and could discern a narrow path of destruction marked by broken branches, torn up soil, and snapped logs where the bear had barreled away. The pathway kept going until it faded out of sight, cresting a rise and then descending towards the river.

During the rest of August and through September and October I made eight more trips to Duck Hole. During these visits I struck up casual conversations with campers, delicately asking them to not burn down outhouses, cut down live trees, pollute water sources, or feed wildlife. I inquired if they had seen any bears. No one had. The bear had moved on to another patch of Adirondack woods, hopefully avoiding people and living like a real bear.

Thirteen years after meeting the bear at Duck Hole, I still have my copy of *The Island of Doctor Moreau*. The missing pages, the holes in the covers, and the chewed-up corner remind me of that bear's teeth. Those big, white incisors I saw so close.

Molehill Bagger

In the United States bigger is always better, not only for homes, vehicles, and presidential campaign budgets, but for mountains as well. Simply put, it's all about the elevation. For example, most hikers have heard of 14,494-foot Mount Whitney, highpoint of California and the Lower Forty-Eight. Washington State's Mount Rainier, which also tops the 14,000-foot-level, is immensely popular. Each year 10,000 people attempt to reach this summit. East of Washington State the names Idaho and Montana conjure images of monstrous snow-capped peaks.

Utah, though having a reputation for being dry and desolate, is also regarded as a mountaineering destination, possessing nearly twenty peaks above 13,000 feet. Utah's name itself describes the original mountaineers of this land, the Utes: "people of the mountains." Ice survives summers at 13,000 feet in the Wind River Range of nearby Wyoming. Continuing eastward, Colorado is encountered. More than fifty 14,000-foot mountains reside within the Centennial State's borders.

Once you travel east of the Rockies, the elevation drops consistently and considerably. By the time you get to the Adirondack Mountains 2,000 miles from the Rocky Mountains, you have high country that Westerners call hills. No summits dare to rise above 6,000 feet, and only two, Mount Marcy and Algonquin Peak, are brave enough to break the 5,000-foot-level. Every other single square inch of dirt and rock inside the six-million-acre Adirondack Park is below 5,000 feet.

What we lack in elevation we gain in sheer numbers of mountains: 39 above 4,000 feet, 217 above 3,000 feet, 592 above 2,500 feet. A good guess is that we have more than 2,000 summits above 2,000 feet. Our peaks are low but, boy, do we have a lot of them. And you know what? No pun intended, it doesn't make a hill of beans difference to us if our beloved Adirondacks are foothills compared to the "real" mountains of the American West. Our mountains are worth climbing.

What makes perfect sense is that the more summits you reach, the tougher your journey will be. For example, climbing the two Adirondack 5,000-footers is easy. Complete two day hikes totaling less than 25 miles of hiking and 7,000 vertical feet of climbing, and you will be done. Tens of thousands of people have reached both summits, and it was first done in 1837.

Dropping to a 4,000-foot-level increases the difficulty of your mountaineering quest. Cover around 250 miles of hiking and 70,000 vertical feet of climbing, and you have bagged these 39 peaks. About 10,000 people have successfully met this challenge. Three men, Herb Clark and Bob and George Marshall, finished hiking every single 4,000-foot peak in 1925. They had begun their pursuit of these high summits seven years earlier. All 4,000-footers can be reached via day hikes.

Shortly after these three men's journey a phrase was coined: peakbagger. Guy and Laura Waterman, in their book *Forest and Crag*, define these people and their pursuit.

Peakbaggers are people who aim to climb a large number of peaks, usually a list of specific peaks, such as the 4,000-footers of a particular range, state, or region (the Adirondacks, New Hampshire, New England). Peakbagging is the pursuit of this activity. The term is used by some with connotations of disdain for the activity but by others as simply descriptive, with no value judgments implied.

After climbing the 4,000-footers, whether you like it or not, you are a peakbagger. If you decide you want to reach every Adirondack mountain above 3,000 feet, you're going to have to do an awful lot of hiking. It's estimated that you will have to cover 1,000 miles of terrain and climb nearly 250,000 vertical feet, which is equal to hiking half of the Appalachian Trail. Operating below the 4,000-foot-level you will have to navigate up 140 mountains that have no trails to their tops. You'll learn why traveling off-trail is called "bushwhacking." Fewer than ten people have reached all 217 3,000-foot peaks. The first two to do so finished during the late 1990s after ten years of hiking.

To hike every mountain above 2,500 feet is a serious journey that no one has completed. You will have to cover somewhere around 2,000 miles and climb a whopping 400,000 vertical feet, which is equal to hiking the Appalachian Trail. What will be the pebble in your shoe is that 500 of the 592 peaks have no trails to their tops. If you successfully reach every summit you won't just be king of the mountains. You'll be king of the molehills.

My molehill addiction started during the mid-1990s. I was on top of Mount Abraham in Vermont, enjoying a gorgeous winter day. A blue sky stretched from horizon-to-horizon.

Three state highpoints—Mount Marcy of New York, Mount Mansfield of Vermont, and Mount Washington of New Hampshire—could be seen to the west, north, and east, respectively. The sun reflected off the snow pack, roasting my face red.

The other resident of the summit was a man with an ice-encrusted beard whose well-worn gear spoke of his experience. He came over and politely inquired about the patch on my pack that declared I had climbed the 4,000-foot mountains of the Adirondacks. I told him that with the completion of that hiking goal I was on the prowl for a new list of mountains and wanted to stay in the Northeast.

This summit partner of mine suggested I take up hiking on an accelerated level, a task best completed, he insisted, on mountains lower than what I was used to climbing. He suggested I contact a man who had a directory of the 770 3,000-foot peaks of the northeast United States. He mentioned not to get too excited though. Only two people had successfully climbed all 770: the guy who had the list and a friend of the guy who had the list. The gentleman on top of Mount Abraham said both of these guys were "crazy." I was given an address.

When I returned home from my Vermont hike I wrote the list bearer in New Jersey, asking if he would mail me a copy. Two weeks later I opened a large manila envelope containing thirteen crisp white pages listing every mountain above 3,000 feet in Pennsylvania, New York, Massachusetts, Vermont, New Hampshire, and Maine. I scanned page after page and realized that I had not hiked much in the Northeast, at least compared to the guy who mailed me the list.

I calculated that to summit all 770 would require me to hike 2,400 miles and ascend 700,000 vertical feet. More than 400 peaks had no trails to their summits. Seventy were unnamed. Many possessed reputations as "slag hills," "heinous bushwhacks," and "miserable, little peaks," along with names unfit for print. By 2004 I had reached peak number 770, a trailless summit 22 miles from the nearest piece of pavement, deep in the wilds of Maine. The modesty of the lower mountains I chased when completing "the 770" was a welcome change from the high-profile 4,000-footers. On the moose paths and briar fields of my little ridges it wasn't about "summit bids," "base camps," and "topping out," along with all the other glory terms. No dramatic rhetoric is needed to describe a 3,000-foot hill that has no name and no view and is located in an unincorporated township that nobody lives in. I fell in love with molehills.

"Give me more mountains!" I said when I got back to New York. But no one would give them to me. That is, nobody had a list of every single Adirondack peak between 2,500 and 2,999 feet, the next level of mountains I would pursue. I had to find them myself.

Once I located a mountain on one of my many topographic maps, two qualifiers had to be determined: height and rise. Concerning height, a peak must be at least 2,500 feet tall and less than 3,000 feet tall. To make my work more difficult, not all maps are portrayed in feet. Some are metric. For the metric maps I did conversions for every peak that may have qualified as a legitimate 2,500-footer. I multiplied all metric summit measurements by 3.2808 (the number of feet in one meter). For metric readings a peak must range from 762 to 914 meters in height. Concerning rise, in the Northeast a mountain needs to rise at least 200 feet on each side to be regarded as a "real" mountain. Like with height, metric measurements were converted to feet. For metric readings a peak must rise at least 61 meters. After spending weeks scouring nearly every acre of the Adirondack Mountains, I determined there are 592 summits 2,500 feet and higher. The ones I now care about, and the ones this story is about, are the 375 summits between 2,500 and 2,999 feet. These are the ones that no one man (or woman) has climbed.

Since I have always been interested in toponyms, that is, the names of natural features, the names of my new-found peaks have been of particular interest to me. But first, out of the 375 mountains, more than 100 are officially unnamed. Having to name them all to keep these anonymous hills straight in my mind, I often named them for already-named features they are close to. "White Birch Lake Peak" is near this lake, "Robbs Creek Peak" is near this creek, "Hell Devil Dam Peak" is near this old logging dam, and "Kings Pond Peak"is next to this pond. The only mountain I did not name for a localized, already-named feature is "Thirteen Summit Bumps Peak." A mountain with more than a dozen summits clustered together has earned its own unique name.

The nearly 275 named mountains fascinate me because each name has a story behind it. I recorded the historical significance of place names in my *History Inside the Blue Line.*

That's what the history of the Adirondack Mountains is: a history of the people behind the names. The hills, streams, and lakes were there before we were. . . . But when we eventually arrived in the wilderness, an arrival as sure as the rising sun, our existence was then known. . . . And we left our mark on the land wherever we went, most notably through place names.

2,500-foot mountains named for fauna are common. Beaver Mountain, Buck Mountain, Panther Mountain, Pigeon Mountain, and Bearpen Peak are but a few. Mountains named for flora are common, too. Oak Ridge, Long Pine Mountain, Blueberry Mountain, and Black Ash Mountain are some.

Many names are transparent concerning their conception: Ragged Mountain (a jagged peak), T Lake Mountain (above a lake that's shaped like a "T"), Big Burn Mountain (experienced a wild fire), Pitchoff Mountain (has steep sides), and Windfall Mountain (experienced a windstorm that knocked down the forest). Others pay homage to people who were so connected to the land that they now live among their hills eternally. Washburn Ridge, Stacey Mountain, Kate Mountain, Jones Mountain, and Hayes Mountain are examples.

Told here is a trip to five unnamed 2,500-foot peaks deep inside 172,000-acre West Canada Lake Wilderness Area during

October 2013. Being the second biggest wilderness area east of Minnesota and north of Georgia, the only bigger Northeast wilderness area is our High Peaks Wilderness Area. Through this story of a two-day climbing trip up a collection of summits, I'll show what it's like to be a molehill bagger. By this end of the story perhaps you'll be the one saying "Give me more mountains!"

I pulled up to the Haskells Road trailhead in the Town of Piseco in south-central Hamilton County. It was a perfect day during my favorite season. The last two weeks of September and first two weeks of October present the best thirty-day period in the mountains. Characterized by low humidity, cool temperatures, fall foliage, and no biting bugs, autumn is hard to beat.

The Haskells Road trailhead is the southeast entrance to West Canada Lake Wilderness Area, the trail leading from this trailhead being a portion of the 133-mile Northville Placid Trail, the oldest long-distance trail in the Adirondacks. I backed my 1995 Toyota Camry, with a proud 370,000 miles on it, into the dirt parking area, my tires crunching the tight sand and gravel. I downed the rest of my Stewart's coffee, popped the trunk, and got out to sort through my pack one last time.

No matter what time of year I'm in the mountains, I go light, though winter requires me to go the least-light of all seasons. My 2,800-cubic-inch day pack was only two-thirds full, even with my food bag inside. My home for the night consisted of a ground sheet, which was a contractor's garbage bag with the bottom seam and a side seam cut so it laid its full size flat. On this I would lay my seventeen-ounce down sleeping bag, which I called "the eggplant" both for its shape and its color. Over this bed, if the night sky was not clear, I would string my six-foot by eight-foot light green tarp up in the shape of an A-frame. With below-freezing temperatures rare during October, even in the mountains, I didn't bring many clothes. I carried a lightweight set of thermal underwear, an extra thermal top, a down vest, a winter hat, a Gore-tex jacket, and an extra pair of wool socks. Since I was going to be out for just one night, I didn't bring food that required cooking. Little odds and ends went into my ditty bag: extra cord, fire starter kit, extra map and compass, headlamp, extra batteries, journal, whistle, bandana, baby wipes, toothpaste and toothbrush, foot powder, compression bandage, and a roll of athletic tape and tiny container of petroleum jelly in case of blisters.

I brought two cameras. One was my 2010 GoPro Hero high-definition video camera, which also takes great stills, and the other was my worn-out Sony Cyber-shot digital camera from 2005. The Sony camera was barely operational. We had been through a lot together. By the time I walked into West Canada Lake Wilderness Area that fall day, this camera had taken more than 11,000 photos. We couldn't part ways just yet.

The contents of my food bag were calorie-dense and durable, food a dietician or dentist would warn against: peanut butter, Jolly Ranchers, extra sharp cheddar cheese, chocolate chips, dried and sweetened cranberries, Pop Tarts, Cheezits, bagels, and a small stick of pepperoni I had cut up into bite sized pieces. I brought half an apple pie for dinner. In the woods I drink only water, except during winter when I make tea or cocoa. But that's just flavored water served hot. Contrary to most backpackers' practice, I do not treat any of my woods water.

I donned my pack and started down the trail, due north towards the interior. I encountered a Department of Environmental Conservation informational kiosk. At the kiosk was a map as well as a whole host of warnings to keep hikers from becoming lost or injured. Like at all of these kiosks, there was a register where hikers recorded where they were going. This registration process helps measure trail use and assists forest rangers in locating overdue hikers.

I signed in. "Date: 10/13. Name: E. Schlimmer. Address: Oneonta, NY. Total number in group: 1. Length of stay (days): 2. Where do you plan to go, and what trail or route will you take: Spoon Lake." I flipped through the 100 or 200 entries prior to mine and saw that no one had written "Spoon Lake" as their destination. I was not surprised.

Spoon Lake is truly in the middle of nowhere. No trails lead to it. But to be honest, I wasn't going to Spoon Lake. I was going to "Spoon Lake Peak," which is a quarter-mile south of, and 500 vertical feet directly above, Spoon Lake. Since this peak is officially unnamed though, it made no sense to write Spoon Lake Peak since no one would have known where and what that really was. For a recorded destination the lake was close enough.

If I reached Spoon Lake Peak during this trip, I would reach one of the most remote mountains in the Adirondack Park. There is no easy, short, or quick way to it. From the trailhead Spoon Lake Peak was more than twelve miles away. Nearly half this distance, and nearly all of the climbing, would be off-trail. Since I would be climbing two other 2,500-foot peaks on my way to Spoon Lake Peak, I'd have to climb more than 3,000 vertical feet this first day.

I finished signing in and hit the trail. I walked north, feeling my pack settle onto my shoulders, the laces on my boots stretch across my feet, and the cool, fall air strain through my beard. I had gotten a late start—10:30 A.M.—but I knew I could hike quickly on the Northville Placid Trail. I covered the seven miles' worth of trail in three hours, a respectable pace. I felt good. I had my bushwhacking legs under me for Spoon Lake Peak and its neighbors.

My checkpoint for leaving the Northville Placid Trail was Bloodgood Brook, which crosses the trail. Being fall, a dry time of year, this modest stream was particularly low, and I saw it before I heard it. It's usually the other way around. I stopped before the brook, dropped my pack, and dug out my compass. I also took out my detailed topographic map, which replaced the overview map I used to navigate down the Northville Placid Trail. I ate a handful of chocolate chips and a big dollop of peanut butter, knowing these fat-saturated calories would give me sustained energy. I already wanted to eat that apple pie.

Since I had many, many miles to bushwhack across and many, many vertical feet to climb, Spoon Lake Peak was not on my mind at all. If I were to have stood next to Bloodgood Brook and thought about all the spruce thickets I had to push through, the young American beech stands I had to fight through, and the cliffs I had to circumnavigate to get to Spoon Lake Peak, the journey would have sounded too daunting. For the moment I had but one brief, attainable goal. I had to get to the top of my first mountain of the trip, "Bloodgood Brook Peak."

I left the west—left—side of the Northville Placid Trail, leaving all footpaths behind for the next 24 hours. It was liberating to get off the trail and into wild land. I've always felt most alive where there are no traces of humans. But there were traces of humans on my way to Bloodgood Brook Peak, at least at the beginning. I paralleled Bloodgood Brook on an old logging road, which could be discerned only with a sharp eye. I followed this wet pathway of mud, ferns, and muck to my first off-trail checkpoint: an unnamed wetland, the source of 1.5-mile-long Bloodgood Brook. After filling my water bottle at this small pond I started climbing. I would not see Bloodgood Brook for the rest of the trip.

An open hardwood forest of American beech, yellow birch, and maples bounded towards the top of Bloodgood Brook Peak. The ascent of less than a half-mile took twenty minutes. Upon reaching the apex of this 2,628-foot peak, the top wearing a cap of evergreens, I sat down and reached into my pack to grab what I always grab on top of a summit, which was my water bottle, something to eat, and my journal.

When I started climbing mountains in the mid-1990s, I didn't carry a journal. I also didn't carry a camera. With youth and overconfidence on my side, as such two go together, I figured that I would remember every mountain I climbed. I actually did. Until about mountain number fifty. Then I learned that all my experiences and all the things I saw would be lost to time; runaways never to return home. Since 1998 I have recorded my thoughts on every summit of consequence, that first entry recorded on Dorset Peak in Vermont. This was before any inkling of climbing anything other than high peaks

crossed my mind. I have filled nearly a dozen journals s
that trip up Dorset Peak sixteen years ago. With each jou..ıaı
holding 125 entries, as of this writing (March 2015) I have recorded my time on more than 1,600 mountains. That's a lot of
memories that would have been lost otherwise. I wouldn't let
Bloodgood Brook Peak slip away.

*Thank God for fall. Light breeze, sun, no humidity, no bugs,
65°. Wow. What a waste to come in here during June or July.
3.5 hours from Haskells Road and NPT trailhead. Not bad
at all. Nice summit of mixed woods. Quieter than a death
row cell. Light pack—no kitchen, no sleeping pad. Don't
need 'em. 2:10 PM. 10/13/13. Can't beat October. Not tired.*

With Bloodgood Brook Peak in the books, I put my pack
back on and made sure I had my watch, compass, and map;
my three tools of navigation. I then began descending due
south towards my next mountain.

If bushwhackers were forced to choose one mammal to dislike it would likely be the American beaver. Why? Beavers
flood forests that bushwhackers want to hike through. Living
in nearly every conceivable type of wetland, beavers are very
good at expanding these lakes, ponds, and swamps to flood
acres of surrounding forest. Hikers like me find their compass
bearings dead-ending in wetlands that are not portrayed on
maps. Beavers are good at what they do. They can gnaw
through five-inch-diameter willows in less than three minutes
and can even gnaw underwater. Some Adirondack beaver
dams are quite impressive, measuring more than fifty feet long
and over seven feet tall.

My bearing took me straight into beaver country. At least
three expansive wetlands threatened to interrupt my course,
the first two unnamed, the final one being Belden Vly. I
stuck to high ground and wound my way around these following a course south, then southwest, then south again,
then southeast, and south again. Arriving at the base of my

next mountain, 2,707-foot "Amos Lake Peak" with dry boots, I was happy with my navigation and luck.

In the world of molehill bagging, what comes down must go up. I followed the eastern ridge of Amos Lake Peak, climbing in the deep shade of a spruce and fir canopy. When I reached the top of mountain number two, I was halfway to Spoon Lake Peak. I pulled out my journal.

Spoon Lake Peak bound! Shit, that's remote. But it's on the list—and near the top of it in elevation—and it is logical to go there when I am back here. Wish I could go up Grass Mountain, too, but that's too far. Mr. Blue Jay and Mrs. Hairy Woodpecker keep me company. Tippy top is a jut of rock and spruce. 3:40. Sunny, 65°, and calm.

Spoon Lake Peak, the one and only, was southwest of my perch, but to avoid a series of wetlands I headed due west. Fascinated with remote, named features, I also detoured to visit Amos Lake, a feature whose toponym history remains a mystery.

Amos Lake looked like every other remote Adirondack lake I had been to. I was not disappointed. Puffy white clouds had moved in, elbowing their way across the blue sky. The mix of white and blue looked like a watercolor painting when I viewed it in the reflection of Amos Lake. A dark green spruce forest formed the borders of the canvas. A woodpecker tapped on a dead tree in the distance, his "tut-tut-tut" echoing across the lake. I thought to myself, "This is why I do this." It was likely that no one had been to Amos Lake during the past 100 years. The last visitor was probably a logger, back then called a lumberjack, during the great Adirondack logging era.

I was tired. I finished my quart of water and then filled up my bottle and drank the whole thing, making sure I was hydrated for the final climb and night of camping. I topped off my bottle with Amos Lake water and began the last climb of the day, which was a grinding 1.5-mile push up 700 vertical feet. Towards Spoon Lake Peak I climbed, first through the hobblebush and brambles, then through the hardwood forests, and finally into the pure spruce and fir forests of the upper elevations. The nearest trail was miles behind me. A vast bank of gray clouds had moved in and took my blue sky away from me, which I thought was unfair. My mood fell like a stone. I was tired at the bottom of the climb, very tired halfway up, and exhausted by the time I hit the 2,600-foot-level. I stumbled up the incline bumping into trees and tripping over downed branches like a reveler who had one drink too many.

At 2,700 feet, where I crossed from the Town of Arietta into the Town of Morehouse, I was officially whupped. I stopped, took my pack off, and sat down for a moment. I dug out my food bag and found the bag of Jolly Ranchers. I picked out a grape one, unwrapped it, and popped it in my mouth. If only it was sunny out. I'd feel better then. The hard candy didn't give me the energy I needed.

Like a good soldier, I got back on my feet. As the ridgeline leveled off after I had crossed two false summits, I was confident I was on top. And none too soon. It was dusk. I was worn-out, but I wanted to make sure I was on the tippy top of my most remote mountain yet. Without hesitating I plowed straight across what I thought was the 2,923-foot top. I kept heading west, stretching my burning legs over downed trees, ducking under spruce branches, and trying to find the path of least resistance in a land with no trails. After a few minutes I started descending. I stopped. All that stood in front of me were the tops of spruce trees poking up from the ridge that dipped down, down, down in front of me, bottoming out in the Indian River.

On the horizon was sunset. No reds, oranges, or pinks could be found in this one. With the low cloud bank and gray light, the sunset was only a lighter shade of gray than the sky overhead. The gloomy light made the trees, dirt, and boulders look like they were painted in a chalky matte finish. My eyes grew tired trying to imagine the normal glossy finish of a high summit.

I climbed back east and found the exact highpoint, which was a nondescript mound of moss. I savored the feeling of being isolated. If I had hiked north or east I would have not encountered a road for eleven miles. If I had headed south or west it would have been five miles before I hit a road.

I looked north towards Spoon Lake, and this body of water was hidden, nestled below the steep north side of my mountain. Due north, through the trees, I could make out the two-mile-wide mass of Spruce Lake Mountain, a 3,000-foot peak that's surrounded on all sides by water. Lakes, streams, and marshes guard its base like a string of moats. Views south were filtered by the evergreen forest, but I could distinguish high country. I found Twin Mountain, Grass Mountain, the Metcalf Range, and more peaks I had never been up.

I looked around my beautiful, remote summit one last time. Chances were very good I would never be there again, and I figured that no one else's boot print would be on this summit for a long time. I left the summit and descended east for a few minutes back down my ridgeline. Finding a flat, open area I threw my pack down. God that felt good. I looked around. Silent is not a strong enough adjective to describe how quiet it was. Nothing could be heard in the distance. No logging trucks, no planes, no chainsaws. The terrible racket from man's loudest creations couldn't reach the top of Spoon Lake Peak. Nothing stirred. The needles on the evergreens, the ferns that grew in little plots, and the leaves on the handful of hardwoods were motionless. It was as if the whole mountain was sleeping, and I was the only one still up. I tiptoed around.

I took off my sweat-soaked shirt and hung it on a branch. Then I dumped the contents of my pack in a pile on the forest floor. I found my ground sheet and laid it down. My sleeping bag—the eggplant—was picked out next. I neatly piled my clothes onto the side of the ground sheet and tossed my down vest at the top of my sleeping bag. The vest would later be my pillow. Before it got too dark I found my headlamp and tested it. My work done, I sat down and wrote in the fading light.

Spoon Lake Peak! Wow. One of the most remote peaks I've been up. Cool. Forgot my spoon though. Will have to eat all this apple pie with something else. Top at 6:40. Now on summit ridge at ~2,910'. Pretty top. Pretty damn tired. Was walking like I drank two beers. Cloudy, 60°, calm, quiet.

My food bag was heavy, but I could have devoured every single morsel before bedtime. I burrowed my hand inside of it. From hundreds of nights in the woods I can tell the difference between foods just by touch, even telling the difference between, when I have them, couscous and textured vegetable protein, gummi bears and Swedish fish. I found what I was looking for: a Tupperware container. I pulled it out, eased back the lid, and there it was, half of an entire apple pie. My smile beamed a bright light through the dreary forest. With no utensil to eat with (what are the chances that I would forget to bring my spoon to, of all places, Spoon Lake Peak?), I found my travel-size tube of toothpaste and crimped a fold down the middle of it to make it rigid. With the tube of toothpaste I dug into the pie, which was pulverized into a pile of delicious, soggy crust and gooey, sweet filling.

Between bites I took off my filthy leather boots and re-moved the insoles to dry. I took off my dirty, stinky wool socks and hung them from a branch. "Ah, what the hell?" I thought. I took off my pants and hung them on a branch to dry. All of naked me ate and drank and was suddenly very merry. I could not have cared less about all those Western states with their gigantic mountains. Spoon Lake Peak was all I needed. So what if I was 450 feet below the lowest point in Colorado? I was naked and eating an apple pie on top of a peak that no one had climbed in a hundred years, if ever. No 14,000-foot moun-tain could beat that.

After dinner I powdered my feet, took a baby wipe shower, got dressed in my clean long underwear, and made sure my gear was neatly organized. With the clouds now dark, I knew there was a chance for rain. I noted where two spruce trees were nearby. If it started sprinkling in the middle of the night, I could quickly string up my shelter and crawl underneath it.

In a sleep so deep that only exhausted bushwhackers can enter it, I heard a few raindrops "pit, pit, pit" on the eggplant around 10:00 P.M. I leapt up, put on my headlamp, and, making sure not to poke myself in the eye with a spruce branch, strung up my tarp in a low A-frame. I grabbed hold of the bottom of my ground sheet and gently slid the entire package under the tarp. I went from sleeping in the open to protected by my shelter in three minutes. I fell back asleep happy with my efficiency.

Many hours later, first over the Granite Mountains of Maine, then the White Mountains of New Hampshire, and finally the Green Mountains of Vermont, the sun rose. I could not note when the light of day hit the top of Spoon Lake Peak. With a sea of immobile clouds over my head, there was no real sunrise. It just got less gray until my world was off-white. I sat up scrunched under my tarp and rubbed my eyes. It was raining, though lightly. The tip of my nose was cold.

My warm, dry sleeping bag felt so good. The ground underneath my tarp was bone-dry. Outside the protection of my tarp the ground was soaked, the evergreen needles and hardwood leaves laid flat on the wet ground like they crawled out of a lake and died in my camp. Hiking on trails when the woods are wet, even when it's raining, is not that bad. You put on your rain jacket and cinch a waterproof cover around your pack, and everything inside, including you, stays dry. Bushwhacking through wet woods, whether it's still raining or not, is miserable. The only comparison is if you hiked through a car wash. The branches continually swipe across your legs, torso, and face, each swipe bringing fresh, cold water.

I didn't want to get up. The off-white color, the pitter-patter of rain on my tarp, and that drowsy, warm, soft feeling in my bag. It was too heavenly. I shut my eyes and dozed for ten minutes, then sat up again. It was time to go. I ate a Pop Tart, finished what remained of my quart of water, put on my cold, damp hiking clothes, and then packed while hunched on my knees under my tarp. I packed everything inside a trash compactor bag that lined the inside of the pack. A pack cover is useless to bushwhackers. The branches will shred it or rip it right off your pack without you even knowing it. I mashed my gear deep into my pack and tied off the top of the trash compactor bag. Now I could throw my pack into a lake and the contents would remain dry.

I crawled out from underneath the tarp and stood up. It had stopped raining. I pulled my pack out from under the tarp and stood it under a spruce tree. Its bark looked like flakes of burnt potato chips. I took down the tarp, shook most of the rainwater off it, and then stowed it in an outer pocket on my pack. The tarp was already soaked. It didn't matter if the forests' branches swiped at it all day.

I put on my pack and set my compass east, down the ridgeline I came up the evening before. I descended and came to a flat area on the ridge, my checkpoint for adjusting my bearing towards my next mountain. I dropped off the side of the ridge heading southeast, the steep grade challenging first thing in the morning. Below me, through the mist, I could see my next checkpoint: an unnamed lake at 2,600 feet.

I reached the lake and fresh water. This body of water looked like Amos Lake, which looked like all the rest of the Adirondack lakes. That is, beautiful. This one held an open spruce forest on its northwest shore and I strolled through it, no branches touching me or my pack, the ground under my feet dry due to the dense canopy over me. It was like hiking through the evergreen glades I had explored around Lake Tahoe, the Rocky Mountains, and New Mexico. If all the woods in the Adirondacks were this open, this bushwhacker-friendly, I'd hike even more.

I hopped across the inlet of the lake, climbed and topped a small hill on the other side, and began my long descent towards the headwaters of the South Branch of West Canada Creek. The forest was inexplicably varied with a quarter mile being hardwood forest, then a quarter mile being wastelands of hobblebush and second growth, then a half-mile being as-thick-as-it-gets evergreen forest. As I pushed intrusive branches away from my face, cold water ran down the inside of my jacket's sleeves. By this point my Gore-tex jacket was more for looks than anything else. I was soaked.

At the bottom of my hill I reached the upper reaches of the eighteen-mile-long South Branch of West Canada Creek. It was just three feet wide. At its mouth where it meets the Mohawk River in Herkimer it's 500 feet wide, and you can't see the bottom. This little unnamed source stream curled and swept down bare bedrock, carving a path through the dead hardwood leaves. The stream was nearly silent, running on smooth slabs with neither rocks nor pebbles to interrupt its flow. I hiked downstream and heard, and then saw, a waterfall. An enormous yellow birch, the largest hardwood species in the Adirondacks, leaned over the six-foot-tall waterfall.

Underneath the massive trunk was dry ground. I sat on this three-square-foot patch of dry leaves and dirt and leaned back on my pack, my knees pulled up to my chest. As far as I could see were wet woods. Stumps, leaves, moss, trees, branches, rocks, logs, boulders, needles, bark, lichen, ferns, and grasses were all soaked, as if sprayed by some giant fire hose. I wiggled out from my pack and ate a bagel, cheese, and pepperoni sandwich.

I drank another quart, gathering it from the stream. The water was cold and heavy and sat in my stomach like chilled mercury. I could feel it jostling around inside of me as I stood up and grabbed my pack. Peak number four awaited my arrival.

I reached the top in less than a half hour, climbing steeply at first and then following a barely perceptible grade to the tippy top, which was a wet patch of leaves in a wet patch of woods. I humored myself and looked for somewhere dry to sit. I actually found it. A spruce tree had blown over but was hung up in other trees. Balanced three feet off the forest floor, the spruce provided an eighteen-inch wide roof, wide enough for my butt. I scooted under the trunk and took out my journal. 2,595-foot "Buck Ponds' North Peak" had been reached.

Rain, rain, go away. Cloudy with occasional light drizzle. Not too bad, but the bushwhacking is wet. Just before prior stream, found my biggest burl ever (probably): 70" tall and 140" wide. Wow! Wrapped around a big yellow birch. Open woods ascent, thank goodness. Sitting under a blown-over, old, dead spruce—this is the only dry spot up here. 9:50. A bit over two hours over from camp.

A burl is a cankerous growth on the side of a tree, looking kind of like an enormous, grotesque peanut. Burls the size of goldfish bowls are common. Ones the size of microwaves are rare. Burls the size of La-Z-Boys, like the one I found, are extremely rare. Despite hiking 10,000 miles, most of it in the Northeast, I had never seen one that big. Burls are the treasures of woodworkers who like to remove them from trees and then hollow the burls out to make bowls. If a woodworker could somehow haul this burl out of the wilderness, he wouldn't carve a measly bowl out of it. He'd be the first to produce a burl bathtub.

Four peaks down, one to go. I crawled out of my dry spot and set a due east bearing straight away from the peak I was on and straight towards its twin, 2,556-foot "Buck Ponds' North-northeast Peak." It was a short traverse. Down 250 vertical feet, up 250 vertical feet, and across one mile, and I was at the top.

Last peak of the day and the trip. Overcast all around, sprinkles of chilly rain now and then. The ascent was not bad at all—just a little beech-whacking and hobblebush-whacking. Wish I had another night out here. Build a big fire and dry out. Mixed woods with some maples on top. 10:50 AM. 55°. Calm. Wet feet, wet pants, wet pack. Good times.

Buck Ponds' North-northeast Peak was my 377th of the 592 peaks. At the end of the trip I'd still have more than 200 mountains between 2,500 and 2,999 feet to go. It was a comforting thought, not overwhelming. Though I was wet, tired, and cold on top of Buck Ponds' North-northeast Peak (a name that never rolls off the tongue), I was already thinking about my next trip up more molehills. The thing I am most concerned with while climbing the peaks on this long list is that one day I may finish. Then I won't know what to do.

I took my boots off and wrung out my socks. Stinky, warm water squished out of them. The peaks were climbed, but there was no easy way back to the Northville Placid Trail, which was two miles as the crow flies. But I'm no crow. A puzzling complex of ridgelines, peaks, swamps, valleys, and lakes stood in the way of hope for a straight shot to the trail. I descended northeast, then went east, southeast, and east again and met a pretty stream. I recognized it.

The unnamed stream drained off the north side of "White Birch Lake Peak," a 2,500-footer I had climbed that past July. During that trip the blood-sucking insects had more fun than I did. In my journal that summer day the writing was all about bugs, not the beauty of the forest or the route I took. Wearing a bug hat, bug head net, long pants, a long-sleeved shirt, and my Gore-tex jacket (with the hood up) in the hot sun of that day, I was very much looking forward to fall. And here I was.

I followed the stream down to the lake it drained into, an unnamed body of water in the northern shadow of White Birch Lake Peak. I had never been to this remote lake. Like the rest of the lakes on this trip, it was beautiful. And like the rest of the lakes on this trip, I imagined building a small cabin along its shore and living there far from technoindustrial society. "Only the hermit is completely free."

Skirting the south shore of the pond, fighting my way through thick spruce forests that thrived in the direct sunlight the shoreline provided, I eventually left the pond behind. I popped up on a ridge, crossed it, and descended. Within an hour I hit the Northville Placid Trail. I turned southeast—right—on the trail. The footpath felt solid under my boots. I hiked ten minutes down the trail to Fall Stream, crossed it by hopping from rock to rock, got to the other side, and took off my pack. It had stopped raining. Blue sky was definitely not going to visit me this day, but being on the trail and out of the wet woods almost made me feel dry. I grabbed a snack and polished off my quart of water. I sat down, took off my boots, and wrung out my socks. Sticky brown water squished out of them.

Boots back on, pack back on, and back on my feet, not hungry, not thirsty, I strolled down the trail thankful for many things. The trail itself. Success on reaching all five peaks. Not getting hurt. Not getting lost. Being healthy enough to be out in the hills. Having the passion to explore the far flung, unnamed corners. The list could have gone on. I was just thankful to be there.

Two hours later I reached the Department of Environmental Conservation trailhead kiosk. I opened the register to put a check in the "out" box next to my name. People had signed in since I had the day before. Most were traversing the Northville Placid Trail. Some were going to Spruce Lake for the night. Others were exploring the trail a short distance to get away, walk their dog, or take some photos. No one was signed in to go to Spoon Lake.

The Navigator

Sophus Von Dorrien. What a name. Strong. Dark. Purposeful. Von Dorrien, born in Germany on August 10, 1832, sometimes recorded his name as "S.V. Dorrien." But this abbreviated version doesn't have the oomph of his full given name. Von Dorrien's influence on the Adirondack Mountains as well as the Adirondack Park was indirect yet meaningful enough to have his name bestowed upon a mountain: 3,012-foot Van Dorrien Mountain. And, yes, it is *Von* Dorrien but *Van* Dorrien Mountain. In the Adirondacks, as well as any other mountain range one well might imagine, mountaintop eulogies have gone awry in a wilderness of misspellings. For example, Wakely Mountain is named for William *Wakeley*, Pillsbury Mountain is named for Louis Dwight *Pilsbury*, and Lamphere Ridge is named for a member of the *Lanphere* family.

Such misspellings are more commonplace than one may think. In today's age of high-fidelity communication, typographical errors become obvious quickly. There are source works that can be accessed, and plenty of people can be met, called, written, or emailed to make sure a person's name is spelled correctly before it's put on a map. Not so during the 1800s, the heyday of the naming of Adirondack features. Many place name histories and local cultural histories were passed down through light conversation by immigrants with strange accents or recorded in sloppy cursive handwriting, sometimes by people who were barely literate.

Thus when Mr. Wakeley was eulogized someone likely guessed the spelling of his name (to make matters worse in this specific case, Wakeley himself was illiterate). Pillsbury (with the double "l") is a much more common spelling than Pilsbury. Right now my spell-check program is encouraging me to change it to two l's. "Lanphere" sounds a heck of a lot like "Lamphere," and a cursive "n" is a near twin of a cursive "m." Concerning the naming of our peak, "Von" sounds like "Van," and a cursive "o" looks like a cursive "a." The misspelling on Van Dorrien Mountain goes unnoticed though. Only a handful of Adirondackers have heard of Van Dorrien Mountain. If they have, they probably don't have a clue as to who Sophus Von Dorrien was.

He was a forester. More important than just that, he was a forester from Germany. The modern practice of forestry—"the science of planting and managing forests"—was refined in Germany and has been practiced there since before 1700, long before the first North American forester existed. The first Adirondack log drive was held in 1813, New York State had 7,000 sawmills by 1850, and the Adirondack Forest Preserve was created in 1885. Despite this, there was only one trained forester working in the Northern Forest by the late 1800s. That lonely forester worked in the White Mountains of New Hampshire, not in the Adirondack Mountains of New York.

When the prominent Adirondack surveyor Verplanck Colvin started petitioning the State of New York to create "an Adirondack park or timber preserve" during the late 1800s, he had the sense to consult with Mr. Von Dorrien to see how Germany managed their forests. What Colvin received was a November 4, 1878 document, fifty pages long, that explained how forestry works. This document carried an impressive title: "Forests and Forestry: A Letter Addressed to Verplanck Colvin, Esq., Superintendent of the Adirondack Surveys, on the Importance of Forests, Their Management in Germany, with a Short Review of the Historical Development of Forestry."

Von Dorrien's literary contribution provided a detailed review and tutorial in forest management. More importantly his work supported Colvin's reason for wanting to preserve the Adirondack woods. Forests are a major, important component of healthy ecosystems, especially when it comes to controlling runoff. Without the great Adirondack forests, snowmelt and rain would wash down from the mountains with fury, flooding everything from small towns to large cities, smashing bridges, clobbering mills, and choking fish with swirling sediment that spilled from eroding riverbanks. Sediment would build up in the Hudson and Mohawk rivers as well as canals, bringing the Empire State's shipping economy to a stuck-in-the-mud death. Without forests cradling the dirt and rock of our planet, the sensible German pointed out, such catastrophes would be encountered on a worldwide scale, not just in Upstate New York.

Five years prior to receiving Von Dorrien's letter, the 23-page *First Annual Report of the Commissioners of State Parks of the State of New York* was submitted to Lieutenant Governor John Robinson and that state Legislature. Colvin, serving as secretary of the committee of six others—Horatio Seymour,

Patrick Agan, William Taylor, George Raynor, William Wheeler, and Franklin Hough—tendered this paper. Even this report, prepared years prior to Von Dorrien arriving on the scene, made it clear that not preserving the Adirondack forests would result in nothing less than disaster: "Down hill sides the furious turbid waters rush to the streams and rivers, cutting and carving ravines through grain fields or gardens, and then, with united swollen volume, sweeping before them and destroying bridges, dwellings, cattle, and human beings."

Von Dorrien's 1878 publication effectively supported Colvin's later causes, and both of these astute men knew it. Without Von Dorrien's document, would the Adirondack Park ever have been created? Surely. Without Colvin lining up his preservationist allies, men like Von Dorrien and the commissioners, would the Adirondack Park ever have been created? This is uncertain.

Before passing away on July 26, 1907 at the age of 74, Von Dorrien had our formerly-unnamed 3,012-foot peak named for him. "Van Dorrien Mountain" appeared on the United States Geological Survey's topographic maps by 1904. Von Dorrien witnessed creation of the largest park and forest preserve in the Lower Forty-Eight: the Adirondack Park.

When I set out to climb Van Dorrien Mountain during the summer of 1996, I didn't know anything about Sophus Von Dorrien. At that time I had little interest in why mountains were named the way they were, though from the limited Adirondack reading I had done I knew why the more popular peaks were named so.

Van Dorrien Mountain, the 210th highest peak in the Adirondack Park, is remote. I had to plan my route to the top carefully since no trails touch this mountain. First I examined the possibility of accessing this mountain from the top of the nearby Ampersand Mountains. I could hike the three-mile-long trail to the top of this range that tops out at 3,330 feet. From there I'd crash off the east side of the Ampersand Mountains towards Van Dorrien Mountain, dropping 1,000 vertical feet into a rugged notch before making the final mile-long climb to my peak. Too long. Too rugged. Besides, I had already climbed the Ampersand Mountains.

I considered accessing Van Dorrien Mountain from the south, hiking down Blueberry Trail, leaving the trail to follow a property boundary around private Ampersand Lake, and then making a final push to the top. This extended journey would require me to spend the night somewhere near the top of the mountain since this route was sixteen miles long and included 2,000 vertical feet of climbing. Way too long. Way too rugged.

The only practical route lay via the east, from the end of Averyville Road. There were several advantages to tackling Van Dorrien Mountain from whence the sun rises. One, I had already explored some of the streams, valleys, and other mountains in this area. I knew where I was going. Two, this approach is scenic. At times my route would parallel four-mile-long East Branch, a sleepy waterway that is in no hurry to slink through the woods. At its bottom, East Branch joins seven-mile-long Cold Brook, an aptly-named stream that begins high in the Sawtooth Mountains to the south. Three, there is an old woods road that stretches five miles from east to west towards Van Dorrien Mountain. I could follow this road all the way to the base of my mountain. Then it was a three-mile bushwhack to the summit. It would be a long bushwhack—about five hours roundtrip—but it was only that: long, not impossible.

With the eastern approach settled upon, I planned my hike. I sorted through my gear and assembled a day pack suitable for a full day of bushwhacking, something I had done dozens of times by 1996. In my small, black backpack went clothing; extra layers and socks to keep me warm in case of cold rain or an unexpected night out in the mountains. I packed a tarp and small ground sheet, also for if I were forced to spend the night out. Odds and ends included my journal, maps, compass, headlamp, extra cord, first aid kit, and camera. Water straight from streams would quench my thirst. Calorie-dense foods such as Pop-tarts, Snickers bars, cheese, pepperoni, bagels, and M and M's would curb my hunger.

Combining hiking with another sport is fresh, fun, and matchless. For example, I have skied into the base of a mountain, snowshoed up and down it, and skied out at the end of the day, and I have canoed into the backcountry, climbed a mountain, and gracefully glided back to my start point. For Van Dorrien Mountain I would combine hiking with mountain biking.

But my mountain bike was far from the town I was living in at the time, Lake Placid. It was in storage in the Hudson Valley. The prospect of a bike-and-hike day was too appealing to abandon though. I rolled through a mental rolodex of friends who may have owned mountain bikes, and I thought of Amy, my good friend and outdoorswoman crush. Amy, with her long, sandy hair, freckles that bloomed during summer like roadside sunflowers, and love of the out-of-doors made her a mountain woman of many a mountain man's dream. Amy could navigate with a map and compass, zoom down mountains on skis, paddle a canoe, tell the difference between a sugar maple and a red maple, and cook something mighty tasty in the woods with only a handful of crude ingredients and a fire-scorched pot. And she owned a mountain bike.

Upon politely asking if I could borrow her bike, Amy kindheartedly consented. Her bike was nearly new. Taking pride in her recently-acquired ride, she reminded me, "But don't go breaking the thing. I just got it, okay?" Assuring her I would treat her bike as if it were my own (that is, very well), I told her I would pick up her bike the following morning, the day of my Van Dorrien Mountain trek.

I arrived at Amy's home in Saranac Lake the following morning. An addition to my traditional packing list was a repair kit for a mountain bike. Inside a stuff sac I carried enough tools to get me through a bicycle breakdown. My devices included tire levers, inner tube, chain breaker, multi-tool, pump, cable ties, and small crescent wrench.

Amy, who lived on the outskirts of town, resided in a geodesic dome, probably much like the one in one of my favorite books, Ed Abbey's *The Monkey Wrench Gang*, which I knew Amy also had read and enjoyed. In Abbey's tale of smashing logging and mining equipment that attempted to enter the wilderness of the West, one of the main characters, Bonnie Abbzug, described as "a young sexualized female assistant" to her housemate and soul mate, Doc Sarvis, MD, lives in a geodesic dome. The entrance to their fictitious home hosted a sign that read, "Welcome to our Happy Little Dome." Ah, if I was only a retired surgeon like Doc Sarvis, perhaps Amy could have been my Abbzug.

I tiptoed inside to see if Amy was up. She had always been an early riser. She sat at her kitchen table, her head leaning down, her eyes casually scanning a magazine, likely an outdoorsy periodical like *Outside, Backpacker*, or *Mother Earth News*. Amy was still in her pajamas, her soft, sandy hair flowing down to the table, framing a steaming mug of tea. The mug read, "I Don't Do Perky." Her two dogs, Maple and Sage, were at her feet. They completed her mountain woman persona (every true mountain woman owns a dog). We commented that the weather was going to be perfect for my hike (when they meet, every true mountain woman and mountain man talk about high country weather). I thanked her again for the bike. Amy reminded me not to break it, and then I was out the door.

I looked under her back deck, and there was her bike. It had some mud on it from recent rides, but it still looked new. The black paint, where not covered with splotches of black mud, gleamed in the early morning sun. I wheeled it to my Subaru wagon, removed the bicycle's front wheel, and then plopped the one-wheeled bike along with its lose tire into the back of my wagon, the back seats perpetually folded down to accommodate typical cargo of skis, backpacks, canoe paddles, and trail-building tools. I closed the hatch, and drove away with a happy "beep-beep."

Traffic was nil during the twenty-minute drive to Averyville Road. I drove under a blue sky with only a few white clouds skirting high overhead. It was breezy, which was good. The breeze, if it kept up, would help keep hordes of biting insects—deer flies, mosquitoes, black flies, and no-see-ums—away from me. I also wore my armor to do battle with Adirondack bugs: long pants, long-sleeved shirt, and a wide brimmed, floppy hat. I brought a bug head net, and I brought insect repellent. Specifically, Ole Time Woodsman insect repellent.

Ole Time Woodsman, which I discovered during the early 1990s, is, in my opinion, the only natural bug repellent that works. Sure, N,N-diethyl-meta-toluamide, aka "DEET," works, but I have been staying away from DEET products ever since I saw a splash of DEET bug repellent spill onto the dash of a sport utility vehicle and then eat the paint off that dash. The Environmental Protection Agency assures consumers that "the normal use of DEET does not present a health concern to the general population, including children" but that "consumers are advised to read and follow label directions when using any pesticide product, including insect repellents." I still can't get that caustic effect on that dashboard out of my mind. Hence Ole Time Woodsman. I like the name. When I wear this insect repellent I feel like an ole time woodsman myself, wise enough in my years to wear a product that represents who I am.

Ole Time Woodsman has a long "get them damn bugs away from me!" pedigree. Two fishermen, Obie Sherer and Don Adams, while on a trip in Maine in 1910, were driven crazy by bugs, and they intended to do something about it. They returned to their camp and, working off a repellent recipe from way back in 1882, came up with a new concoction they hoped would keep the bugs away.

Their potion worked. Soon, Maine loggers heard about this miraculous batch of "fly dope." The loggers became regular customers, and Obie decided to name his product after them, the actual "ole time woodsman" of Maine who were out there swinging axes, yanking crosscut saws, and driving logs downriver with the antagonistic insects. Ole Time Woodsman became the first commercial insect repellent in America. Today's marketing includes that this repellent will make everyone's wilderness experience "more comfortable, peaceful, and memorable." That's exactly the type of experience I wanted to have.

I pulled into the Averyville Road trailhead, also known as the Pine Pond trailhead, and, like most other times, the trailhead was empty. The only time I had seen vehicles parked there was during deer season from late October to early December. I parked under the long shade of eastern white pines and carefully pulled Amy's bike out. After reattaching the front tire, checking the brakes, adjusting the height of the seat, and taking it for a quick spin around the trailhead, the bike was as ready to go as I was. I donned my backpack, hid the car key in the woods, and pedaled into the wild forest.

The old roadway connects the Averyville Road trailhead with Oseetah Lake seven miles away, and this road has been around a long, long time. United States Geological Survey maps from 1904 portray this road, and its course has not changed since. What is most interesting is that these old maps portray homes along the road, likely pioneer families who eventually found the North Country woods too cold and dark, the soil too cold and rocky. With their foundations and cellar holes long gone, swallowed by the woods, today the road winds past trees and bushes where seemingly no one had ever lived.

The road started out rocky and eroded, obviously used by high-clearance four-wheel-drive vehicles and ATVs. As I rode farther and farther west, deeper into the woods, the road narrowed. Two miles in only an ATV could pass through the tunnel of greenery hemming the fading roadway. I pedaled around rocks and scooted around the deepest mud holes filled with murky brown water. As I pushed farther west towards my checkpoint, where Cold Brook joins East Branch five miles from the trailhead, I became lost in the fun of it all. I rolled down the muddy track at what I guessed was ten or fifteen miles per hour. The bugs couldn't catch me, though they tried, and I had seen not a soul all morning. The sun shone above me, and the breeze blew. Life was very good.

A half-hour from the trailhead I knew I was nearing Cold Brook, which I intended to follow south, away from the old road. After following this waterway upstream for two miles I would leave it and then head southwest to gain the summit ridgeline of Van Dorrien Mountain. But without a cyclometer (a small handlebar-mounted device that reports distance traveled, among other things) I had to guess where I was only by time, and that was based on guessing how fast I was riding. Around the forty-minute mark I pulled over and stopped to listen for Cold Brook. No luck. I continued, biking a minute, stopping, listening, biking another minute, stopping, listening.

At one point I thought I heard Cold Brook. I left the bike on the side of the trail with my backpack and scurried down a steep embankment to the shore of East Branch. No feeder stream was in sight. My fear was that I had biked past Cold Brook. If so, then I'd be flung towards Flag Brook, which climbs towards the Ampersand Mountains, not towards Van Dorrien Mountain to the southwest. I decided to stop then and there and search for Cold Brook on foot. Surely I had not passed it yet.

I wheeled Amy's bike off the trail and laid it on the soft forest floor, out of sight of the trail. I took off my pack and dug out the bicycle repair kit. It would do me no good on Van Dorrien Mountain. Convinced that my mountain woman's mountain bike was hidden, I returned to the trail, crossed it, and then scrambled back down the embankment to East Branch.

The stream was bubbling by hemlocks, birches, and maples, free to roam where it wanted to as long as that was within its two pebbly shorelines. I rock-hopped across East

Branch. I filled my water bottle with cold water, put on my wide-brimmed bug hat, and wetted it with a liberal amount of Ole Time Woodsman. After a Snickers bar I was ready to begin hiking. The smell of Ole Time Woodsman spread into the surrounding area like a fog, its pungent smell of part pine pitch, part wood smoke, part citronella, and part creosote-encrusted railroad ties put out a burning, woodsy smell.

Examining my topographic map, I was confident that I had yet to reach Cold Brook, the ticket to my peak. I set my compass due west. With less than a mile of off-trail hiking I'd hit the stream. Then I'd turn left—south—and climb into the high country. I left East Branch and all trails behind. I headed due west towards Cold Brook, which I had traveled up and down three times before. Those forays were during the depths of winter, when the brook was frozen nearly solid, and at least a foot of snow insulated it. Then the woods were silent save for the few hardy species of birds that wintered over, like black-capped chickadees, blue jays, and downy woodpeckers. Cold Brook was going to look a lot different during summer.

The off-trail hiking towards the west was easy. I could not have called it bushwhacking since there were so few bushes to whack. I strolled under a quilt of green leaves of American beeches, maples, and ashes, my boots smushing and crunching a mixture of dead leaves, greenery, and mud. Every once in a while I noticed deep scratches on the bases of young striped maples. These signs let me know I was in a big buck's territory, the scratches gouged out by his beefy antlers.

I continued for ten minutes. Then fifteen. Then twenty. Was I going the right way? I checked my map and compass, and, sure enough, I was going the right way: west. But I should have hit Cold Brook already, shouldn't I have? But distances on maps can be deceiving when compared to real world distances through the woods. I was convinced I was being overly optimistic. I surely could not have been hiking as fast as I thought. That was it. I was covering less ground, hiking slower than I thought I was. "Patience, young one," I said to myself.

I hit the thirty-minute mark without hitting my stream. Where in the hell was Cold Brook? It was out there, somewhere, in front of me. I decided to push on, fueled by confidence, good woods sense, and the thorough planning of my route. I continued for another fifteen minutes, and with each step I questioned myself. Things did not feel right. I promised to give myself another ten minutes before stopping and seriously reassessing where I had come from, where I was, and where I was headed. Three minutes later I crested a small rise and heard it. A stream! A smile creased my face. I had found Cold Brook.

It took a hell of a lot longer than I had anticipated to reach this waterway. I calculated that I hiked west for at least a mile, not the quarter mile I expected. But then I sorted out all the confusion. It was not that I was *hiking* slower than I had thought I was. It had been that I was *biking* slower than I had thought I was. I got off Amy's bike too soon, at least a mile before Cold Brook. Mystery solved.

Back on track and still on schedule, I was free of the possibility of being disappointed in myself for navigating poorly. I shot down the embankment and hit the shore of Cold Brook. I checked my compass to make sure the brook was flowing the correct direction: south. It was. At its top Cold Brook peters out between the Sawtooth Mountains to the southeast and Van Dorrien Mountain to the southwest. All looked good.

The brook was beautiful, just as I had imagined it when I was walking on top of it during winter. I prefer wintertime over summertime because there are no bugs, among other reasons for this preference. Yet during that Adirondack summer day the bugs were completely tolerable, even absent from time to time. Or maybe it was my Ole Time Woodsman, repelling bugs since 1910.

For the next two miles, two hours' worth of hiking, I would not have to look at my map or compass. All I had to do was follow the stream uphill, picking the east shore when it looked clear, picking the west side when it was more appealing to travel along. It would have been much easier to travel this waterway during winter. Then I could have strolled up the center of it.

Patches of woods in the Adirondack Mountains look more like jungles from Borneo or Vietnam than your classic Northern Forest. The forests that are tough to travel through have branches intertwined above downed trees, stumps, holes, and knee-high undergrowth. The woods lining the shores of Cold Brook were hiker-friendly, with trees spaced apart, downed trees sprinkled in conservatively, and undergrowth thin. Good times.

Like a little goblin that wouldn't leave, moments of doubt continued to creep into my mind as I followed Cold Brook up-hill. Granted I had only been to this chunk of woods during the middle of winter, but still, the stream appeared wider and marshier than I had recalled. At times the brook looked more like a slow-moving wetland, with all its slackwater and small marshes. But, I reasoned, winter is as different as you can get from summer. Cold Brook just changed outfits for the season. Therefore, it was difficult to recognize Cold Brook with the debut of green replacing familiar white.

I covered two miles of stream-following in two hours as I had predicted. It was time to leave Cold Brook and head for the high country. What would dictate my pace was how dense the woods were. As one climbs higher and higher the trees get shorter and shorter. They also grow next to each other tightly, at times letting no sunlight touch the ground. With each dwarfed tree competing for the best realty—spots out of the wind yet exposed to the sun—bushwhacking above 2,500 feet is akin to pushing your way through a Christmas tree farm that has ten times more trees per acre than it should have. When it's raining, bushwhacking through a forest like this is like pushing yourself through a car wash, the soft cloths being re-placed with pine-scented scouring pads. Bushwhacking isn't for everyone.

I downed a quart of water, ate some food, refilled my water bottle, and prepared myself for the slog towards the top of my mountain. Up I went at a steady pace. From years of hiking, especially off-trail, I've learned that the tortoise and the hare fable is true. Slow and steady wins the race. In the world of hiking it wins the summit.

Upward I climbed, slowly transitioning from a northern hardwood forest of beeches, birches, ashes, and maples to a mountain conifer forest of fir and spruce. Only one species of fir—balsam fir—can be found high. Spruce come in either black or red species.

Above me I could see the horizon getting closer and closer, lower and lower, until the horizon was below my feet. According to my map I had topped out on Van Dorrien Mountain's unnamed north peak, a scrappy knob covered in blowdown. The dense forest filtered any significant views from this little summit, but through the trees I could make out the hulking mass of Van Dorrien Mountain a mile away.

Like I had the luxury of doing when I followed Cold Brook, I could again put my map and compass away. I'd let the northern ridgeline that spills off Van Dorrien Mountain guide me to the top. As long as I didn't drift off to the left or right—east or west, respectively—this graceful ridge would take me right to where I wanted to be. I checked my watch. I still hadn't come close to my turn around time yet, the time when I must start heading back to the trail.

My path was occasionally open and easy to traverse, but then blowdown and evergreen thickets would try to stop me. I pushed, heaved, crawled, and forced my way through the stunted forest, branches and needles grabbing at my clothes and pack, trying to convince me to go no higher. For more than an hour I ascended the ridge. At times I enjoyed filtered views of the surrounding mountains. I looked east towards the Sawtooth Mountains. By knowing the elevations of the peaks in that range, I could look out and see how high I was in comparison to them. My God, they looked far away. Though according to the map the Sawtooth Mountains were only a little farther than a mile away as the crow flies, they looked way farther than that. I peered towards this range trying to get a feel for how far away they really were. It was hard to guess. Three miles? Self-doubt crept in again. Was I really on Van Dorrien Mountain? But wait. I didn't have to guess how far away the Sawtooth Mountains were. Confidence! I knew the answer. They were little farther than a mile. My map told me so.

Or did it?

With a finger I traced my route on my topographic map from the trailhead, to where Amy's bike was hidden, to East Branch, to Cold Brook, to the climb, to the knob, to the ridgeline, to where I stood at that moment. It all made sense. I felt annoyed for not trusting my skills, and I remembered the advice my field instructors gave me when I was a wilderness leadership student a few years earlier. Trust your map and compass. "What is wrong with you?" I asked myself out loud. "Put that shit away and get to the top of this fucking mountain." The stern talk smacked some reassurance into me. "Let's do this!"

My body pushed higher while the trees pushed back harder, putting up defenses of prickly needles, coarse branches, and sappy trunks. The ridge seemed to go on and on and on. Nearing the 3,000-foot-level, the trees were only ten feet tall, the height of a basketball hoop. More light shone down on me. The sun was warm, not hot. Bugs were minimal. I had picked a good day to go hiking.

The ridge narrowed. The top was near. I burst onto a slab of bedrock into the full brightness of the sun. God, it felt good to be out of the scrappy woods for a moment. I peered south along the last remains of the summit ridge and saw plenty of other slabs of exposed bedrock. Sweet! From years of bush-whacking in the Adirondacks I had learned that one out maybe fifty Adirondack peaks offers any kind of view. Van Dorrien Mountain had more exposed bedrock than I had seen on any trailless peak up to that day. I was suddenly in a hurry to get to the top to drop my pack, peel off my sweat soaked shirt, take off my boots, and roll off my stinky, wet socks. I was definitely going to lie down. Maybe I'd take a nap.

Back into the bush I dove, more than willing to tackle the final 300 feet to the summit. I disappeared into the forest and then resurfaced on slabs of bedrock, looking like a whale that disappears and then surfaces to catch its breath. The slabs of bedrock poked their massive bodies above the forest more often. I was strolling in the sunlight. No branches grabbed at me. My work was done after five hours of hard hiking.

I looked ahead to the tippy-top and took in my surroundings. Scanning left to right I saw the Sawtooth Mountains, the Seward Mountains, the Santanoni Mountains, and the dense forests growing on the east side of my mountain. Panning right I took in the avenue of bedrock straight ahead, south, of me. A few trees gripped the sides of the rocky mountain in defiance of the winds that scour the mountain. Just right of center a pretty girl sat, eating lunch. To the right the mountain dropped steeply. Far below the Saranac Lakes—

Wait.

What?

I yanked my head back to the center of my panorama. I squinted. I looked back down to where I had climbed from. I looked back ahead. I was . . . speechless. What would a pretty girl be doing on top of Van Dorrien Mountain, a trailless, far-flung peak that is described in no guidebook? So what if no one had ever heard of Sophus Von Dorrien. I had never met a hiker who had even heard of Van Dorrien Mountain. And then it occurred to me.

This was fate.

The second-best thing in the world is a pretty girl. The best thing is a mountain. I had waited 23 years for this day to come. My two loves coincided. My planets were aligned. My horoscope must have been very good that week. The gods were looking down upon me. However you want to word it, I had my mojo! Thank you, God, oh magnificent one, for bringing this beautiful bushwhacking beauty into my life. In the distance I could hear the faint din of wedding bells. Out of all the days of the year and out of all the thousands of mountains to hike, we both chose to hike this mountain on this day. Fate! When two young bushwhackers' paths cross on such an obscure mountain, it is meant to be.

I tucked in my shirt, straightened out my muddied pants, and adjusted my pack. I brushed the evergreen needles off my mud splattered face and beard. I couldn't fix my hair because I had a shaved head, but if I had hair to fix I certainly would have fixed it.

Taking care not to scare her, I coughed to alert her of my presence. I felt like a bull elk during rutting season. She looked up from her peanut butter and jelly sandwich. "Hi. I didn't see you over there."

What a smile.

I strolled towards her. "Yeah, I came up from Cold Brook. Man, what a summit, huh?" I looked around.

"Oh," she replied with twinkling eyes, "it's wonderful. This is one of my favorite mountains." Nonchalantly she added, "This is my third time up it."

Third time up it? This girl was hardcore. I had never met anyone who had bushwhacked up an Adirondack peak three times. I was in love.

"Three times?" I asked. "Which way did you come up this time?"

She looked at me with a puzzled expression, yet her smile remained. "I came up the trail. Didn't you?"

"Trail?"

I was frozen like a waterfall in January, especially when I looked fifty feet ahead and saw a blue Department of Environmental Conservation trail marker. It all made terrible sense so quickly.

When I was on Amy's bike many hours earlier I biked *past* Cold Brook. I didn't stop before it. I was oblivious to this mistake at the time, and zooming past Cold Brook became the first domino that tumbled the rest. When I hid her bike and crossed East Branch and began bushwhacking west, I was actually headed straight towards Flag Brook while walking away from Cold Brook to my back. And that was why it took so long to reach Flag Brook (which, again, I thought was Cold Brook). Flag Brook is over a mile west of where I hid Amy's bike. Without a clue, but doubt here and there, I had followed Flag Brook to the base of the Ampersand Mountains. And then I climbed them.

I was on a mountain farther, taller, bigger, and tougher than I had intended to climb. I looked southeast and there it was, Van Dorrien Mountain, nearly two miles away from me. I had really messed up. Van Dorrien Mountain, that 3,012-foot-tall mound of dirt and rock and bark and branches and boulders, would be in this world long, long after I was not. I could climb it any day, any year, any decade. I had the rest of my life to get there. But what about my mountain woman here? I was hurt. Out of all the days of the year and out of all the mountains to climb that day, it was not fate that brought me and my supposed new mountain woman together. It was bad navigation, which doesn't make for a good love story.

I had to save face and salvage our chance meeting. "No," I said in the most casual voice I could fake. "I didn't take the trail. You see way down in that valley over there?" I pointed to where Amy's bike was hidden four miles away. "I came from there. Yeah," I added, "I bushwhack."

She looked impressed. Or surprised. Or confused. "Oh," she said. "That's a really long way. How long did it take you to get up here?"

"Five hours."

"Wow. I got up the trail in an hour-and-a-half."

Getting to the top of Van Dorrien Mountain was not going to happen. It was already 2:00. The forests I fought my way through? I didn't want to fight my way back down and chance getting turned around on Flag Brook again. My confidence was shot, and my motivation was hidden in a deep, dark well. But I'm quick on my feet. "You know, I was hoping that when I got up here I would run into someone who could give me a ride back to my friend's house. She lives in Saranac Lake."

She looked up and replied in a "go on" tone. "Uh-huh."

"Well, no pressure, 'cause I know I'm just some guy who stumbled out of the woods. But you wouldn't happen to be going back towards—" I interrupted myself. "Well, I don't need an answer now. You know, uh, just let me know if I can catch a ride with you. If not, I'm sure I'll find someone else." My sentence ended awkwardly. "No problem there."

"No, I can give you a ride," She said. "It looks like you've come a long way."

I thanked her and then found a lunch spot a bit away from her. No one likes being crowded on a summit. I dropped my pack and dug out my water. I took off my boots and let my pale, damp feet dry in the sun while my boots and socks did the same. I ate a Snickers bar, which always makes me feel better.

I looked over at Van Dorrien Mountain and gave myself a mental finger pointing. I failed by paying no attention to the voices that had popped inside my head, serving as little alarms. "Danger! Danger! Erik Schlimmer! You are blindly walking off the face of the Earth!" Huh? Can't hear ya'.

Twenty minutes after our meeting my mountain woman came over. "Want to head down?" she asked.

"Sure."

I was beat. My new hiking partner had spring in her step. Once past the steeper parts of the trail we traversed the flats that lead to the trailhead ten miles from where my car was parked. We descended the three-mile-long well-maintained trail in a little over an hour. We threw our packs in the trunk of her silver Honda Civic and turned left out of the trailhead parking lot, quickly gaining speed on Route 3 towards Saranac Lake. We talked about the mountains, such as which ones we had hiked and which ones we wanted to hike. Teasing myself and finding humor in my misadventure I told her I wanted to hike Van Dorrien Mountain someday. She had never heard of it.

When we pulled into Amy's driveway a few white clouds were still skirting across the sky, and the breeze still blew. I realized it was a fine day to be in the mountains even if I ended up on the wrong one. I thanked my new friend for the ride, grabbed my pack, and walked towards the happy little dome. She drove away, never to be seen again.

Inside, Sage and Maple were happy to see me. I was happy to see them, too. I opened the door to the back deck and they flew out the doorway, sprinted down the stairs, and ran around the backyard like it was their first taste of freedom. They loved good mountain weather, just like me, Amy, and my Ampersand Mountains girl did.

I decided to call Amy at work, something she said was fine at any time because she found work boring. I located the phone book, found her workplace listing, and called. A cheery voice from a bubbly female employee answered. I knew it wasn't Amy. This girl was perky. "Eastern Mountain Sports! This is Angie! How I can I help you get outside today?"

"Oh, I don't really want to go outside today, Angie. Can I speak to Amy instead?"

The perkiness disappeared. "Hold on."

She picked up. "Hello, this is Amy."

"Amy. It's your buddy Erik Schlimmer."

"Oh, hey. What's up? You're back already?"

"I am back." I think I even sounded a little perky.

"Great," she said. "Is my bike back in one piece, too?"

I paused. "Well . . . not . . . exactly."

"Not exactly?"

Before Amy blew her top by learning that I had abandoned her bike in the great Adirondack wilderness, I assured her it was well-hidden and safe from prying eyes. Within a few minutes I recapped my asinine hike up the Ampersand Mountains. Instead of scolding me for leaving her bike to fend for itself overnight, I got goodheartedly teased for being sloppy with my map and compass work: "You did what? Dude, how does anyone do that? Hey, Rob!" she exclaimed to a colleague, a mutual friend of ours. "Dude, it's Schlimmer! He went to bushwhack up some mountain near the Sawtooths and ended up on Ampersand!"

In a distant voice I could hear, "*Ampersand*? Are you serious?"

Amy put her hand over the phone. I couldn't make out what the conversation was about, but muffled laughter is easy to recognize. Rob spoke into the phone forcefully. "Dude— how do you even *do* that? You *suck*!" A man of few words, he handed the phone back to Amy.

I was at Amy's house when she got home. It was great to see her. I guessed she was my only mountain woman after all. I showered and ordered a pizza for us, and then we relaxed on the back deck and casually made a plan for the following day. An ascent of Van Dorrien Mountain was out, but I needed to get her bike. That night I slept on the couch. Maple and Sage slept with their mountain woman mother like they always did.

At 8:30 the following morning Amy and I left the house, me with my day pack and her with her lunch for work. She dropped me off at the Averyville Road trailhead where my car had spent the night. I found my car key where I had hidden it. I began my walk to East Branch to find Amy's bike. The two-hour, five-mile-long hike was boring. It was way more fun on a bike. I recovered the mountain bike and pedaled back east, away from the mountains.

Amy's bike was unloaded in her driveway. I felt bad about leaving it out overnight, and it came back a lot muddier than when it had left her house. I went inside and found a bucket, brush, and dish soap. I did a hell of a job scrubbing her bike while Maple and Sage lay on the grass nearby, watching me work. They yawned and sprawled, their bellies soaking up the warm Adirondack sun. The bike squeaky clean, I put it back where I had found it.

During the summer of 2001, nearly to the day, I gave it another shot to get up Van Dorrien Mountain. Approaching from the same direction, the east, and riding my own bike this time,

I reached the top of my elusive mountain. I recorded my time on the summit that I had waited five years to reach.

Black flies. Started late. Now 5:00. Half-hour bike ride in on the old road. North knob has blowdown, thickets, blowdown, thickets, and blowdown. And no view. Wearing sneakers. The true summit has a great view of Ampersand Lake, Sawtooth Mountains, Seward Mountains, Ampersand Mountains, and all the way to the MacIntyre Mountains.

Like the name Sophus Von Dorrien, strong, dark, and purposeful, the mountain named for him is as well. Strongly guarded by blowdown and thickets, covered in inky firs and spruces, and serving as home to over a thousand acres of forest. Van Dorrien Mountain is still one of my favorite peaks. In 2012 I returned to climb it in winter. The first time I attempted to climb it, in 1996, I fell in love. Not with a mountain woman on top of the Ampersand Mountains, but with a mountain named for a man who helped preserve the mountains I love.

One is the Loneliest Number

I am down to one hiking partner: Taylor. I like to think the reason I don't have more than one hiking partner is because of the terrain I explore: trailless, viewless, far-flung mountains. People simply aren't interested in these types of peaks, I tell myself. After all, these are the low hills of the Adirondacks that you bust your butt all day climbing up only to be rewarded with a nondescript spruce forest, the same exact looking forest that was at the bottom of the mountain. So why climb a mountain merely to end up back in a patch of woods that you were apparently standing in hours ago? It's difficult to come up with a good answer.

What I don't like to think is that I am down to one hiking partner because of who I am. I once told an outdoor education colleague of mine, "I know I'm not the easiest person to get along with in the field."

He had a two-word reply: "You're right."

My biggest fault is that I am a perfectionist. It must be the German in me and because I was raised by an overbearing father who accepted nothing but perfection. I *love* doing things perfectly. I mean, why would you not want to do something perfectly? Anything less than perfect is . . . well . . . not perfect, and that is no good. As I've grown older, however, perfection has become a demon of mine. Instead of standing in the light of successes I have attained or goals I have met, I rarely find time for celebration. Instead, more often than not I am giving myself a *reprimand*.

When I reach the top of a mountain, for example, I'll be happy with that success. Happy is such a wimpy word though. It's light and transparent and gets blown around like a feather in the wind. Instead, I use firmer words that form sturdy critiques of my performance on the mountain, and these define who I am: inattentive when I don't note all the different species of trees, ignorant when I can't identify animal tracks, uneducated when I can't place that bird call. In short, imperfect. If I'm this hard on myself when I hike an innocent mountain, imagine the internal scolding I get when I screw up something at work, say the wrong thing to a pretty girl, or hurt someone in a relationship. You can well imagine the expectations I put on hiking partners.

I *love* being right. However, I do not find any satisfaction in being right and someone else being wrong. Intellect has never been a competitive pursuit of mine. I want to be right because being right instills a possession of intelligence, reasoning, and decision making ability. It shows that I think before I speak or write. That I am precise. A fault that steps on my perfectionist's coattails is that I often think I am correct. As a former mentor once said to me, "Erik, you're right a lot of the time." He then paused. "But not all of the time." Not even my stubbornness could have me disagree with his observation.

Combined with perfectionism, the pursuit of being correct is now a cycle I have difficulty stopping. If I'm not being perfect, then I must have made an incorrect decision at some point, and if I'm making incorrect decisions, then I'm not perfect, and if I'm not perfect . . . This self-critique goes on and on like a wash cycle that won't end. The water never drains, the rinse cycle is never reached, and the machine never turns off. It just agitates.

Taylor is young. That's likely one of the reasons I enjoy his company. If youth was a career, cheerfulness would be its salary. Partly due to his youth, and certainly due to his personality and upbringing, Taylor is a lovable guy. He likes to laugh, he doesn't take life too seriously, and he doesn't take himself too seriously. His personality is infectious. When I'm around Taylor I tend to take myself less seriously, which is a welcome vacation.

Taylor is no slacker. Like most of us, Taylor has goals. Dreams. He has ambition. For his age (Taylor's in his mid 20s) I think he has a superb feel for where he has come from, where he is, and where he will next go. And, boy, is he fun to be around, especially off-trail in the woods. You need to be cheerful and carefree when you bushwhack. If you take bushwhacking too seriously you'll soon grasp how miserable this sport is. If Taylor gets serious and realizes how strenuous many of our hikes are, he may not be cheerful anymore. Then I won't have a hiking partner at all.

Thankfully, during January 2010, Taylor was not too serious to pass on an invitation to complete a three-day trip into Moose Pond. This remote body of water buried in the northwest corner of High Peaks Wilderness Area is photogenic. Mountains surround Moose Pond. To the north stands Three Peaks, which rests just below the 3,000-foot-level. To the east towers Street Mountain. At 4,314 feet it is the 24th highest peak in New York. To the south stands an innocuous 3,002-foot hill, a shoulder of immense Street Mountain. Behind this hill rises MacNaughton Mountain, its highpoint fourteen feet below the 4,000-foot-level.

To the west stand the Sawtooth Mountains with their unique claim: largest mountainous region in the East without trails. To find a bigger area of mountainous land with no trails you will have to travel 2,000 miles to the Rocky Mountains. The Sawtooth Mountains complex—thirty square miles of woods, streams, lakes, and cliffs—is home to eleven mountains over 3,000 feet, all officially unnamed. They're locally named in descending order, the tallest peak, at 3,855 feet, being "Sawtooth Number One" and the lowest peak, at 3,002 feet, being "Sawtooth Number Eleven." The range is aptly-named. These serrated peaks reach towards the sky in disorganized fashion.

I emailed Taylor an itinerary for the proposed Moose Pond trip.

Day one (Saturday): Hike into Moose Pond via the old and original segments of the Northville Placid Trail from the end of Averyville Road. Dump gear at the Moose Pond lean-to. Hike up "Street Mountain's southwest peak." Head back to the lean-to for the night. 7.5 miles, + 1,400 vertical feet.

Day two (Sunday): From the lean-to, hike "Sawtooth Number Eight" (aka "Boulder Peak") via eastern drainage to wetland at 2,870 feet. Then straight up the peak. Return same way. Stay at lean-to. 5 miles, + 1,200 vertical feet.

Day three (Monday): Pack up and head out. 5 miles, + 500 vertical feet.

In my email I assured Taylor we'd have fun. "It will be awesome. Snowshoe some peaks, eat some dinners, drink some cocoa, eat some chocolate, and then head back and eat pizza."

If anything can sell a winter camping trip, it is food. Plus the mileage and climbing for this three-day trip were conservative. Having a full 48 hours in the mountains (we'd start late on day one and would be done around lunchtime on day three) we would need to hike nine miles and climb 1,500 vertical feet per day. Piece of cake.

Taylor did not hesitate accepting. I was elated. Though nearly all of my hiking is done solo, during winter I enjoy the company. Having a partner during the coldest months of the year adds a level of safety. If I were to have an accident in the mountains—a sprained ankle, a twisted knee, a wrenched back—my partner could help me. If he couldn't help me, he could at least go get help. Having a partner also makes things more enjoyable. Since I find winter, even winter in the mountains, relatively depressing, having a partner like Taylor cheers things up. Finally, having someone to help break trail is invaluable.

Breaking trail, that is, being the first one to travel down a trail or cross-country through virgin snow, is tough work. Though snowshoes (and skis) help keep you on top of the unconsolidated snowpack, they have only limited effectiveness at keeping you "afloat." With each step you sink down no matter how long or wide your snowshoes (or skis) may be. Depending on the firmness of the untracked snow, you could sink in a few inches, or you could sink in to your calves. Add to this a mountainous slope in front of you, and you may be trying to break trail through snow up to your thighs. When hiking through untrodden snow in the mountains, a pace of one mile per hour is nothing to be disappointed with. A half-mile-an-hour pace is slow, but not uncommon. A quarter-mile-an-hour pace is demoralizingly slow but not unheard of.

With Taylor on the Moose Pond trip with me, we could alternate who would be breaking trail and who would be snowshoeing in their wake. A common tactic teams use is to have someone break trail for a certain amount of time (perhaps twenty minutes) or a certain distance (perhaps a quarter-mile). This lead person can also remain out front simply until he cries uncle—until he becomes tired and has slowed the team to a snail's pace. Then the guy who was second goes first. The guy who was first is now last. When it's time to go downhill, like when the team is descending from a summit, the lead snowshoer can last much longer out front. Breaking trail while going downhill—the steeper the better—is not exceedingly difficult.

I had a very nice stove (reputed to boil water faster than any other backpacking stove on the planet) to bring for us as well as a shelter (a unique floorless tent that is a cross between a teepee and a circus tent). Those two pieces of gear were key. Winter backpackers love nothing more than hot drinks and hot food, and no winter backpacker likes to sleep outside exposed to a snowstorm (we planned on staying in the Moose Pond lean-to but would bring our own shelter in case the lean-to was occupied). I also had a tarp to bring to use as a ground sheet inside our floorless shelter.

Like on all of my winter trips, I planned on using ski poles and wearing a pair of snowshoes that measured thirty inches long by nine inches wide. For the 190 pounds that these snowshoes would support, their dimensions were adequate. Then I remembered that Taylor did not own snowshoes. I offered to lend him these snowshoes, and I would wear my smaller pair that measured 25 inches long by 8 inches wide. Since Taylor outweighed me by thirty pounds, it would make sense for him to wear the bigger of the two pairs I owned.

He asked me not to go to any trouble. He planned on borrowing a pair from the outing club of his college. So I was back to wearing my bigger pair of snowshoes, which put my mind at ease. The less I sank into the trackless snow around Moose Pond, the happier and less exhausted I would be.

We would bring our own personal gear. This consisted of sleeping bag, sleeping pad, mug, spoon, extra warm layers, toiletries, extra wool socks, and insulated booties to wear around camp. We wore similar clothing, which included waterproof jackets and pants, thermal long underwear, winter boots, thick wool socks, gloves, mittens, and winter hats.

We chose foods that packed the most calories per ounce. The more calories a winter backpacker consumes, the warmer he will be. Calories equal heat. Fatty foods dominated our menu. Extra sharp cheddar cheese and chocolate in many forms—M and M's, chocolate chips, chocolate bars, and cocoa—would be carried into the woods. We also brought butter. While preparing our freeze-dried dinners each night we planned to drop a big dollop of butter into them. This would boost each dinnertime meal with 200 calories and 22 grams of fat, clogged arteries be damned. We also planned to use the butter as part of a winter camping ritual. Into our steaming mugs of cocoa we would drop pats of butter to make our sugary drinks fatty. Do not knock it until you try it.

Group gear, individual gear, and food squared away, we each began to reflect on our destination. The two mountains near Moose Pond we had set our sights on were the 3,002-foot southwest peak of Street Mountain and Sawtooth Number Eight, the taller of the two at 3,396 feet. I had been up both of these peaks while climbing the Adirondacks' 217 3,000-foot mountains, but I had not been up either during winter. To breathe new life into an already-completed peakbagging list, many mountain climbers attempt to complete their lists of mountains a second time: in winter. It's a fresh challenge. It's also a stiff challenge. Of the first 3,000 people to hike every 4,000-foot peak in the Adirondacks, fewer than 100 of them hiked them all during winter. By 2001 four people had finished hiking every 3,000-foot peak in the Adirondacks, but no one had completed this list during winter. I had a strong chance at becoming the first to do so.

Both peaks we intended to climb have no trails to their tops. The southwest peak of Street Mountain is a bland hill. No cliffs guard its sides, no views can be found from its top, and, unless you are specifically pursuing a goal to climb every 3,000-foot peak in the Adirondacks, you'll never notice it. It's a bump on Street Mountain's southwest ridge, a mole on an enormous face. Sawtooth Number Eight, on the other hand, has personality. Of the eleven peaks in the Sawtooth Mountains, Sawtooth Number Eight, which I had nicknamed "Boulder Peak" nearly a decade earlier, may be my favorite.

I first reached this mountain during July 2001 while working as a seasonal backcountry ranger. That summer day I fought my way up the scrubby southwest ridge through clouds of biting insects only to be confronted with a fifteen-foot-high cliff just short of the top. I traversed right, following the cliff, looking for a crack in its walls so I could scramble to the top. I found a fault in the peak's defenses. A steep, narrow, chunky crack was my way to the top. I shimmied up it, and at the top of this beefy climb I encountered another cliff. "Wait. No." I said to myself. "You can't have a cliff on top of a cliff."

I looked around and realized that two gigantic boulders rested on the top of the peak, certainly two of the biggest rocks I'd ever seen. I would have to find a way up at least one of them. I scrambled my way up the larger and higher of the two. It was a tough climb since I had to keep swatting black flies away from my face while ascending.

I burst from the dense spruce forest and above gray rock into the sunlight. I was nearly speechless at the view from my remote roost. I stood there in my wet, muddy clothes, soaked and sore from climbing through the wet forest for hours (it rained the night before). I decided to let my writing do the talking for me, recording my thoughts in my journal.

What a great peak. Difficult, thick ascent from beaver meadow. Tons and tons of old logging equipment down there. Two bus-sized boulders near this cliff that I'm sitting on. These rocks give possibly the best view of the whole range. A little rain in the A.M. Wicked thick woods. Bugs!

I took it all in. To the north, like sentinels, stood the two highest peaks in the Sawtooth Mountains, their rugged faces looking down on minuscule me. To the east stood the highest peaks in the state, an impressive jumble of 4,000- and 5,000-foot peaks, a few of them tall enough to fracture the sky, no trees whatsoever growing on their tops. The southern view was wild. It had no end. Mountain after mountain was heaved, piled, and bumped upon the other, a mixture of blue, green, and black silhouettes fading to the horizon a hundred miles away. To the west stood the Seward Mountains. The north side of this range dropped sharply into the headwaters of the Raquette River.

With a view like that during summer, the panorama from the top of Boulder Peak during winter would be even more impressive. The absence of humidity during winter is the reason you can see so well, so far, so crisply. I figured I would be able to take in at least half of the Adirondack Park.

I drove to Taylor's parents' residence from my village of Oneonta, arriving at their house in Saranac Lake around 10:00 A.M. Taylor and I had not seen each other in months, and it was good to meet again. We knew this trip was going to be awesome. The day was clear and cold, perfect for snowshoeing. The temperatures were predicted to drop to near 0 degrees during the dark Adirondack nights coming up, but we had the gear to survive this cold front.

I came inside to change into my hiking clothes and visit with Taylor's family. His parents, Katherine and Ted, had always been especially kind to me, like I was an adopted son of sorts. At times I wished I had parents so sensitive when I was growing up. They seemed so calm, loving, and reasonable. Their mannerisms explained Taylor's warm demeanor.

Soon dressed and ready to go, we bid Taylor's family good-bye, telling them we would see them Monday afternoon. Since I had driven nearly three hours from my home in central New York, Taylor offered to drive us to the Averyville Road trailhead just outside of Lake Placid twenty minutes from Saranac Lake. We trudged outside in our heavy winter boots, grabbed my gear out of the trunk of my car, and heaved it in

Taylor's little Honda Civic. The small backseat and even smaller back compartment was soon filled with gear, reminding me of a little clown car.

We pulled up to the old Northville Placid Trail trailhead at the end of the road, foregoing to begin our trip at the "new" Northville Placid Trail trailhead, which was three miles before the end of Averyville Road. During the 1970s this very northern section of this trail was rerouted. The new portion is scenic (it runs right next to the Chubb River) and may have already been broken out by snowshoers and skiers the day of our hike, but we chose the old, abandoned trail for good reason. One, Taylor had never been on it. Two, it's two miles shorter than the new trail. Three, we like doing things differently. If everyone is taking the new trail, we'll take the old trail.

We parked at the small trailhead at the end of the road. Surrounded by tall, bright white snow banks, Taylor's car looked even tinier. No other cars were there. Most people, even locals, didn't know about this old trailhead. As I threw my snowshoes onto the ground next to Taylor's snowshoes, I did a double take. His snowshoes were small. Very small. *Tiny.* They looked like kiddy snowshoes, the little plastic ones that a toddler would wear in a backyard. I couldn't help but notice Taylor's ski poles, too. They had no baskets. Baskets, circular pieces of plastic that attach to near the bottoms of ski poles, keep the poles from sinking into the snow. Think of baskets as little snowshoes for ski poles.

"Taylor, uh, where did you get those snowshoes?"

"Oh, I got them from the college." He looked over at me from making last minute adjustments to his pack. He brightened his smile. "For free."

"Well," I broke in slowly and politely, "they're awfully small. Are you sure those are going to be okay? I think the snow's going to be really deep back there."

In his universal cheerful tone, Taylor was unconcerned. He looked down at his snowshoes and admitted, "Yeah, I guess they're kind of small. I'm sure they'll be okay."

We donned our packs, our breath visible. The day was still clear and cold, about 10 degrees. When it warms up to 30 degrees during winter, the woods tend to feel muggy. When you traverse pieces of land that are fully exposed to the sun, such as frozen bodies of water, a 30 degree sunny day can feel downright stifling. The crisp weather was certainly on our side.

Since I had traversed this old section of the Northville Placid Trail a few times before, I led the way. With our snowshoes on and our ski poles held tight in gloved and mittened hands, we headed south along the edge of an expansive field. We hiked under the canopy of an evergreen forest, the mix of Scotch, red, and white pines obviously planted by human hands. The rows of trees were too neat, too tidy for nature. We hiked fast. Our toes and fingers were cold from standing around the trailhead getting our gear ready.

I told Taylor we would soon be drawn away from the field and into the woods and then the old trail would curve east as it ran away from the farmland. Within a few minutes we met a feature that was not on our maps and that I had never seen before: a plowed road. I stopped short of the road and took out my map. I was baffled. Taylor must have noticed my confused expression. "Yeah," he said, "I think someone built a house back here. Someone said something about that. This must be their driveway."

The problem was that the driveway headed south-southeast, the same way the old trail went. It appeared that the homeowner, when constructing his driveway, ran right over the old Northville Placid Trail. Perhaps the homeowner didn't even know this unmarked trail existed. I explained to Taylor that I was having trouble figuring out if the driveway was west of the old trail, east of the old trail, or right smack dab on top it. If it was summer, this guessing game wouldn't have had such intrigue. But with two feet of snow covering the forest floor and any trace of our trail, and the giant snow banks lining the driveway, it was hard to make a good guess as to where our route lay.

After walking north on the driveway back towards the trail-head and then south on the driveway towards the new house, wherever that may have been, we decided we should continue walking towards the house and keep our eyes peeled for the trail. Our plan worked. Two minutes down the driveway we noticed a faint break in the tree line on the right: the corridor of an old trail. We climbed the high snow bank along the drive-way and plunged into the woods. We were still hiking fast and making great time. Now I could feel my toes. The feeling of warm, thick blood flush into my fingertips. I looked behind me to see if Taylor was still with me. He was hot on my heels.

The trail leveled, then descended gently, then climbed gently. At the top of a small rise we caught glimpses of Street Mountain and the Sawtooth Mountains far to the south. The sun beat down on us. Our spirits were high. We began to descend a big hill. At this point I had doubts that we were still on the old trail. It was fading in spots and was becoming difficult to follow, not being maintained in over thirty years. I didn't want us to go down this hill only to realize at the bottom that we had made a mistake in navigation. Then we'd have to hike back up. I told Taylor to wait where we stood in case I was taking us the wrong way.

I descended and bottomed out in a wetland. It was frozen, its white surface shimmering in the sunlight and bouncing the sun's rays up into my face. I squinted. Knowing I could not find the trail without being in the forest where a cleared corridor could be noticed, I crossed the wetland. My snowshoes made neat, precise imprints in the firm snow that had been baked during days and froze hard during nights. I entered the woods on the far side and found the continuation of our trail. I gave a whooping yell up to Taylor. "Woo-hoo! Come on down!"

As I watched Taylor complete the descent I noticed he was coming down out of balance, as if his snowshoes were on loosely or that he had never snowshoed before. This wasn't like him. He had a lot of experience snowshoeing. Besides, if you snowshoe only a few miles you'll be an expert by the end of such a short trip. It's only walking with much bigger feet.

As he got closer I saw what the problem was. While I was riding on top of the snow, sinking in six to ten inches, Taylor's snowshoes were "post holing" into the snowpack. On some of his steps the bottoms of his snowshoes scraped the frozen ground, which was buried two feet below the bottoms of my snowshoes. His ski poles, without their baskets, penetrated the snow like spears. This was not good. Taylor looked tired, which was also uncharacteristic. We had gone not two miles.

Taylor pulled up beside me, obviously frustrated. "I'm sinking in like crazy. I really should have brought bigger snowshoes."

"Well," I asked, "what do you want to do? Should we keep going?"

I knew what the answer would be. In his typical charm, Taylor replied with self-deprecation in his voice, "Nah, I'll be fine." Then with a smile he concluded, "This sucks."

And so we continued. The pitiful performance displayed by Taylor's snowshoes and poles, combined with his lunges down that hill, confirmed something I was not happy about. There was no way Taylor was going to be able to break trail during our trip. How imperfect! If he was sinking into his knees following the trail I broke for him, how was he going to get along in front of me? It wasn't going to happen. I slowed my pace and concentrated on slow, rhythmic breathing as I led the way. I had a whole lot of trail breaking ahead of me.

We covered the three miles of the old Northville Placid Trail and met up with the new Northville Placid Trail, meeting it at a faint intersection. At the intersection was a footbridge over an unnamed stream that begins high on Street Mountain miles away. We could barely hear the stream running, its wintertime power governed by blocks of ice and muffled by a foot of snow.

Our final mile to this subtle intersection had been quite scenic. Adirondack beavers had been hard at work flooding sections of the headwaters of the Chubb River. With their little ponds frozen solid, we glided across them. Taylor didn't have trouble on these sections since only a few inches of snow covered the ice. I tried to keep to the ice whenever possible. The sun beat down on us, giving us strength.

Lo and behold there was a broken ski track along the new Northville Placid Trail coming in from the left. Unfortunately, it began at Averyville Road and ended at our intersection. The original section of trail extending towards Moose Pond was untracked. The snow was deep. We turned right, continuing towards the pond. I continued to lead. Taylor tried to keep up. Though I was breaking trail, it didn't help Taylor at all. We might as well have been on two untracked trails that paralleled each other. A mile down the Northville Placid Trail I stopped. I was getting tired. I also had an idea.

"Taylor, how about we switch snowshoes?" I asked. "Then you can break trail and I can follow you. I'm lighter than you." I looked down at his snowshoes. "Maybe those won't be so bad on me."

Taylor looked up as he leaned over his ski poles, breathing hard. He probably would have wanted to chew on a dead cat rather than take on trail-breaking duty. But the idea made sense to me. As it was, we were both breaking trail.

"Okay," Taylor said, "but give me a minute."

We took our packs off and drew out snacks and water. We looked haggard, which was not good considering we still had to cover two miles to Moose Pond and then snowshoe up a peak with no trail at all. The snack eating and water guzzling gave us resolve. We could do this.

We switched snowshoes. Packs back on. Taylor took off like a man who had stolen something. Things were looking up, and quickly. With my big snowshoes on he mashed down the snow in front of him, leaving big imprints for me to walk in. Taylor's little snowshoes and I still sunk down more than I cared to. I couldn't believe Taylor had worn these rinky-dink things for nearly five miles. I would have quit. The kid is tough.

Our pace slowed. Taylor was working hard breaking trail, but his determination could not overcome the miles of virgin snow in front of him. Our breaks became more frequent. We were both getting cranky. Then we stopped talking to each other. It took too much energy to talk. Besides, what were we going to say? "This sucks"? On one particularly long break, I offered to go ahead with my tiny snowshoes. Taylor stepped to the side.

I made it sixty feet before I gave up. Wearing those little snowshoes was like wearing no snowshoes at all. Standing in snow up to my knees, I looked back at Taylor. I said matter of factly, "This isn't going to work. If you come up here, I'll put my snowshoes back on and break trail."

Taylor came forward. He felt bad, I could tell. Taylor is not a perfectionist like me, but he knew he was better than this. He realized that the moment that kid at his college's outing club handed him those wimpy snowshoes, he should have pushed them back and asked for a real pair. And when that kid tried to give Taylor a pair of ski poles without baskets, he should have eased them back over the counter. But the kid from the outing club was not with us, lucky for him.

Finally we reached the Moose Pond lean-to but only after Taylor's right leg busted through a frozen stream that I had walked across without any hint of breaking through. "Awwwwhhh!" he grumbled. He fought his way out of the stream, pulling hard to free his snowshoe, boot, and pant leg gripped by ice water, snow, and slabs of broken ice. Taylor appeared not sure what to do or say. With a sour expression he reported, "My boot just filled with water."

Then I wasn't sure what to say. "Okay." It sounded like I was reading from a book.

"What should I do?" he asked. It was probably the closest I had ever seen Taylor to being pissed off.

"Take your boot off, wring out your sock, put your boot back on, and keep moving." It sounded like insensitive advice, but it was actually sound. I knew we were close to the lean-to and that his foot would not freeze before we got there.

We arrived. The lean-to was empty, and no tracks led to it from the south. The area was desolate. Across Moose Pond snuggled below us rose the Sawtooth Mountains. They looked very snowy, very far away. I don't think I could have managed to climb any of them that day. We put our packs in the lean-to and sat on the edge of it. We didn't say much. Taylor dug a dry sock out of his pack and exchanged it for the sopping wet one on his foot. He wrung out his soaked sock. Gray ice water drained out the bottom. We laughed at Taylor going into the woods with kiddie snowshoes and ski poles without baskets. We laughed at me insisting on taking us down trails that are not broken and up peaks that have no trails. It felt good to laugh at ourselves. If Taylor wasn't there I would not have been able to laugh.

Daylight was getting short. It had taken us much longer to reach the lean-to than we had anticipated. We emptied our packs onto the lean-to floor and then repacked survival gear in our packs—down jackets, down booties, my sleeping bag, the tarp, and a good chunk of our food—and set out for the southwest peak of Street Mountain, leaving the rest of our gear in the shelter. We knew it would be sunset when we reached the top of our mountain. We put our headlamps in our jacket pockets so we wouldn't have to dig them out of our packs later.

The Northville Placid Trail south of the lean-to was in terrible condition. Dozens of downed trees crisscrossed the trail, and piles of snow hid the trail tread. Evergreens bent over the trail, heavy with snow. At times it felt like we were hiking through a tunnel more than down a trail. A half-mile along the trail we stopped. It was time to leave the path. Our peak rose to our left.

Leading the way off-trail with my compass, we started climbing. The snow was even deeper than it was on the trail. After twenty minutes I looked back and Taylor was nowhere to be seen. I waited. I was only at 2,600 feet. He arrived with slow steps. "Erik, I'm sorry, but I'm really tired. I can't go up this thing."

I felt sorry for Taylor. All his problems stemmed from his snowshoes. He looked bummed. "Hey, man, that's cool," I said, trying to put him at ease. "There's no view on top of this thing anyway."

"Yeah, I just don't think I should go up." Then he mentioned the continuing consequence of busting through that stream. "My right foot's frozen, too."

Taylor had an aura of gloom. "Hey, you don't have to convince me of anything. If you don't want to go up, then don't go up. It really doesn't matter to me. I mean, I'd like you to climb it with me, but if you don't want to, that's fine." Taylor didn't chime in. "Why don't you head back to the lean-to, get in your bag, get warm, and eat? That'll be better than going up this thing."

Taylor entered an only slightly better mood. Perhaps he wanted me to approve of his decision. When we had met a few years earlier he had been one of my outdoor education students. I was his field instructor. Maybe he still looked up to me that way. I wasn't sure. But I felt bad for Taylor, for there are few feelings worse than regret.

We parted ways after I told him, "If you don't see me three hours from now, you're gonna have to put your gear on and come find me. But I'll be okay."

"Okay."

Taylor began his descent. I was on my own. I missed having him with me, but most mountains I had climbed in winter I had climbed on my own. Besides, the hardest part is the beginning of the hill where you have the least amount of ground covered and the least amount of vertical feet scaled. The top seems so far away. It's demoralizing if you think about it. At the bottom of the climb you can't get your pace right, too. You're too slow, wasting time, or too fast, wasting energy. The higher you go sometimes the easier it is.

The fading light made me feel like a special guest in the forest. Likely no one had ever experienced sunset from this peak. Though I've not done it many times, snowshoeing to the top of a peak on a cold winter evening and then watching the sun set is a striking experience. It's the closing of one world and the opening of another. It is light to dark, wind to calm, motion to stillness, cold to colder. There's just something about winter twilight.

I climbed and climbed, my snowshoes giving their soft "plop, plop" back and forth, right then left, right then left. Methodical motion. I was in a groove. Below the summit was an open area that swept upward, both sides of this incline rising in graceful, rounded angles. It was like entering a small half-pipe. The snow was baked bright pink by the sunset far off to my right. It all looked like cotton candy. With the color, the cold air, my beating heart, and the sweat in my hair, I felt like I was in another world up there. I suppose I was.

After breaking trail up the final 100 vertical feet I reached the top. The summit was a dense patch of spruce trees, and there was no view even when standing on the three or four feet of snow. In the last light of day, just enough to see what I was writing, I penciled my thoughts in my journal. It was calm and 20 degrees.

An adventure with Taylor. Followed old NPT to the split, the section near the Pine Pond trailhead now a plowed road. A very nice ski track on the new NPT to near the split. Wish we were on skis. Sun, sun, sun to lean-to. Taylor's snowshoes are small. He turned around below. Open forest to scrappy top. Area just below was gorgeous! The light, the shape, the snow, the silence. Such beauty.

I didn't eat or drink. There would be time for that back at the lean-to. Besides, it was getting cold fast. I fought my way through the spruce forest and back off the summit. Then I slid down my cotton candy snow, which had already changed color. During the descent it looked like a slate roof. The sun had already set behind the Seward Mountains. Down I went, gracefully sliding down the steep spots and trudging across the flat spots. Halfway to the bottom I clicked my headlamp on. Its beam shone on the snow and my tracks, the blue-white light looking foreign in the dark forest. The natural light from the sunset had been much prettier.

Taylor heard me before he saw the beam of my headlamp, the harsh "crunch, crunch, crunch" of my snowshoes biting the hard nighttime snow. I rounded the back of the lean-to, swept around the side, and pulled up to the front, shining my light on Taylor in his sleeping bag. He looked content and cozy. Taylor had brought a book on this trip, which surprised me. A book had never crawled out of his pack during the few other overnight trips we had done. In the two hours he had been hanging out at the lean-to he had something to keep his mind off not getting up our first mountain. Like any reliable winter camping partner, Taylor had gone down to Moose Pond and managed to bash a hole in the ice so we could have fresh water. Despite being downtrodden, Taylor had been motivated and kind enough to solve the question of how we would get water. Thanks to Taylor we would not have to melt snow and ice over the stove, which takes a long time and uses a lot of fuel.

I recounted my hike and told Taylor how beautiful the cotton candy snow had been. I assured him there was no view from the top. He said, "I'm so happy you came back down. I really didn't want to have to go up there and find you if something happened. I'm so comfortable."

I tossed my pack in a back corner of the lean-to and then took off my snowshoes, resting them against the front log of our little home in the wilderness. I emptied the contents of my pack on the cold, wooden floor and dug out my warmest clothes, the clothes I was looking forward to when coming down the mountain.

I took off all my frosty clothing, much like Taylor had done a few hours earlier, and hung them on a series of nails and wooden pegs on my side of the lean-to. I put on mid-weight and heavy-weight long underwear tops and a pair of heavy-weight long underwear bottoms. I took off my cold, damp socks and replaced them with a dry pair of thick Merino wool socks that stretched up to my knees. They were heavenly. A fresh, dry winter hat and my big, puffy down jacket topped things off. It was down to 15 degrees.

I crawled into my sleeping bag and started rummaging through our kitchen gear. We boiled a gallon of water, some for making cocoa right then and there, some for our freeze-dried dinners, and some to put into water bottles that we then put in our sleeping bags to keep us toasty. We guzzled down butter-choked cocoa and gobbled butter-boosted freeze-dried dinners, which heated us from the inside out. Show me a winter camper who doesn't like butter, and I will show you an imposter. The temperature steadily dropped, and we inched down into our sleeping bags without even noticing. Overall, day one sucked, but tomorrow was another day. After hours of good night's sleep, durations that would easily stretch towards twelve hours, I was confident we would be raring to have a go at Boulder Peak.

Being in the western shadow of Street Mountain, our little lean-to hid in the shade the following morning. At 7:00 A.M. we ate breakfast. Then we put on our frozen clothes, repacked some survival gear, pulled our boots on, and snowshoed down to the pond by 8:30. It was 5 degrees. The surface was brilliant in the bright morning light, the flakes on Moose Pond dancing in the sun. We squinted intensely and wished we had brought sunglasses. Most days in the mountains aren't so sunny.

We crossed Moose Pond heading west, wrapped around a southern peninsula that jutted out, and then turned south to enter a long, deep bay. That was the easy part. With only a few inches of snow covering Moose Pond, Taylor had no problem scooting across this body of water. However, once we hit the woods at the end of the bay the snow lay deep. In the lead I took us across a flat area nestled between two compact hills. The sun tried to filter down but was blocked by a thick canopy of branches and needles, heavy with snow. It was very cold. We descended into a wide drainage to an important checkpoint where another, smaller drainage comes in from the west. With three feet of snow in the woods burying anything that may look like a drainage, we had to pay attention to our navigation.

We found our turn onto the secondary drainage, thank goodness. One mile into our hike we were heading west and nearly straight towards Boulder Peak. I had talked up the view from this peak to Taylor, and I'm sure he was interested to see what all the hoopla was about. I knew he would not be disappointed when we reached the top after two or three hours of bushwhacking. But I was the one who felt disappointed. While we took a short break to drink some water, Taylor spoke up. "Erik, I'm exhausted. You should go on without me."

I didn't know what to say. But Taylor's expression gave me direction. He looked spent. "You don't feel good, huh?" I asked.

He leaned on his ski poles. "Yeah, I don't know what it is. I'm so tired. I think that hike in yesterday really took it out of me." In his usual affection for others he apologized for feeling this way.

Like the day before, I tried to put his mind at ease. "If you want to head back to the lean-to, that's okay. But are you sure you want to head back?" I asked. I made a wimpy attempt at motivating him. "This is Boulder Peak, man."

"Yeah, I know," he said. "I know it's gonna be awesome up there, but I can't do it. I don't think I'd make it." He added, "And I can't feel my right foot. My boot's still frozen."

I let Taylor know that I would be comfortable with whatever he decided to do. What I didn't want him to do was spend his day bushwhacking up towards the peak to make it only half way, or three-quarters of the way, or almost all of the way yet not reach the summit. It would be too disheartening. I was also concerned about frostbite on his foot that sunk into the stream the day before. Before Taylor left, like I did on the southwest peak of Street Mountain, I asked him to come and try to find me if I did not return before dinnertime. He agreed.

Wishing me luck, Taylor started hiking back towards the lean-to in a hesitant stride. I was on my own again. I continued up the unnamed drainage. It carried only a little water, which I could barely hear underneath my snowshoes. Since I was tracking west the sun brightly shone on my backpack and the back of my legs. My front froze. I crept higher up the streambed but the sides crept in closer and closer, steeper and steeper, until I was trying to scramble up small, icy, awkward canyons. The ice spilled downhill in small, frozen waterfalls, the waterfall pools not being frozen due to the velocity of the impacting water. I almost fell into two pools, the ice right in front of me fracturing and then sinking into waist-deep ice water. I smartly headed for the woods.

The woods were no easier to get through. An extraordinary amount of snow had already fallen in the Sawtooth Mountains that winter. Since I was on the northeast side of Boulder Peak, not a glint of sunlight had reached this hidden forest since November. The snow had piled and piled, confident the sun would leave it alone until May. I plopped my snowshoes in front of me, left, right, left, right. My shoulders bumped into the tightly-packed spruces and firs, which dumped shovelfuls of snow on my head and my pack. Being in the shade was frigid and miserable. Hell is likely very cold, not hot.

To escape the cold I broke straight uphill, shooting for Boulder Peak's eastern ridge. That's where the sun was. It was a fight to get there. The climb of less than one mile and 700 vertical feet took more than two hours, the pace of a turtle. Even with my big snowshoes on I sank into snow up to my knees.

I hit the ridge flooded by sunlight, the light coming like a flash. The sun did nothing to warm me. It was cold, white light. Where I stood at 3,200 feet it was 15 degrees. By the time I reached the ridgeline I was cold more than anything else. Not tired, not thirsty, not hungry, not frustrated. Just cold. It was already noon. However, the sun put me in good spirits. This was Boulder Peak! I had been dying to get back to this mountain since I had climbed it in 2001. The view from the top was going to be worth every branch smacking me in the face, every plop of snow falling on my head, and every muscle burning in my legs.

Thank God I had my big snowshoes on. And Thank God Taylor had turned around. He would have been up to his neck in snow. On many parts of the ridgeline only the tops of young spruce trees stuck out. They looked like saplings, not real trees. But they were real, hearty trees, buried for the winter in six feet of Sawtooth Mountains snow. Every once in a while I would step onto a hollow section of snow where tree branches had intertwined with each other to create roofs of sorts. Under their hasty roofs were little, empty caves, free of snow, that I could fall into up to my waist and sometimes up to my arm pits. Dubbed "spruce traps," these secretive wintertime obstacles are well named. When you plunge into a spruce trap you feel like an animal caught is some cruel, ingenious pit. It also zaps a hiker's strength getting out of one. You also get very wet and snowy fighting your way back to the surface. I fell through five of them, then ten. At fifteen I stopped counting. I had to keep moving.

Looking up I asked myself, "Could it be?" Praise Jesus, there it was. The top! Wow. My motivation shot up like a rocket. Boulder Peak! I went to take a step towards the boulders I had not set foot on in nearly a decade and heard a terrible sound. "Bwwwwrrrraaapppp." Then a pause. And then a muffled "snap."

My left foot fell from under me. "Another spruce trap!" I cursed. While my left foot dangled in a dark pit, my right foot and its snowshoe remained on top of the snow. I was motionless, half standing and half sitting. My position was most awkward.

I grabbed a nearby short, stout spruce tree and hauled myself upright, putting all my weight on my steady right foot. Once out, I looked down at my left foot and saw something that made my heart sink: a boot with no snowshoe. I peered into the black hole and, thank goodness, I saw my snowshoe at the bottom. With all the snow up there it would have been easy to have my snowshoe buried to a point where finding it would be difficult, perhaps impossible. There was six feet of snow.

With a ski pole I fished around for my snowshoe like a fisherman poking around a koi pond, trying to catch the snowshoe's binding with the basket of my pole. I didn't want to crawl down into that hole. It was deep and cold and confining. Like with any good fish story, I caught my fish. My heart sank yet again. The snowshoe was broken. Badly.

I felt like a kid whose birthday cake had slid off the table. Here I was on a trailless mountain more than two miles from Taylor, more than two miles from a broken trail, and seven miles from a trailhead. Whatever fun I was having was gone. I went from recreation mode to survival mode, from experiencing Boulder Peak to wanting to get the hell off Boulder Peak. Without two good snowshoes under my feet, I was doomed to remain on Boulder Peak a long, long time. Just that one step without a left snowshoe had sent me flailing. I remembered the armpit-deep spruce traps behind me. If they were armpit-deep with two snowshoes on, well, I could literally be over my head in snow on the way back down. I felt very alone.

Not daring to walk any farther I balanced on my right foot as I gently took off my pack. I opened it and dug out my ditty bag—a bag of odds and ends. Part of the odds and ends always includes fifty feet of strong cord, a pocketknife, and, usually, large Zip ties. I bring Zip ties specifically for repairing snowshoes. I opened my ditty bag. No cord. No Zip ties. No repair kit. I couldn't believe it! For years—no, decades—I had carried cord in that ditty bag. I'll admit I didn't always carry Zip ties, but cord? It was always there. But it wasn't there on Boulder Peak.

I had to come up with an alternative fix for my snowshoe. If I ever needed to be a perfectionist, this was the moment. I stalked through the contents of my ditty bag. All I found that resembled cord were two bandanas (this resemblance was a real stretch). They were leftovers from my summertime packing list. I brought them to help dry off when I went swimming on hot summer days.

I removed my overmitts and gloves. The cold felt like flecks of glass in my skin. I managed to tie the two bandanas together and then wrap and tie one end around the stout aluminum frame of the snowshoe. I then wove the other end through the thickest, most reliable part of the plastic binding that remained, which wasn't that thick and did not look that reliable. I wasn't satisfied with my work, but my hands were so cold. I tried to warm my hands by placing them between my thighs. I put my gloves back on.

I dug my pocketknife out of my ditty bag and made a sacrificial cut to my backpack, severing a strap that I often didn't use. I cut the eighteen-inch-long piece of black nylon webbing off and then wrapped it and weaved it, binding to frame, frame to binding. It improved the makeshift fix greatly. My hands felt like they were being held in an open flame, burned by the cold even with my gloves on. Between my thighs my frozen hands went again.

I gently slid my boot into the floppy snowshoe binding, quickly pulled my overmitts on, and then, without the weight of my pack on, tested the snowshoe. It held. I dared not let out a sigh of relief though. I was not one step closer to Taylor. I didn't want to move. It wasn't about not fixing the snowshoe perfectly. I just didn't want to see it, feel it, or hear it break again. I was worried. And lonely. I felt like a kid who didn't want to jump off his first high cliff and into an Adirondack swim hole.

I wouldn't take one more step towards the summit despite seeing the boulders thirty feet ahead. Their sides and tops were neon white in the sun. I remembered the clouds of black flies that flew into my eyes and bit the back of my neck, ears, and hands during the summer of 2001. My cheeks, forehead, and even my eyebrows were gnawed red by those bugs. I would have given anything for oppressive July heat, humidity, and bugs instead of six feet of unconsolidated snow and a snowshoe held together with two bandanas and a strap.

Like a snowshoer trying to not wake a giant, I turned around and gently pressed my left snowshoe down into my ascending track. Again the binding held. I slid my right snowshoe forward after easing my weight onto the left. It still held. I tiptoed off the summit like that. Testing, bracing, sighing, relaxing, stepping, testing . . . All I wanted to do was get off the summit and down the eastern ridge. I stopped and realized I had not written in my journal. Out of sight of the boulders, I wrote quickly.

Solo on this peak as well. Taylor is whupped. Moose Pond, to drainage, to turned SW before bog, to spruce and snow hell. Very thick woods + enormous blocks of snow and ice + nasty snow pack = a good challenge. Shady, cold climb. Hit the top and my snowshoe broke. Badly! "Fixed" with two bandanas and a strap from my pack. Not fun. No boulder top for me. Sunny.

Down the mountain I went. Thank God I had my ascent track to follow. The snowshoe held, but every left step was awkward. The snowshoe flopped around as it saw fit, and the weight of descending strained the cob job repair. With two good snowshoes I would have covered the summit-to-pond retreat in an hour. With only one good snowshoe it would take me nearly triple that time.

I descended the northeast face. The temperature hadn't budged down in the shadows. I stumbled down the upper drainage, connected to the lower drainage, and then entered the flat patch of woods nestled between the two compact peaks. I could see where Taylor had trudged back to the lean-to. I hit the bay. By this time long shadows stretched across Moose Pond. The surface didn't have the brilliance it had in the morning, and no snowflakes danced. The snow looked pale and exhausted. Like me.

The "crunch, crunch, crunch" of my walk echoed across the pond. Walking on the few inches of snow on Moose Pond felt like walking on a sidewalk compared to breaking trail up and down Boulder Peak. Strolling in easy strides, I stopped. Could that be wood smoke I smelled? Taylor had a campfire going, and I felt like I was coming home.

There was Taylor in his big poofy down jacket and in his sleeping bag reading his book, his back up against the back wall of the lean-to. It looked like he had not moved an inch since the night before when he retreated from the southwest peak of Street Mountain. He looked up from his book with a big smile. "Yeah! How's it goin'?"

"Holy shit." I said. "There is so much fucking snow up there."

"Erik, I'm glad you're back."

"Why's that?" I asked.

"I think I have frostbite."

"Are you kidding me? Dude, did you see my snowshoe?" I took it off and held it up for Taylor. It looked like a chimp had repaired it. The frozen bandanas drooped off, and the black strap, now loose, was encrusted in so much snow and ice that he couldn't tell it was black. The binding limply hung on for whatever remained of its life.

"Holy shit!" Taylor said with a laugh. "What happened?"

I told him about the stream ice fracturing and sinking, the frigid northeast side of the mountain, the snow, the sun, the summit ridge, the spruce traps, and, finally, the broken snowshoe and how I didn't make it to the boulders though they were so close. Dry and toasty in his sleeping bag, Taylor said, "Thank God you came back down. If you didn't come back I don't think I would have gone up and helped you. It sounds like I would have died trying." We laughed. It felt great to laugh. It felt great to be next to my friend, a man who bashed a hole in the Moose Pond ice when he was at his lowest the night before and a man who got a fire going when he was at his lowest this day. Maybe all I do need is one hiking partner.

We addressed Taylor's frostbite, which was actually frostnip, the big toe on his left foot being jaundiced, a deep yellow color like honey. I prepared a hot water bottle and thawed his big toe slowly with it. Feeling returned within an hour or two. We also thawed Taylor's boot by the fire and forced a hot water bottle inside of it. I also put my broken snowshoe by the fire. I thawed the bandanas and strap and retied them with better care.

We passed the night staring into the fire, looking at the stars that held in the black night, eating, drinking cocoa, and mocking people who aren't cool enough to bushwhack. "Hey," we thought, "we may have gotten our butts kicked on these two trailless peaks, but at least we're out here trying." We've always felt that being beaten back by a peak with no trail is more honorable than summiting a peak with a packed trail. Not having your way in the mountains is a humbling experience that reminds us that mountains are older, tougher, and taller than we are. Mountains don't need us.

We slept the sleep of winter campers. We woke early. It was 5 degrees again. Another sunny day greeted us. We knew what each other was thinking. It was a shame to have to leave such a pretty place, even if it was cursed. Taylor looked off at Boulder Peak like he wanted another go at it. He also looked so content in his sleeping bag that perhaps I was mistaken. Maybe we'd be back. Maybe not.

On our hike out we made better time than on our hike in. Our day-old snowshoe tracks were frozen hard, and there was little trail-breaking duty to be done. Taylor kept up with ease but hobbled a little, his partially-frozen right boot refusing to bend. Back along the Northville Placid Trail, to the faint intersection, down the old Northville Placid Trail, across the beaver ponds, and across the driveway we hiked under a blue sky. Then finally, the trailhead.

Taylor's Civic was frosty from the past two nights' single digit readings. His car looked even colder than I was on Boulder

Peak. The snow banks still towered above the lot. Nearly three days of sun had not melted an inch of them. It was like we were in a continent-sized freezer. We threw our packs on the snow, dropped our poles, and removed our snowshoes. My damaged one was still in one piece. Remarkable. Perhaps I had repaired it "perfectly." We looked at each other and smiled. Our self-deprecating smiles were hard earned.

I thought I had lost Taylor as my only hiking partner on this cursed Moose Pond trip. But a man like Taylor can be down, yet he can never be out. Taylor called two weeks later and asked where we were going next. I told him about a perfect little trip I had in mind.

Booty Call of the Wild

I'm a scrounger. Always have been. Likely always will be. Even when I have money in the bank and cash in my wallet, I scrounge. A month ago I found two old, wooden chairs in an industrial dumpster down the street from my home. A house was being gutted. I fished the two chairs out at night. I didn't want my neighbors see me climb into a dumpster. The chairs' old white paint was peeling and stained with runny splotches of black and brown, like they had been resting on the bottom of the Hudson River before they were reeled in and tossed into the trash heap. I scrubbed them, washed them, sanded them down, and then caringly brushed on two thick coats of Behr Premium Plus Ultra interior satin enamel in soft daffodil yellow (no junk paint for me). I love my new chairs. These chairs are an example of "street booty."

The acquisition of street booty is rare for me because I spend so little time on the streets. I spend an awful lot of time in the woods though, and this is where I find "trail booty." Booty, as defined by my favorite reference book, a 1968 *Reader's Digest Great Encyclopedic Dictionary*, which clocks in at a hefty 2,094 pages, is: "The spoil of war; plunder. Goods taken by violence or robbery. Any prize or gain." Wedged below "boot tree" and above "booze" in this heavy reference text, booty is derived from the French *butin* and influenced by the Middle Low German *boot*. Middle Low German was a language popular in the Germanic regions between 1100 and 1450.

Booty has, well, a more popular but less innocent meaning today. Via a non-scholarly online dictionary that's primarily used by people half my age, a "booty call" is defined as "A late night summons—often made via telephone—to arrange clandestine sexual liaisons on an ad hoc basis." You can imagine what the "booty" part is. So when I tell a person quite younger than me that "I got some trail booty" in the Adirondack Mountains the weekend prior, he gives a sheepish, sometimes suspicious, grin and asks, "Did you get her name?" I'm cautious to not openly label the two chairs above as "street booty." In the Capital Region of New York, where I live, street booty has a clear, familiar definition: one that involves ladies of the night, Johns, a meeting place, and an exchange of money or drugs.

My street booty is limited to a few pieces of furniture here and there, but my trail booty pedigree is something to be respected. When I am in the woods I'm constantly on a casual search for free stuff. I've acquired quite a bit of it.

My quests for "any prize or gain" began during the summer of 1999 when I had my first real outdoor job as caretaker and ridge runner for the Maine Appalachian Trail Club. It was a simple, pure life. I lived in a tent, did my laundry in a five-gallon bucket, and took a shower with a five-gallon bucket. I had no access to phone or the Internet. I received occasional mail at the post office, a three-mile hike down 2,000 vertical feet of rugged trail and a six-mile drive into civilization. My diet was as simple as my life. Ramen, peanut butter, instant black beans, tea, powdered milk, cereal, cookies, cheese, pepperoni, crackers, and honey kept me full with plenty of ice cream on days off. During my five months in Maine I climbed a whopping 89 mountains, an average of nearly twenty a month. While not at work my journeys took me to the Presidential Range, the Canadian border, Baxter State Park, Mahoosuc Notch, and just about everywhere in northern New England.

During workdays at my base of operations, my campsite at Horns Pond, I greeted day hikers passing through and registered backpackers staying at one of the eight campsites or two lean-tos near Horns Pond. I also tended two composting outhouses that, long and fetid story short, turned poop into potting soil.

Horns Pond is the most used campsite in Maine outside Baxter State Park. Nestled below The Horns—twin peaks that look like two bald knuckles rising out of a fist of woods—Horns Pond is one of the highest bodies of water in the state. In addition to greeting, registering, and tending, I made sure the two lean-tos were free of two things: graffiti and garbage.

Many people hear a unique call of the wild. It is a voice that, for whatever reason, propels them to carve their initials in shelters to prove to someone, but who we are not sure, that they were there. In addition to initials, the more popular lean-to art I see includes a pot leaf, the triangle symbol for the band Pink Floyd, and the word Phish. Boy Scout symbols are not uncommon, which further literally displays the public relations woes this organization has. Graffiti inside the lean-tos at Horns Pond was absent. Why? Because I was there. No day hiker or backpacker dares to carve something into a lean-to when others are around. But such are cowards.

Even worse than those who carve initials into lean-tos are the degenerates who carve initials into trees, which only happened in my patrol area on the rarest of occasions. William Harlow, in his 1942 *Trees of the Eastern and Central United States and Canada*, a real gem of a book, describes the tree carvers, particularly American beech carvers, well: "Because of its smooth gray bark, beech usually has a great attraction for that species of forest park vandal, the initial carver. Nothing good can be said for the practice of trying to attain a cheap immortality by scarring an otherwise attractive tree trunk." Amen, Mr. Harlow.

Garbage was rare for the same reason graffiti was rare. People generally only litter when no one is around. And the farther you hike into the woods and the tougher the hike is, the more trustworthy and thoughtful people are. Most littering, and more serious offenses such as rape, robbery, and murder, nearly all take place within a half-mile of a road. The farther in you go, the safer it is and the cleaner it is. Litter bugs me.

Occasionally Appalachian Trail thru-hikers would purposely leave belongings in the lean-tos. I regarded this abandoned stuff as garbage. Their point was to leave items so other thru-hikers, likely acquaintances of theirs who were days behind them, could stop by the Horns Ponds lean-tos and pick up items they needed. Items were innocently yet deliberately left behind for the common good. People who left junk in the lean-tos were also thinking that a poor backpacker passing by or staying at the lean-tos would say with thanks, "Ah-ha! That's what I need. A can of tuna! A bookmark! A broken lighter! Glad someone left it for me in these lean-tos." Hikers left behind toilet paper, matches, candles, maps, duct tape, tarps, tin foil, cord, and an assortment of other things, most of them useless.

I snagged all these items from the lean-tos. Most of it was junk that got thrown out when I hiked down from my campsite and into civilization. But there was one item in particular that summer that I found and kept and cherished. It was a book by an author I had never read before.

This was not any old book, and it did not tell any semblance of a normal tale. No, when someone reads Hunter S. Thompson's *Fear and Loathing in Las Vegas: A Savage Journey into the Heart of the American Dream*, an adjective that never, ever passes lips is "normal." From this book I learned that no one who knew Hunter S. Thompson would call him that either.

Thompson was known for three things: writing, guns, and drugs. Combine Stephen Ambrose (award-winning author of thirty books, all of them good), Ted Nugent (gun lover who once told President Barack Obama: "Suck on my machine gun") and William S. Burroughs (noted drug fiend), and you'll have someone like Hunter S. Thompson. *Like* Hunter S. Thompson.

First, no one wrote like Thompson. No one ever will. In an obituary he wrote about Richard Nixon, who he hated, he reasoned that "If the right people had been in charge of Nixon's funeral, his casket would have been launched into one of those open-sewage canals that empty into the ocean just south of Los Angeles." But Thompson could compromise when he needed to. If being hurled into a Los Angeles cesspool was not a viable option, then Nixon's corpse "should have been burned in a trash bin." He liked Regan though. "I had a soft spot in my heart for Ronald Reagan, if only because he was a sportswriter in his youth, and also because his wife, [Jane], gave the best head in Hollywood."

He wrote that Palm Beach is a place where "millionaires gnaw the brassieres off the chests of their own daughters in public." He called a man "a shameless thieving whore with a bad whiskey jones and the morals of a slut on acid." He called another man "the whole Mason family compressed into one person like a huge tube of blood sausage with a head and two legs."

Like any decent American, Thompson loved guns. The first image I ever saw of the author was a black and white photo of him getting ready to blow away an electric typewriter with a large-caliber revolver with a scope mounted to the top of it. This was in response to a bout of writer's block. (I sometimes want to do something like this with my Mossberg 590A1 combat shotgun, but laptops are expensive.) As the *Economist* wrote in their obituary of Thompson, "There were always way too many guns around at Hunter S. Thompson's farm in Woody Creek," his Rocky Mountain compound outside of Aspen. He took his own life with a revolver, either a beefy .357 or a beefier .44.

Thompson felt comfortable around two things that usually don't go well together: guns and drugs. The *Economist* put it simply: "He did not give 'a flying fuck' what he smoked or ingested." In *Fear and Loathing in Las Vegas* Thompson is weighed down during his travels by "two bags of grass, seventy-five pellets of mescaline, five sheets of high-powered blotter acid, a salt shaker half-full of cocaine, and a whole galaxy of multi-colored uppers." On a brief fishing trip with two others he packed "four cases of Heineken beer, two quarts each of Chivas Regal and Wild Turkey, two bottles of gin and a gallon of orange juice, along with six bottles of their best wines and another six bottles of champagne for the cocktail party that night." Add to that powdered heroin, marijuana, and synthetic mescaline.

Drugs, not guns, are the centerpiece of *Fear and Loathing in Las Vegas*. When Thompson wrote this book in 1971, he had already proven he could arrive at a venue with an assignment but get drunk and forget why he was sent there in the first place. Thompson was sent on assignment in 1970 to cover the Kentucky Derby. When he got to the derby he was too drunk to accurately cover the event. Instead, he rambled on about himself and his drugs and his whiskey, the final article titled "The Kentucky Derby is Decadent and Depraved." This *Rolling Stone* article was a hit.

When Thompson was sent to the Mint 400, a 400-mile-long off-road motorcycle race, in 1971, he did the same thing he did at the derby. Instead of writing the 250-word summary assigned to him by *Sports Illustrated*, he wrote about drugs and fat cops and stupid people and patriotism and demolishing hotel rooms. His 50,000-word piece became *Fear and Loathing in Las Vegas*.

Finding that copy of *Fear and Loathing in Las Vegas* in one of the Horns Pond lean-tos made my summer, and it turned me on to Thompson's "gonzo journalism" writing style. Later I read his *Fear and Loathing (On the Campaign Trail in '72)*, *Generation of Swine*, *Hell's Angels*, *Hey Rube*, *Songs of the Doomed*, and *The Curse of Lono* (he has another seven titles). These publications, though quite good, pale in comparison to that first Thompson book I read in Maine. I had never laughed so hard. I had never seen such writing. I could not put it down. This was Thompson's favorite book to write, he regarded it as his best work, and he knew it would be the most financially successful of his books. He summed, "*Vegas* is a book that no other living writer could have written." Thompson's writing is unremorseful, brash, sincere, zany, grim, and ungoverned. It's gonzo.

This first-ever piece of trail booty was cursed though, leading to a confrontation with an Appalachian Trail thru-hiker. It was late morning at the Horns Pond lean-tos. This was typically the quietest part of the day since backpackers were moving between campsites. As I sat on the edge of the shelter reading my trail booty book while the sun climbed over Sugarloaf Mountain to the south, a thru-hiker pulled into the campsite. Hearing him approach, I closed my book and laid it at my side to greet him.

He looked like the rest of them. He had a scruffy beard, scruffy hair, chiseled legs, a deep tan and wore a pair of shorts and a t-shirt worn for so long that they looked part of his body. We exchanged light conversation, me asking him how his thru-hike was going and him asking me what my job was like.

Two men in the woods talking about the woods. At times I admired these thru-hikers. Though I was spending five months in the woods myself, the average time it took a thru-hiker to cover the Appalachian Trail, being a long-distance hiker myself I would have rather been hiking hundreds of miles than being corralled into one specific area. But I loved my job. I was getting paid to do what the thru-hikers were paying to do.

The thru-hiker dug into his pack and pulled out his food bag and water bottle. It was turning out to be a hot day. As he took care of himself, I let him be. I picked my book back up.

Soon I felt the thru-hiker's eyes upon me. I tried to ignore him but couldn't. I thought he must have been wondering what I was reading. I looked up from my book and smiled at him. He was not smiling. "What's up?" I asked.

"Um," he started, choosing his words carefully. "Where did you get that book?"

"Oh," I said. "I found it in the lean-to a few days ago. Great book."

The thru-hiker thought for a moment and then chose a tone which communicated I had made a mistake but didn't realize it since I was naive. "That's a *trail book*, brother."

I knew what he meant. A thru-hiker had left this book for another thru-hiker. I didn't possess the tolerance to get into a philosophical conversation about thru-hikers leaving stuff in lean-tos I vowed to keep clean. I was four months into my season. I think the thru-hikers were beginning to annoy me. Most were cool. Some had spent too much time in the woods. The thru-hikers who started going off the deep end, vowing to never rejoin evil capitalistic society, morphed into something more than backpackers. They became wandering hippies.

I was having such a nice day. Why was this guy giving me flak for reading a book I found and then enjoyed? "Sorry about that, but it's not a trail book. Someone left it here. It's my book now."

His condescending tone deepened. "Well, you see, I know someone left it here for another thru-hiker to enjoy. So . . ."

He raised his eyebrows and smiled at me with his head tilted, his "So . . ." communicating something to the effect of, "So . . . I'll forgive you if you stop reading it and put it back where you found it."

"So . . ." I responded, "I don't know what to tell you. It's a really good book. And it's mine." We were at a stalemate like two sword-wielding warriors trying to cross a log over a deep gorge. Neither would let the other warrior pass.

Disgusted with me for breaking an unwritten Appalachian Trail decree, he soon packed up his belongings and left with a critique: "That's so not cool, brother." I picked up *Fear and Loathing in Las Vegas* and continued where I had left off.

When I returned to the Adirondack Mountains at the end of my 1999 Appalachian Trail season, I brought my love for trail booty with me. During the past fifteen years of hiking all over the Adirondack Park, I have found great trail booty, good trail booty, and not so good trail booty. I also started classifying finds into two subcategories: "bushwhacking booty" and "lean-to booty" (in hindsight, my copy of *Fear and Loathing in Las Vegas* was technically lean-to booty).

Not everyone is attracted to booty. They regard it as garbage. One man's trash is another man's treasure. So when I was teaching a backpacking leadership course in Pharaoh Lake Wilderness Area and came upon a lean-to with an old fleece jacket hanging on the wall, my students thought it was kind of weird, and gross, that I went bananas over it. "Yeah, baby! That's what I'm talking about. Lean-to booty." I pulled the fleece jacket down, held it up to my body, and, seeing it would fit, asked if anyone else wanted it. After all, a good leader puts himself last. With shakes of heads from side to side instead of up and down, the jacket was mine. I shook it off and inspected it. "I'll take it." Later that night I balled it up and stuck it under my head. It made a great pillow. The students assured me I was going to get lice. The fleece jacket hangs in my closet today. I wear it around the house when it gets chilly.

Most things I find in lean-tos are rather innocuous items. But they do add up. I haven't bought cord during the last fifteen years. I find ten feet here, twenty feet there, fifty feet there. I haven't bought matches since I don't know when. I have nearly run out of candles. For years I was finding lots of candles in lean-tos. I'd repossess them and use them during winter camping trips. I have only a few left. Luckily, I don't go on many winter camping trips these days. I have found cans and bottles of bug repellent in lean-tos. I haven't used them. Most I threw out. Usually I bring my trusty Ole Time Woodsman with me. I have found a couple of maps. One portrayed a section of the Northern Forest Canoe Trail while another detailed the northwest region of the Adirondack Park. I still have those maps.

For a while I was on a tarp-finding spree. Brown, blue, or green, most of them were in excellent condition. These often ended up at lean-tos via inexperienced backpackers who thought they'd need a tarp, but then they got to the shelter and learned that they didn't need a tarp. So they left them. I have three tarps. The others I gave away to friends so they could cover their woodpiles during winter.

Beyond these incidentals, I have only a couple of big scores at lean-tos. *Fear and Loathing in Las Vegas* was a big score. The only other book I found and read and enjoyed was *Noah John Rondeau: Adirondack Hermit* by Maitland DeSormo. Fittingly, I found this book in a lean-to along the Cold River, where Rondeau used to live. I gave it to a friend when I was done with it. In the Cold River valley I also found an old-time felt hat like the ones old-time loggers and woodsmen would wear. I wore it for a while and lost it. Now it's someone else's booty.

While hiking in High Peaks Wilderness Area I visited the back of a lean-to to pee. When I looked down I saw a pocket knife. I stepped to the side, relieved myself (I really couldn't wait), and then picked up the knife. It was brand new, not a scratch on it. This SOG Autoclip model AC20-CP knife, valued at $30, was a hell of a find. I carried it w... for years until it got stolen out of my car one night. Someone got some "car booty."

The only other Adirondack lean-to booty of note is a small pair of binoculars and a fancy lighter. The binoculars are not powerful enough for any kind of serious viewing. I gave them to a friend of mine. She uses them to view the birds at her feeders near her kitchen window. She says they're good for that. The lighter seems powerful enough to smelt iron. It's a fantastic device that puts out a tiny, blue flame yet sounds like a welding torch. I haven't used it though. I just bring a regular lighter into the woods. Additional straight-up Adirondack trail booty includes a lightweight pair of Manzella gloves, which I found on Lower Wolf Jaw Mountain in the High Peaks.

I have found food at lean-tos, but I have to be careful with that stuff. Nothing ruins a backpacking trip like food poisoning. The only two foods I have eaten are a can of seasoned re-fried beans and a "self-contained stove-top popping pan." In other words, Jiffy Pop. The can of beans was found in a lean-to in High Peaks Wilderness Area towards the end of a three-day backpacking trip with a friend of mine. We combined the beans with what we had left in our food bags: instant mashed potatoes, cheddar cheese, and hot sauce. Then we slapped this steaming, messy, tasty mush onto our remaining tortillas. We were in heaven.

The Jiffy Pop was found in Pharaoh Lake Wilderness Area by me and my girlfriend. The popping container was hanging on a branch at an illegal campsite. We disassembled the site's fire ring, hucked the rocks into the lake, scattered the ashes in the woods, and then dropped leaves over the site so as to conceal it. For our volunteer conservation work we enjoyed popcorn for dessert that night while overlooking scenic Pharaoh Lake.

Most of my booty found directly on trails has come from outside the Adirondack Park. I found a lightweight balaclava in the

White Mountains of New Hampshire; a folding arm chair in the Catskill Mountains; a water bottle in the Smokey Mountains; a boonie hat in Nantahala National Forest; and a North Face four-person tent on the highest peak in New Mexico.

Bushwhacking booty has been limited since few people bushwhack. Outside of the community of Speculator I found a makeshift campsite far from any trails. The woods were trashed, the slobs leaving a lot of their gear behind. I salvaged a fleece sleeping bag, four fuel containers for my backpacking stove, and a coffee mug.

There is a third subcategory of woods booty beyond lean-to booty and bushwhacking booty, one that doesn't offer much. But the one item I found in this realm of booty is probably the best thing I have ever found in the woods. Now we enter the rare yet profitable world of "river booty."

Looking for treasures in a river is usually not worthwhile for one reason. Most things in the world sink. Wallets, sunglasses, cameras, phones, knives, and so forth; once they go overboard they go down like little *Titanics*. Most items, if retrieved, are ruined. But an item from the brief list above turned out to be my greatest booty find of all.

I paddled my Old Town Pack canoe down a section of the 120-mile Raquette River on the western border of High Peaks Wilderness Area. It was August. Most of the bugs were dead, thank goodness. My pack was tied into the front of the twelve-foot dark green solo canoe, my backpack straps clipped to the thwart with a carabiner. My PFD was snug around my torso while my callused, woods-roughened hands gripped the paddle that propelled me forward.

It was another day "living the life" by getting paid by the Department of Environmental Conservation to hike and canoe in the Adirondack Park. As the only seasonal backcountry ranger in the Western High Peaks, it was nice to be doing my favorite thing and getting paid to do it. Early to meet my boss, Earl, the local law enforcement ranger, I decided to put my paddle away and let the sluggish current carry me all the way to my take-out point. My hand draped over the side of the boat, gently trolling downstream with my little canoe. It was a hot day, and as the river widened towards Trombley Landing, my and Earl's meeting point, shade became scarce. The day was nearly silent. A few birds called in the distance and an occasional breeze rattled the leaves, but no manmade noise penetrated the river valley. I had not seen anyone since the ranger outpost at Raquette Falls early that morning.

Coming upon a small, sandy take-out on the right side of the river, I pulled over to stretch my legs and check things out. I pulled the lightweight boat on shore, took off my PFD, and hiked up a steep, short hill away from the river. A lean-to, hidden in the pine forest, was empty. I sat in the shelter and looked down on the river and my tiny boat. I was thankful for having a job I loved.

Not much else to do, I hiked back down, hopped in my boat, and shoved off. As I backed the boat off the shore and went to paddle forward, downriver, I noticed something gleaming on the sandy bottom. I coasted downstream a little, did a wide sweeping turn back upriver, and again passed the section of water where I had thought I had seen something. I peered into the rust-colored water and saw it: a kitchen knife on the bottom.

I pulled back into the take-out, slid my boat on the shore again, and then took off my boots, socks, and shirt. The sun felt good on my bare shoulders. I was going in after that knife. It wasn't that I needed a kitchen knife that was lying on the bottom of a river for who knows how long. That's pretty lousy booty. What I didn't want was to have someone staying at the lean-to jump in the river for a swim and cut their foot on a knife. This was a diving mission of purest cause. This was public protection.

I submerged into the crawling current. It was amazing how blurry things were when compared to peering down from my boat. I came up for air, went under again. Nothing. I pulled myself out of the river, my soaking pants weighing me down.

Warm river water ran out the bottoms of my pockets, down my legs, and onto the shore.

I paddled out again and spotted the knife again. This time I made surer of its location, which was ten feet from shore and straight out from a baby pine growing near the shoreline. Back to shore and into the river I went again. No luck. Again. I dived down three times, scanning the sandy bottom with each descent. Without luck, I got onshore, climbed the embankment a little and tried to peer down into the river. It was impossible to see below the surface. The sun, clouds, and silver maples that hung over the shorelines were mirrored on the river's surface.

One more trip out in the boat, and that was it, I promised. I was still a bit ahead of schedule in meeting Earl, yet I certainly didn't want to be late. Once we met and I got a ride back to our base of operations in the Village of Long Lake, my weekend would begin. Chances were good I'd end up hiking on my days off, but it was still my weekend. I would kick it off with a hot shower, clean clothes, and a can of beer.

Out on the river I spotted the knife and again noted its location. I was closing in on my knife like a destroyer closing in on a U-boat. Back to shore and back in I went. Success! On the first dive I swept down to the bottom and saw my knife. It appeared to be an old, nasty, cruddy kitchen knife, something you'd see in a domestic violence call on Cops. I grabbed the slimy, slippery handle and headed for the surface. I burst out of the water with my prey.

Stumbling onto the shoreline, my heavy pants spouting water everywhere, I looked at the knife. This was no kitchen knife. It looked unique. It was . . . beautiful. The handle looked wooden, but I couldn't tell with it being waterlogged and covered with slime. I scrubbed the slime off as best I could in the river and tossed the knife in my boat. Shirt and shoes back on, I dug a bandana out from my pack and went to scrubbing the knife more thoroughly. As each little layer of slime and river smudge was wiped away it became clear that whoever lost this knife was probably really bummed that they had lost it.

Upon conferring with Earl when we met, for he knew more about knives than I did, we were in agreement that it was a handmade knife. It was the first handmade knife I had ever seen. It's still the last. The nine-inch long knife has a silver five-inch blade that looks much like the end of a sword. It's thin. The blade's spine (the thickest point of the non-cutting side) is just four millimeters thick. A front bolster (the section where the blade joins the handle) is of brass, while the rear bolster (the bottom of the handle) is brass as well. Though I retrieved this knife more than a decade ago, and have it still, I am not certain as to what the 3.5-inch handle is made of. Some feel the handle is part of an antler, which ups the "cool factor" of this knife. Some think it's made of wood. I personally feel it is wood of a hard species such as locust, hornbeam, or oak, though I don't know if these species are commonly carved.

I like to think that the owner made it himself and that the knife had traveled with him for years through the Adirondack Mountains. The knife has great balance to it. It is well-designed to rest in a man's grip. It's hard to drop. But someone, sometime, for some reason, dropped it into the Raquette River. Such a unique item to drop, the only reason I can see for someone not stripping down and diving in like I did was that it was dropped during late fall, when making or buying a new knife seemed smarter than jumping into icy river water. It also could have fallen overboard without the person knowing this until they unloaded their boat at their take-out. What a frown that must have been.

The discussion of booty; that is, taking something from the out-of-doors that is not yours (yet no one else's), was introduced to me by my Wilderness Leadership professor, Jack Drury. When I became a student of Jack's during the early 1990s, he had already made a name for himself as one of the best outdoor educators in the Northeast, perhaps in the U.S.

Jack has been an Adirondack guide, as of this writing, for 42 years. That's one year more than your author has been alive. He founded the Wilderness Leadership major I completed at North Country Community College, is former president of the Wilderness Education Association, climbed Denali decades before it was cool to climb Denali, and has traveled across most of our continents. He has authored two books. Jack is a backcountry mentor of mine who stands shoulder to shoulder with other mountain mentors like Guy and Laura Waterman.

One thing Jack likes to discuss is ethics. Specifically, back-country ethics. The choice to remove or not remove something from the backcountry comes down to a singular question he would ask his leaders-in-training: "What makes something an artifact and something else junk?" I'm proud of the answer I gave him, and it's an ethos I follow today. To be an artifact it has to not be available today. All the rest of the stuff is junk. A field instructor of mine framed this discussion more succinctly when talking about the presence of all things in the backcountry human-made: "When the entire human race is dead and gone and aliens land on this planet, they're going to look at each other and say, 'My God! These people put shit *everywhere!*'"

Therefore, I have come across "bushwhacking booty" in the form of woodstoves stamped as early as 1814, ancient bottles, and horse-based logging remnants such as horseshoes, cables, and sled runners. I don't touch any of these because they are irreplaceable components of the Adirondack historical land-scape. They don't make stoves like that, they don't make bottles like that, and they don't make metal like that anymore. Though I stumble across items like these hidden deep in trail-less regions that no one else will likely ever enter, I leave them, just as I would a bird's nest, a moose antler, or a turtle shell. Instead, I record what I find in my journals. I record what I see with my camera. On my maps I record where the most notable artifacts are.

The items in lean-tos? The matches, candles, tarps, cord, books, and cans of refried beans? There's nothing special about them. I could go "by the book" and remind backpackers that one of the Department of Environmental Conservation's regulations is that "any tent or other camping equipment left unoccupied for more than 48 hours may be taken down and removed." I have never liked going by the book, and ethics can't be controlled by ink and paper. Ethics are controlled by us—the people out there leaving the place a little tidier than how we found it. It is our duty. Especially when it involves taking a really good book home.

Cops

"Bad boys, bad boys, what 'ya gonna do?" It's a lyric so famil-iar to so many people that chances are good that you, like me, sang the following line with it: "What 'ya gonna do when they come for you?"

You may know the lyrics, but I doubt you know the band: Inner Circle. I only know who sings this song because, being an astute viewer, I read the credits at the end of television pro-grams and movies. Despite popular assumption, Inner Circle was no one-hit wonder, though their biggest hit was indeed

"Bad Boys," the theme of the longest-running reality television series ever: Cops.

Formed in 1968 and first known as The Inner Circle Band, this Jamaican reggae group has released thirty albums. The one that started it all was Dread Reggae Hits in 1973, and their most recent album, Hawaii Sings Jacob Miller, was released in 2013. To put this band's pedigree into perspective, the Rolling Stones have been around just six years longer than Inner Circle has. Fellow Jamaican Bob Marley died at age 36. Inner Circle has already rocked a decade longer than that dreadlock-wearing, guitar-strumming, pot-smoking reggae god lived.

Inner Circle shows no signs of stopping despite working with nine different record labels and replacing band members about two dozen times. The current lineup includes Ian Lewis, Roger Lewis, Lancelot Hall, and Bernard Harvey. This foursome has led Inner Circle since 1986, the year before their 3-minute, 49-second "Bad Boys" was released and adopted by Cops for their first episode in 1989.

"Why reggae?" is a question I have asked. After all, this genre is about kicking back with a bong, bowl, hookah, joint, spliff, water pipe, or vaporizer full of weed (of course I'm only aware of these illicit terms from what I've read on the Internet), perhaps following your smoke session by a drink or two, all the while the lights turned down and the music never running aground. The music is mellow, the chords soft. The lyrics encourage introspection, social justice, and peace and harmony.

By using reggae, the producers of *Cops* have created a paradigm. The graceful and groovy music plays while we see a helicopter swooping down on a neighborhood, sheriffs pointing guns at people sprawled on the pavement, and mean-looking German Shepherds being released on suspects. Such a confusing encounter between auditory peace and visual violence—tranquility and mayhem—could only be replicated by listening to Enya while working at a slaughterhouse. Whether or not you find Inner Circle's "Bad Boys" appropriate to introduce such a program, the music still gets us fired up for choke holds, shootouts, high-speed chases, and drunk mistresses.

A good question should be asked when viewing any reality television program: *Is it really real?* Think long and hard or do your own research on this subject, and you'll start calling reality television "reality" television—when writing it, putting the first word in quotation marks or, when saying it, framing that first half with air quotes.

During 2008 I actually worked on production of a reality television episode for MTV's second-longest-running series: *Made*. It's a disgraceful piece of my past that most do not know about until now. Citing that I worked with MTV for an entire month to produce this show, I can assure you that most reality is lost in television. A lot of times it was never there to begin with.

To produce one episode of Cops, field producers record approximately 15,000 minutes of tape. The editors and producers use only 42 minutes of it—one-quarter of one percent—to construct a reality that offers an appealing storyline. In reality television programs few references are made to times and dates since taped segments are later cut and pasted to form alternate timelines. But it's hard to keep track of 15,000 minutes of events. Sloppy editors have people getting into certain vehicle makes and models and then pulling up to destinations in different makes and models, for example. Watch any reality television show with concentration, and you will pick out more inconsistencies than cops pick out in clumsy burglars' cover stories.

Despite my obvious reservations about authenticity claims from reality television proponents, I never helped produce an episode of Cops. I've never been a cop. I know a couple of cops, but we rarely talk about their work. So when I found myself camped in a lean-to in a remote corner of the Adirondack Park with two cops from New Jersey, I had to ask: "Is your job anything like what I see on Cops?" I wanted to know if the reality of police work was as ill-placed as that reggae music itself.

I usually camp pristinely. That is, I wander off-trail and set up my camp in a section of woods that, going with the odds, no one has ever camped in. I make sure no widow-makers are overhead: dead trees and branches that may crash down onto my camp during the night, my cynical politically-correct name for widow-makers being "life partner eliminators." Assured my camp is legal—200 feet from road, water, and trail—and hidden from trail hikers, and not under foliage that could crush me while I sleep, I clear a few sticks out of the way, set up my tarp, and there I have it, home sweet home for the evening.

I ended up sleeping in a lean-to, and thus camping with two cops, for good reason. I was hiking through a rainstorm in the dark after covering a heck of a bunch of miles. By the time I reached this lean-to during an October 2008 hike I had covered 31 miles and climbed 3,500 vertical feet. It was day two of a three-day, 86-mile hike in the central Adirondacks.

During the first day I had hiked seventeen miles from the Northville Placid Trail's southern terminus at Upper Benson to the Hamilton Stream lean-to where I spent the first night. Again, I usually don't sleep in lean-tos, but this shelter was precisely where I wanted to stop hiking for the day. And it was raining.

The morning of day two I continued north on the Northville Placid Trail, winding past Priests Vly and Buckhorn Lake before completing a short road walk through the community of Piseco. Here I left Silver Lake Wilderness Area and entered West Canada Lake Wilderness Area. I reentered the woods at a trailhead at the end of paved Haskells Road. There was only one car, a vehicle with New Jersey plates, parked at the trailhead. I continued on the Northville Placid Trail.

The seven-mile stretch of trail ahead of me, from Haskells Road to a trail intersection before Bloodgood Brook, is dreadfully boring. There is just something about this section of trail—out of all the thousands of miles of trail I do like—that I don't like. I have no strong, specific reason to dislike this stretch. For example, I've never had a terrible experience on this section; never been hurt or lost. I find the trail's grade too flat or too steep, the tread too dry, too wet, too rocky, or too sandy. The path weaves below hardwoods that all look the same, and none are of impressive size. There are no views. I've never seen a critter in this area. No moose, bear, or deer. Not even a sweet butterfly.

Despite the odds of seeing nothing walk, crawl, or flutter along this section, I had been following fresh tracks, those of *Homo sapiens*, since I left Haskells Road. I'm no tracker, yet I deduced (correctly, it later turned out) that there were two hikers ahead of me. Their aggressive waffle cone treads pressed into the black, brown, and gray mud and showed that their boots were hefty; likely old pairs of leather stompers. One of the hikers used a trekking pole. I tried to figure out how far ahead they were, but since it rained the night before and there was light mist falling still, everything on the trail was wet. If it was dry out I could have looked at the mud their boots flung up on rocks and seen if the mud was already dry or still wet. At stream crossings I could have seen where they had splashed water onto the shorelines and rocks. If the water was still there, not evaporated, I would have known they could not have been far ahead.

The wet, lifeless woods hemmed my ribbon of trail and drooped over me and my little pack as I made my way towards my trail intersection. As I ascended a hill that led to this intersection, past briars and bushes drenched from the swirling and falling mist, I spotted my *Homo sapiens* above and ahead of me, barely within sight through the fog. They were hiking slow. Really slow. They moved towards the high-point of our ascent and the intersection like molasses would have moved down that hill during February. Each wore old-school external frame backpacks, and the packs immediately reminded me of my first backpack, which was an external frame contraption I purchased for $7 circa 1988. Frayed and soaked pack covers gently swayed behind them trying to guard the contents of their massive packs. The packs so big, they hid the hikers' torsos. Arms clad in yellow rain jacket sleeves seemed to pop directly out of each side of the backpacks. Legs popped out the bottoms.

They each wore shorts with their wool socks pulled high, and their feet were clad in big pairs of heavy leather boots that had seen duty during at least two decades. The wobbly swaying of their torsos and packs, the mud all over their boots and socks, and the way the lead hiker leaned heavily on his trekking pole showed these two adventurers were having a tiresome time in the woods. Having likely started at the Haskells Road trailhead, they were only seven miles into their trip. I was hoping they would not collapse in front of me.

They may have been slow, but they were too far ahead of me to catch before I arrived at my intersection at the top of the hill. I watched them fade into the fog towards only God knew where. I left the Northville Placid Trail. It would not be under my feet again until the end of the day.

I hiked a half-mile downhill along the south side of Bloodgood Brook to a trailhead that seems to have no official name, called the Jessup River or Spruce Lake trailhead by some. Most hikers just call it "that trailhead at the end of the Sled Harbor road." At the trailhead I hooked up with a lonesome and narrow dirt road that ran along the Jessup River. After passing Belden Vly and crossing the Miami River I connected to an equally lonesome and narrow dirt road at Sled Harbor. At Sled Harbor I ceased heading northeast and started cruising north while the off and on rain continued.

Following the Miami River all the way to its top where it tumbles over tiny stones under the face of Pillsbury Mountain, I crested a height of land and curved west. I was gunning straight towards my destination still seven miles away, a group of remote bodies of water known as the West Canada Lakes: Brooktrout Lake, West Lake, South Lake, and Mud Lake, each one high and remote. All four are above 2,300 feet while West Lake, the center lake of the group, is a six-mile hike from a trailhead at the end of a thirteen-mile-long dead end dirt road that's not plowed during winter. The la beautiful, even if visited in the rain.

By heading towards the sunset somewhere in front of me, I was finishing an enormous north, then east, then north, then west sweep around gorgeous country. I reached the east end of Pillsbury Lake at dusk. By the time I walked the mile to its west end it was dark. I put on my headlamp and clicked it on, its blue beam struggling to pierce the fog. The rain came down in light, little spurts, colored a dazzling light blue by the beam of my headlamp. Most of what kept me wet were raindrops falling from the saturated leaves overhead, the rainwater blown loose by unpredictable breezes.

Whitney Lake, 500 feet north of the trail, was hidden by the darkness while Sampson Lake, just 400 feet south of the trail, was unseen as well, swallowed by the night. My sneakered feet carried me west, and my seven-pound pack, which I was testing for an upcoming speed hike of the Northville Placid Trail, hovered airily on my shoulders. Whether I was carrying seventy, seventeen, or seven pounds, by the time I reconnected with the Northville Placid Trail at Mud Lake, mile thirty of my hike, I was pretty damn tired. Knowing the South Lake lean-to was a mile away, and seeing I was hiking in the dark in a rainstorm, I chose to sleep in this lean-to rather than bother to set up a pristine camp.

A short side trail led off the Northville Placid Trail towards the back of the shelter. The front of the lean-to faced the inky, rainy, cloudy blackness that swallowed all of South Lake. If I had not hiked in this region before, I would have had no idea that I was hiking straight towards a one-mile-long, quarter-mile-wide body of water. A thick blanket of clouds hid the moon and the stars. The only thing illuminated for nearly 600 square miles around me was the ten feet of trail in front of me. The nearest streetlight was in downtown Piseco, ten miles away as the crow flies.

Perched on the edge of South Lake ten feet from the shore, the South Lake lean-to is likely most popular of the four shelters in the area. I figured chances were good that someone was inside. Then again, it had been raining off and on all day and the day before. Rain has a powerful ability to keep people out of the woods. I had seen only two hikers all day. They were probably camped farther south at one of the three Spruce Lake lean-tos. Or they had just dropped dead right in the middle of the Northville Placid Trail. I approached the lean-to quietly, which was not difficult. I carried only two weak warnings of my approach: the restricted beam of my headlamp and my feet emitting little "squish," "squish," "squishes." The wind blew and the raindrops fell, making a rattle through the trees.

I thought back to the tactical movements I had completed through the wee-hours of nights and mornings, often in rainstorms, when I was a paratrooper. I wasn't as tired as a paratrooper that night, but I was getting there. The military travel was way more miserable than this night's hike, but even back in the Army I could see the merit of nighttime movements through terrible weather. It was a great time to move undetected, with my unit hidden, noise muffled, and the "enemy" hunkered down somewhere, thinking no unit would be crazy enough to travel through such inclement weather (since the bulk of my enlistment was during peacetime, my unit often hunted other Army units). But there is little sane about paratroopers to begin with.

I pulled up to the front of the lean-to. To my surprise there were two men inside. Their gear hung on nearly all the nails and wooden pegs pounded into the shelter's walls, little drip, drip, drips of dirty, sweaty, gray water plunking down from their gear and onto the hard lean-to floor. I noticed that two backpacks hanging from a beam across the ceiling were external frame packs. Reasoning that five or six people in North America were still wearing external frame packs by 2008, I went with the odds that these were the two men I had nearly caught by the intersection.

I was glad to see that I was not waking them. They didn't hesitate welcoming me. "Hey, man! Come on in!" man number one, a short, stout man, said. It didn't seem I was inconveniencing him at all. Man number one was eager to host me.

"Thanks," I replied in a soft voice. "I didn't mean to disturb you."

"Are you lost?!" number two, a tall and burly mean-looking guy with a shaved head, asked with alarm in his voice. He was nearly yelling at me, like he was trying to speak above a fierce wind between us.

"Nah." I chuckled a little. "I'm hiking in the rain at night on purpose."

I pulled back my rain jacket hood and stepped into the front corner of the shelter, making sure not to splash their sleeping bags or sleeping pads, or them, with the rainwater that covered me, my rain jacket, and my pack cover. I slipped off my pack, took off the pack cover, took off my rain jacket, and headed back into the storm for a second to thoroughly shake these off. I hopped back in and hung them on one of the few remaining pegs.

Number two followed up. "Where ya' comin' from?!"

"Oh . . . uh," I explained as I stood at the edge of the lean-to soaking wet, "last night I stayed at the Hamilton Stream lean-to."

The two men looked at each other, confused. I guessed they had never heard of the Hamilton Stream lean-to. "It's the shelter way down by the Sacandaga River—where the big suspension bridge crosses the river. At Whitehouse."

They still looked puzzled. Number one spoke up. "You couldn't have come from there! That's twenty miles away!"

I assured them. "No, that's where I came from this morning. But once I hit the intersection by Bloodgood Brook, I hiked out to Sled Harbor and then doubled back past Pillsbury Lake and Sampson Lake." It had been a great day despite the rain. "What a hike" I said with a smile. As forethought I added, "I think I saw you guys near that Sled Harbor intersection this morning."

Number two looked incredulous. "Whoa, whoa, whoa! How far is that?! You did that in a day?!"

Feeling pressure to convince my doubting audience, that for some reason loved to talk loudly, I replied that it was 31 miles. But it came out like I was asking a question since I thought they wouldn't believe me. "It's, uh, 31 miles?"

I looked around the lean-to while they tried to figure out if this mysterious man who sought shelter from the storm was one hell of a hiker or just full of baloney. For certain these were the guys I had seen earlier in the day. Beyond noticing the external frame packs, I spotted their yellow rain jackets. It looked like the jackets had been dumped into a pig pen and stomped by a gang of angry swine. Mud was everywhere: on the sleeves, the hoods, the torsos. Mud was on their stinky socks that hung from the ceiling beam, and, sure enough, their heavy leather boots were caked in mud, too. Soaked shirts and shorts hung from the back wall. I wondered to myself, "Did they hike here or crawl here?"

I spotted a trekking pole. It was broken in half. I cracked the silence by pointing to the pole. "What happened to that thing?"

Number two burst out laughing. "Ah-hah-hah-hah-hah! Oh, you missed that one, dude! "Frank—" The man caught himself in a social faux pas. Even in the wilderness men mind their manners. "Shit! I'm sorry!" He pointed to his friend. "This is Frank! I'm Jason! What's your name?!"

"Erik."

"Well, Erik, you missed it! Frank here went to cross that brook near Spruce Lake, hopped across, landed on the pole, and SNAP! Frank goes down! Hard! Right in the fucking mud! He gets up and looks like Swamp Thing!"

Frank pepped up. "Oh my God, I thought I was gonna die! Just look at this thing!" He held up the two sections of the mangled pole. They were covered in mud. "So now I gotta carry this thing for the rest of the trip!" He shook his head with a self-deprecating smile. "Like my pack's not heavy enough, you know?!" Their accents confirmed that it was their car parked at the Haskells Road trailhead. Jersey plates? Jersey accents.

The above dialog from Frank and Jason, though of course written in traditional English and spelled correctly in this book, didn't sound like how you are pronouncing their dialog (that is, unless you're from New Jersey). If you are having trouble imagining and replicating their thick Jersey accents the following pronunciation guide will help.

Traditional English	Jersey English
New Jersey	New-JOY-zee
Coffee	CAW-fee
Parkway	POCK-way
The	Duh
This	Dis
Father	FAAH-thuh
Farther	FAAH-thuh
Further	FUUH-thuh
Long Island	Lawn-GUY-lind
Motherfucker	Muth-ahh-FUCK-ahh
Where	Wheah
There	Dheah
Fair	Fhaeh
Party	PAH-dey
What do you mean?	WHADDYA-mean?
Cops	Kahps
Peppers	Pep-uhs
Adirondack Park	Ad-ih-rahn-dak-PAAHK

Beyond unique pronunciations, people from the Garden State tend to lop off g's from the ends of words. "Going" becomes "goin,'" "camping" becomes "campin,'" "hiking" becomes "hikin'" and so forth. R's are rarely pronounced, especially towards the ends of words.

People from *New-JOY-zee* are often louder, much louder, than people from the Adirondacks. This must stem from the clamorous auditory competition they face in daily conversation back home. While people from the Adirondack

Mountains may have to raise their voices a hair to be heard over a solitary vireo, breeze, or chipmunk, those from urban environments often have their conversational partners yelling "HUH?" over the racket of car alarms, passenger jets, sirens, and garbage trucks. They tend to swear even more than I do. "Hand me that tent stake" becomes "Hand me that fuckin' tent stake." The difference is subtle when read, obvious when heard.

Frank put the two busted pieces of hiking pole down and got back to the matter at hand. "You hiked 31 miles to get here?! In a day?!"

"Yeah. It's 31 miles from last night's shelter to this one— that is, if you take the scenic route."

I was embarrassed at the attention I was getting. I started unpacking my gear. Both men wore their headlamps, which were on. With my headlamp on, too, the shelter was lit well enough for us to see each other and all of our gear. Beyond our little hovel the wild night was black.

While I was unpacking Jason must have been rolling 31 miles around in his mind, imagining hiking it. He replied, "Dude, that's a long—" and cut himself off again. "Frank! Frank! Look at this guy's pack! It's so small!"

I reached into my 2,800-cubic-inch pack and pulled out what was still hiding in the bottom of it. Frank, a direct man, assessed my gear. "You ain't got shit in there! Holy shit! But Jason's right. That's still far! We did—what did we do, Jason?! Fourteen miles?!"

"Fourteen miles!"

"And we were just about half dead when we got here, weren't we, Jason?!"

"What do you mean 'were'?!" Jason rhetorically asked.

I couldn't help but laugh. Jason and Frank. Laurel and Hardy. Abbott and Costello. The Keystone Cops. The accents combined with their impromptu hand gestures were over the top. The volume only made things funnier. I felt awkward finding things so humorous about these two men. I was careful not to laugh that much, but it was hard. I didn't want them to think I was laughing *at* them. Their urban mannerisms in the middle of the Adirondack wilderness, in a rainstorm at night no less, were so out of place. I don't know why that necessarily meant these two men had to be seen as comical. But they had to be.

"Yeah, but," Jason reasoned, "this guy can hike that far 'cause he's a lot younger than us! How old are you, Erik?!"

"35."

They looked at each other and laughed with embarrassing expressions. "Huh-huh-huh!" Frank bellowed. He looked over at Jason. "He's not much younger than us!"

"How old are you guys?" I asked.

"I'm 39" Frank replied. "Jason's 37!"

They were good enough sports to be teased so early into our meeting. "Oh, man. Come on, guys. You can do 31-mile days. It's really not that hard. Hike with me tomorrow! We'll go everywhere."

Jason thought the suggestion ridiculous. "No way man! Look at all the shit we bring!"

While we carried on conversations about where we had come from and where we were headed the next day, I changed into a dry top, removed the insoles in my sneakers in a hopeless attempt to have them dry, and hung my wet socks on the rafter overhead. I also laid out my sleeping pad and sleeping bag and assembled my little kitchen: stove, pot stand, pot, lid. The men were examining my gear.

"Erik, what do you got with you there?!" Frank asked.

The total weight for this three-day trip, and thus my forthcoming Northville Placid Trail trip, was a little over 100 ounces—7.1 pounds. It was the lightest I had ever gone. My typical pack weight is ten pounds. My gear is organized into four categories: home, kitchen, clothing, extras. Beyond the equipment I carried with me, I wore a long sleeve shirt, a pair of shorts, a pair of wool socks, and running shoes. I had less than two pounds of gear on my body.

My home totaled 3.2 pounds, the heaviest of the four categories. It included my backpack, pack cover, sleeping bag, sleeping pad, tarp, and ground sheet. The kitchen sink was surely left behind when it came to my kitchen. Six solid fuel tablets, my homemade stove for the fuel tablets, titanium cooking pot, homemade lid, one spoon, one lighter, and a soda bottle was all I needed. Total: nine ounces. I didn't need much clothing: 1.7 pounds' worth of down, nylon, wool, and Goretex. The extras couldn't be classified into any of the above categories. My ditty bag (a stuff sac full of all kinds of goodies like cord, batteries, fire starter, and petroleum jelly for blisters), first aid kit, and headlamp weighed 1.6 pounds.

Like all other trips, this three-day trip wasn't about the numbers. It was about two other things. One, it was about that October can't be beat. Biting bugs are dead, fall foliage peaks, the sleeping weather can't get any better, humidity is long gone, and the summertime kids and crowds have returned to school and work. I'll take it.

Two, it was about occasionally feeling the need—the need for speed. After recently reading a series of running books I learned why I have a desire to hike long distances fast. It's the same reason why long-distance runners, and runners in general, like to cover distances quickly. Humans are built and programmed to walk and run far. Full explanation of the psycho-physiological reasons for why we run (and hike and walk) would require more space than this story provides. Many books have been written on the theories of why people travel long distances fast by foot. The best one carries a simple title: *Why We Run*.

Written in 2001, *Why We Run* was written by a most interesting man with a most impressive running record: Bernd Heinrich, Ph.D. Heinrich has been running since he was a kid. He's been running very fast over very long distances since and has won the Golden Gate Marathon and West Valley Marathon and almost made the U.S. Olympic marathon team. Finding marathons too short, which says a lot about a man itself, Heinrich entered the world of ultra-marathons.

His career highlights include world records for r[...] kilometers, 200 kilometers, 100 miles, and tot[...] within 24 hours.

Why We Run is a personal story about a runner finding challenges, researching techniques, testing strategies, preparing oneself, and then going for it, feeling the thrill of victory or the agony of defeat, stages long-distance hikers experience, too. Heinrich sees running as a metaphor for life, an ethos of the human spirit.

> The human experience is populated with dreams and aspirations. For me, the animal totem for these dreams is the antelope, swift, strong and elusive. Most of us chase after "antelopes," and sometimes we catch them. Often we don't. But why do we bother to try? I think it is because without dream-antelopes to chase we become what a lap dog is to a wolf. And we are inherently more like wolves than lap dogs.

Why We Run is a journey into Heinrich's professional world, too. A botanist by day, the man who loves running so much possesses a Ph.D. in Zoology. Heinrich's specialty is researching "the comparative physiology and behavior of insects." He's into why birds can fly such long distances, why camels can go without water for days, why bugs hop and crawl with impressive speed and power, and why a human can run down any animal on Earth but stinks at sprinting. Between the birds, camels, and bugs, he concisely explains how we became built and programmed to travel far and fast by foot. Our ancestors on the plains of the African Savannah ran after prey to eat and ran from prey to live. If you were a lousy runner you died, either by starvation or by becoming a meal yourself. The strong runners survived. End of story.

Me in particular? I believe I am built to hike long distances fast (I also run), and to do so, and to have fun while doing it, I choose to go light. Whether I'm speed hiking to tap into my ancestors' hunter/prey psyche or just bumping around in the woods somewhere, I never go heavy.

When I concluded my enlistment as an Army paratrooper in 1993 I swore off carrying a heavy backpack again (there is no light in "light infantry"). Yet when I completed my first long-distance hike, fittingly for this story, the 133-mile Northville Placid Trail, during the early 1990s, I carried a forty-pound pack and averaged fewer than fourteen miles a day. When I completed field components towards earning a degree in Wilderness Leadership during the mid 1990s I carried a fifty-pound pack, and our group rarely covered more than ten miles a day. Enough was enough. It was time for my "enlightenment."

With each long-distance hike I went lighter and lighter. Five years after my initial Northville Placid Trail journey I thru-hiked the Long Trail with a twenty-pound pack. By mile fifty of that trip I was sold on the "less is more" mantra of other long-distance hikers who, at the time, knew way more about long-distance hiking than I did. During the following years my daily mileage rose while my pack weight dropped. I hiked the Florida National Scenic Trail at 22 miles a day, Metacomet-Monadnock Trail at 22, Cohos Trail at 23, across the Catskill Mountains at 23, Tahoe Rim Trail at 25, around the border of High Peaks Wilderness Area at 26, Baker Trail at 27. I can assure readers I do not list these numbers for my own ego. I write about lightweight backpacking to share an approach that has made the woods more enjoyable for me. With joy and understanding comes happiness.

I rattled off my gear list to Frank and Jason. When I found a piece of gear I was particularly fond of or spotted an item that I thought they'd find neat, I held it up. I did remember the total weight: "Everything but food and water totals an even seven pounds. Some packs weigh that much empty." Like most traditional backpackers, Frank and Jason found what I was doing to be interesting, even inspiring. But I could tell they weren't going to change their ways. Their old packs, boots, heavy rain jackets, and bulky gear had gotten them into and out of the woods for twenty years. Why change? Sure, going light would make their lives in the woods easier, but they'd have to give up their favorite accoutrements, buy new gear, figure out how to use it, and then worry that they forgot something. For them it was easier to bring everything.

Jason asked what I did for a living. "I'm an outdoor educator at a university," I replied. "No one really knows what that means, so, basically what I do is teach students how to plan and lead expeditions. I teach courses in navigation, backpacking, canoeing, leadership, trail design. All the fun stuff."

For the following twenty minutes my two urban shelter mates grilled the professor. Sitting with them in a lean-to in the middle of nowhere was a bona fide outdoorsman! Maybe kind of like reality television survivalists Bear Grylls (who's a fraud) and Les Stroud (who was cool but is now a sell-out). They asked me every conceivable question about the out-of-doors including navigation, pack selection, tree identification, bird identification, trail design, Adirondack history, mammals, weather. On and on the subjects went. I had answers for most questions but not all. When they started asking questions about survival, I was at a loss for good answers.

"Do you know what kind of bugs to eat?!" Jason asked.

"No."

"No?! Why not?!"

"Well," I plainly replied, "I bring my lunch."

Frank asked how to start a fire with two sticks.

"I don't know, Frank. I bring a lighter." He looked disappointed.

Frank asked if I could track animals. I said that not only do I have trouble tracking animals, but I can't identify most tracks. If it wasn't the track of a deer, moose, or bear, I'd tell my students it was a fox track.

My answer to Jason's question about how to build a "survival shelter" with only a knife was boring.

"I don't know. I set up my tarp. In the winter I bring a tent." They looked at me like I wasn't that great of an outdoorsman after all.

I spelled it out for them. "Look, guys, I just bring enough gear with me so I don't have to do any of those things." They fell into thought for a moment. They got the logic.

Frank topped off our impromptu classroom session with a question that had been nagging him. So important of an inquiry, he had to act out.

"Now, Erik, Erik! You gotta help me with this, man!" Frank got out of his sleeping bag wearing only a tight pair of white boxers and an old, ratty t-shirt. "Oh my God, Erik! This is killin' me, man!" He didn't know what to do with himself.

He was stressing me out. "My God. Calm down. What's killing you, Frank?"

"This chafin'! Motherfucker, it hurts! It hurts!" Frank faced me and squatted halfway down to the position he would have gotten in if he was going to poop into his sleeping bag. He spread he knees wide. With his crotch fully exposed and sheathed by only a thin, dirtied section of his boxers, Jason's headlamp and my headlamp were illuminating his penis and scrotum as if Frank's crotch was on stage. There was little left to the imagination.

"I got it here! Right here!" Frank formed his hands into rigid knife edges, like a man who was about to Karate chop a pine board. He gently slid the outer edges of his palms up and down the crease of his boxer shorts, his hands wedged into the inner and upper parts of his thighs on either side of his crotch. "It's all red! And itchy! Motherfucker, it sucks!"

Jason offered his sympathy. "Yeah, that shit sucks!"

Frank held his audience in awe, next twirling about and pushing his ass out towards us. He used the knife edge of his hand this time to caress the crack of his ass while he squatted halfway down towards his sleeping bag.

"And in here, Erik! Right in here! Ah! Right in the crack of my ass!" He pushed his butt out towards me, as if I needed a better look. Frank was a classy guy.

I scrunched my nose like I smelled rotten chicken. But I couldn't take my eyes off Frank's ass and crotch that were both threatening to bust a seam along his taut underpants. The sensation I had while watching Frank caress himself, with two dudes watching, was experienced only once before: when I saw a wreck on the interstate so bad that I couldn't peel my eyes from the carnage.

Turning around once more to remind me that it just wasn't his ass that was chaffed, Frank grabbed his scrotum once more, and before I knew it he hopped back into his bag. His act stopped so suddenly. With an expressionless face he calmly and softly asked, "What can I do about that?" Frank and Jason looked at me, waiting for a good answer.

"Well," I began, but Frank interrupted.

"Erik! You've had this shit right?! Tell me you've have this shit!"

"Uh, yes. Yes, Frank, I have." He let out a sigh of relief.

The moment was surreal. Gaining some composure and power washing the image of Frank's chaffed crotch and ass from my mind's eye—I was the composed professor after all—I suggested Frank bring baby wipes and baby powder next time. Chafing, sometimes called "butt chap," a label as gross as the actual condition, is a grownup version of diaper rash, and backpackers acquire it from hiking in steamy conditions. After explaining to Frank and Jason the conditions for chaffing to rear its ugly, I engaged my audience.

"And what do we do with babies with diaper rash?" I asked. They were stumped. "We clean them, powder them, and then put on a clean diaper. You have to keep the area clean and dry. Do that, and you won't get it again. I never go into the woods without baby wipes and baby powder. Clean and dry. That's all you gotta do."

Frank heartily thanked me for the advice though it wouldn't do him any good until his next backpacking trip. Frank, and Jason, had probably never thought of chaffed backpackers as big babies who need a wipe, some powder, and a diaper change.

I settled in after our academic session and finished my Ramen noodles. Frank told me that he and Jason had been hiking together for the past fifteen years. Once a year they come up to the Adirondacks and go backpacking. They assured me that every year it rains. Beyond bad weather following them, bad luck was always hot on their heels. The broken trekking pole was one example. Stories of rain jackets tearing, the bottoms of boots peeling off, forgetting a key piece of gear, getting lost, planning trips that were too ambitious, and burning every night's dinner were intertwined with highlights of seeing wildlife, meeting other backpackers, watching pretty sunsets, and not having their wives around. Despite misfortune and ignorance, these guys loved the woods. Their only complaint about the mountains was that they're five hours from New Jersey.

I asked how they had met and became hiking partners. Jason had a two-word answer. "We're cops!"

"Cops?" I asked. I followed up this question with a dumb question: "In New Jersey?"

"Yeah, in New Jersey!" Frank answered. "We're cops in Trenton! I've been there sixteen years! Jason's the baby! He's only been there thirteen years!" They were both looking forward to retiring at age 44. By this writing, Frank's been retired for two years. Jason retires next year.

"Man," I said, "you guys must have some great stories."

Frank, speaking for only the second time that night without yelling, said in a somber voice, "Erik, you would not believe it. Really. You would not believe the shit I see."

Jason nodded and agreed in a serious tone. "You wouldn't believe the shit, Erik."

And this is the point in our story where I asked them the question: "Is your job anything like what I see on *Cops*?"

"Hell no!" Jason and Frank said in near unison. Frank concluded their answer, which I thought would have taken much longer to do, with "They don't do any paperwork!"

Jason seconded this observation. "Yeah, they don't do any paperwork!"

Naively I asked, "Do you guys watch *Cops*?"

Jason, with a little disgust in his voice, replied, "No, man! That's like you going home and watching, uh . . . some show about hiking! You'd be so bored watching it!"

"Yeah," Frank chimed in, "I don't bring my work home with me!"

Jason confirmed this approach to cop self-care. "Amen!"

There I had it. My answer. The reality television program *Cops* is not really that real because it doesn't show cops taking on post-arrest paper work. It was a simple answer, kind of boring, but it made sense. I didn't bother asking what they thought of the reggae music.

I slept well, dry and snugly and listening to the pitter-patter of rain on the roof. With a big day ahead of me, I got up an hour before sunrise: 5:00 A.M. I clicked on my headlamp and made sure not to look Frank or Jason's way, lest my light wake them. I quietly crammed my sleeping bag into its stuff sac and mushed it into the bottom of my pack. After packing my kitchen and clothes and extras inside, I folded my sleeping pad and strapped it to the outside. It was raining lightly. With my rain jacket on and my pack cozy in its waterproof cover, I put on my running shoes. They were still wet and muddy. As each foot entered a messy "squish" was forced out.

Jason rolled over and moaned. "Erik, you leavin' man?" He was definitely not yelling.

I whispered back to him so as not to wake Frank. "Yeah. I've got a lot of miles to cover today."

"Good luck, brother."

"All right, man. Have a good one."

South Lake was still hidden, still stuck down at the bottom of the black night. I took the side trail back to the Northville Placid Trail. The end of my day—the trailhead way back in Upper Benson—was an awful long way away: 38 miles. Containing only 3,000 vertical feet of climbing, the trail ahead of me climbed very little, at least when considering the overall distance. It would be my farthest day yet. Six years earlier on the Florida Trail I covered a 31-mile day somewhere between

Pensacola and the Everglades. But 38? Never been there, never done that.

Thinking about that entire distance, which would take sixteen hours to cover, would make the journey appear more daunting than a test of endurance and my love of the woods. I cut the trip into little segments. Rather than the goal being the trailhead in Upper Benson, my goal was merely Spruce Lake four miles away. From Spruce Lake my next destination would be the intersection I turned off to hike to Sled Harbor the day prior. I would keep ticking off mini-destinations a couple miles apart, cutting a 38-mile hike into bite-sized pieces. As I got farther into my hike and started getting frustrated that I wasn't yet in Upper Benson, I'd reduce the distance between destinations. On some hikes I've been so tired that I have had to say to myself, "Just make it to the top of this hill," which may be only 500 feet away. Whether hiking 38 miles, working towards a graduate degree, or, yes, writing a book, I have to buck it up into manageable chunks. Lots of mini goals eventually add up to one big, fat goal that at one time I thought I would not reach.

By 9:00 A.M., three hours after sunrise, the rain stopped. Thick, gray clouds blanketed the woods. I doubted the sun would be coming out this day. The rest of this 38-mile day is lost to time, most memory of it gone. The few things I remember are my feet being wet, my pack feeling light, not seeing a soul during those sixteen hours on the trail, and being happy when I saw my car at the end of Haskells Road. I know I was bushed.

It would be years later before I read *Why We Run*, but on this 2008 hike I deduced what would be confirmed by Heinrich's practical applications to ultra-marathoning. You are, and I am, built to quickly cover long distances by foot. I wasn't impressed with my performance as much as I was impressed that a human could hike nearly forty miles without stopping. If Heinrich had heard about my hike, he wouldn't have been impressed either. My hike would have only confirmed his research and shed light on why he could run up to 200 kilometers without a break. Heinrich's and my conclusions regarding human endurance would be affirmed by my speed hike of the Northville Placid Trail two weeks after this trip. Originally planning to hike the trail in five days, an average of 33.2 miles a day, I ended up hiking it much faster: three and a quarter days, 39.9 miles a day.

During this Northville Placid Trail hike I reached the West Canada Lakes. I made a point to take a break at the South Lake lean-to where I had met Jason and Frank two weeks earlier. While I sat at the lean-to Jason and Frank were somewhere in Trenton, calling in a helicopter to swoop down on a neighborhood, pointing their guns at people sprawled on the pavement, and maybe even releasing an attack dog on someone. Remembering the energy and humor they displayed after being whupped by fourteen miles of hiking, I could see them enjoying their jobs and all the excitement that came with them. I bet even with all the excitement back in Trenton though, they would have rather been up in the Adirondack Mountains with the mud and the rain. I couldn't help but sing Inner Circle's anthem at the shelter. "Bad boys, bad boys, what 'ya gonna do? What 'ya gonna do when they come for you?"

Ruby Mountain Recon

In hindsight, both my Army recruiter and Will's Army recruiter embellished much. If you're an Army recruiter and tell a prospective recruit, typically a naive teenage male, that joining the military as an Army infantryman is really cool, while leaving out all the miserable aspects of being an infantryman, that young man may bite at the offer. Recruiters are salesmen (and saleswomen), nothing less. They're good at what they do. If a halfway decent Army recruiter became a realtor, he could sell oceanfront property in Nebraska. If he became a used vehicle salesman, he could sell a four-wheel-drive motorcycle. Buyers beware.

The pitch Will received from his recruiter in 2001 when he was 19 years old was similar to the pitch I received from my recruiter in 1991 when I was 17. Being in the infantry is pretty much like what you see in the movies. It's totally awesome. Who were the heroes who found Private Ryan in *Saving Private Ryan*? Infantrymen! How about when Chuck Norris and Lee Marvin in *Delta Force* blew away truckloads of Middle Eastern terrorists? Actually, they were in Delta Force. But you know what job you have before trying out for Delta Force? Infantryman! And when Bruce Willis turned German terrorists into minced meat when they tried to take over the Nakatomi Plaza in *Die Hard*? Well, he was a New York City cop. But probably former infantry!

Maybe movie plots weren't the best examples. But the vision of being transformed into a gun-slinging, explosive-detonating, knife-wielding, bone-crushing man is a vision that has, to put it mildly, appeal for young men. The pitch even worked on now-retired General Tommy Franks, the man who oversaw the invasion of Iraq and occupation of Afghanistan. When Franks was asked what he imagined the Army being like after hearing the pitch from his recruiter in 1965, a pitch that began a 38-year military career, Franks was honest about his naivety. In his autobiography, *American Soldier,* Franks admitted that he speculated "The military would probably be a more adventurous version of camping and hunting, which I'd always loved."

Franks was surely disappointed when he got to Basic Combat Training at Fort Leonard Wood, Missouri, which has a great nickname: Fort Lost in the Woods. When a fellow recruit dared open his mouth during his platoon's first day in the Army, Franks's drill sergeant belted out, in typical drill sergeant eloquence, "You recruits will shut the fuck up or your collective ass is grass, and I'm a lawnmower." Meanwhile Franks was thinking, "When are they going to feed us and let us go to bed?"

Being in the Army is no camping trip. Serving as an airborne infantryman is still the hardest thing I've ever done. I found being an infantryman more difficult than mountain biking 2,700 miles from Canada to Mexico, climbing more than 1,500 mountains, and paddling the East's longest rivers from source to sea. Since ending my enlistment 22 years ago, I have never been that exhausted, that sore, or that scared. Since Will ended his enlistment ten years ago, I presume he hasn't been that exhausted, sore, or scared either.

When Will and I met in 2013 while serving as colleagues at a veteran service organization, one of the first things we inquired about each other was if the other was a veteran. We asked for further details, like what branch we were part of and what our jobs were while we were in. It turned out we were both Army infantry. With our common sufferings, though through different war eras and different decades, Will and I naturally felt a bond.

We both know what it's like to run until we puke, stay awake until we hallucinate, and carry a backpack until we think our arms are going to be ripped from their sockets. We've literally walked the walk. We've marched with sixty pounds on our backs until our feet bled. Knowing this about each other built a kind of trust, a "been there, done that" bond that only people in combat arms understand. We got along. Later into our careers we got along so well that we went for a hike together. It was Will's first hike in the Adirondacks.

Will and I enjoy a unique dynamic when it comes to our military experiences. We survived the same initial gauntlets: ten-week-long Basic Combat Training and five-week-long Infantryman School, both courses held at Fort Benning, Georgia. After these schools though, we took different paths.

I stayed in Fort Benning an additional three weeks to complete Airborne School. This parachuting course is divided into three separate weeks of instruction: ground week (how to land), tower week (how to exit an airplane and control your descent), and jump week (five parachute jumps, one of them taking place at night). At the end of this training program I received a pair of coveted jump wings, a small silver parachute badge for my dress uniform.

With nearly five months of training completed I was qualified to be sent to an airborne unit. I was assigned to the 82nd Airborne Division at Fort Bragg, North Carolina. During my two-year enlistment with this unit, the "All Americans," my training was intense and nearly continuous. I completed the SINCGAR Course (how to operate a radio in combat), Driver Course (how to drive a Hummer), Dragon Missile Jump Pack Course (how to jump out of an airplane with a missile strapped to my body), and MOUT training (Military Operations in Urban Terrain). My longest post-Airborne School training took place at Fort Irwin in Death Valley, California. Here I completed the Army's thirty-day Desert Warfare School where temperatures crept to 120 degrees.

The highlight of my enlistment was a four-month deployment to Honduras to guard remote Central Intelligence Agency listening posts. During this assignment I gained a second pair of jump wings for completing parachute operations with the Honduran army. When I left the Army a few days short of Christmas 1993, I had completed 25 simulated combat jumps with up to 130 pounds of equipment and weapons on my body. The only award of note I received was the National Defense Service Medal for being enlisted during the Gulf War. However, the closest I've ever been to Kuwait is when I visited Cape Cod a few years ago.

When Will finished Infantryman School, he was sent to Fort Drum, New York, to join the 10th Mountain Division, and he completed a one year assignment to South Korea. While serving with this unit he deployed to Iraq. Will was enlisted from 2001 to 2005, but from September 2003 to September 2004 he took part in Operation Iraqi Freedom, the U.S. mission to overthrow Saddam Hussein, curb sectarian violence, and get rid of all the bad guys.

Will joined an elite group of men within the 10th Mountain Division: a recon squad. Bad asses who hunted bad guys. While the traditional Army infantry squad has six to twelve men, a recon squad has as few as two and only as many as five, the premise being that the fewer guys there are the faster they can move. Boy, could they move. Will's physical training regimen was on-par with paratrooper standards. At one point his squad was running seven miles at a time averaging seven-minute splits, fast enough to probably win your hometown's next 10k.

Typical missions, if there are such things in war, centered on observation. Will's unit would hide during day and patrol and observe during night, scanning for enemy combatants planting improvised explosive devices. When they observed someone planting an explosive, the combatant was "engaged," a euphemism for getting shot to death or blown up. The squad had the tools to get this done. Will usually carried an M4 carbine (a smaller version of the M16 rifle) with a grenade launcher mounted below the barrel. The squad carried a couple of these rifles along with a .50 sniper rifle (capable of "engaging" a person over a kilometer away), claymores mines (antipersonnel devices that blow 700 steel ball bearings into the enemy), and light anti-tank weapons (shoulder-fired rockets that can punch a hole through eight inches of steel plate). Their missions ranged from one night to two weeks at a time, and, as the reader can well imagine, the missions were hazardous. With only two to five men, running into an armored vehicle or a platoon of enemy would have spelled disaster for the unit. The key was to not be seen, to be smarter than the enemy, to be the hunter instead of the hunted.

Not all of Will's colleagues came back alive. The ones who made it back, guys like Will, left parts of themselves in Iraq. Firefight by firefight, ambush by ambush, the combat chipped away little chunks of hope, humanity, and love. They saw a world turned upside down, where religion was transformed into a manifesto, neighborhoods were reduced to smoldering rubble, and children were caught in the middle of shootouts or enlisted as young soldiers with little chance of making it out alive.

Many of our military members saw friends become wounded or killed, smelled decomposing bodies, saw wounded or dead noncombatants, witnessed serious accidents, got knocked over by explosions, became injured, or sustained head injuries. These experiences, by the way, are the top seven wartime events that contribute to post traumatic stress disorder, a debilitating mental illness that may last decades. It is not impossible to experience all seven events during one hell of a battle or during a peacetime enlistment.

I've looked at photos of Will taken while he was in Iraq. In one he's posing with his squad, rifle in his hands, body armor and a tactical vest overflowing with magazines and grenades cinched on his torso. He's in casual attire, not wearing a ballistic helmet. He wears a standard Army brown t-shirt and camouflage pants that spill over the tops of his tan boots. Will is clean-shaven and looks young, too young for such heavy responsibility involving life or death.

For his work Will was awarded an Army Commendation Medal, two Army Achievement Medals, and the Combat Infantryman Badge. He also completed the Army's ten-day Air Assault School in Fort Campbell, Kentucky, learning rotary aircraft operations and how to rappel out of a hovering helicopter. Promoted to the rank of sergeant after his Middle East tour, he later earned a great infantry honor: the Expert Infantryman Badge. This credential is earned only after completing twenty grueling tasks that include setting up an ambush, calling in artillery strikes, performing combat in urban terrain, shooting at the expert level, carrying a heavy backpack over a long distance at a fast pace, and acing the Army physical fitness test.

Will's two infantryman badges, his Combat Infantryman Badge and Expert Infantryman Badge, communicate two things. First, I was in combat, so don't mess with me. Second, I know what I'm doing, so don't give me any flak. Even if Will didn't have these badges I wouldn't have messed with him or given him flak though. I just wanted to take him hiking.

Each Monday morning during the spring of 2014 I would roll into our workplace, and, like any well-oiled workplace, colleagues would inquire with each other about what they did over the weekend. I usually gave a two-word answer. "I bushwhacked."

Will, who is usually inquisitive but quiet, overall, had his interest rise into verbal expression. "What's bushwhacking?"

I told him all the bad things first. I told him about the spruce thickets, bugs, steep ups and downs, briars, mud holes, blowdown, and rain. But if bushwhacking was all work and no play, I wouldn't do it. I made sure to tell him about the solitude, eye-catching views, wildlife, challenge, and beauty. I assured him it wasn't anything like the infantry. He could tell that the aspect I enjoy most about bushwhacking is that it demands self-reliance, which is psychologically rewarding. No trails, no people, no technology. A man and his wits and his mountains. He liked the sound of the simplicity and had one question. "When are you going bushwhacking again?"

When you take someone into the woods for the first time, you must choose your destination wisely. If you drag them along a hellacious hike with no views, a hike that leaves them grumpy and exhausted by the time they get back to the trailhead, you will likely never see them again. If you fittingly select a hike that is scenic, and is challenging but isn't a death march that leaves them looking like a zombie by the time they make it back to the trailhead, they will likely sign up for more. You only get one chance to make a first impression. I chose our mountains wisely.

2,569-foot Davis Mountain and 2,667-foot Ruby Mountain look like all the other mountains in the far eastern corner of Hamilton County. As one drives west on State Route 28 between the communities of North River and Indian Lake and looks south towards these two mountains, the driver may think it best to call them hills. Both rise less than 1,000 vertical feet above the rivers, streams, and ponds. Neither mountain has jagged lines. They look more like piles of green blankets or gentle mounds of broccoli rather than robust sentinels rising towards the sky. What they lack in extreme topography was seen as an asset though. I didn't want to push Will up two enormous trailless mountains on his first hike.

Davis Mountain and Ruby Mountain are not remote. Davis Mountain is a little more than a mile from Route 28. It takes another mile of hiking to reach Ruby Mountain. The walk back to the road from the top of Ruby Mountain is the most difficult part of the hike, and it would be the longest segment of our hike, which was three miles. The entire five-mile route would climb a paltry 1,600 vertical feet; an amount typically required to scale one mountain.

On Friday, May 16, two days before our hike would take place, I brought something into work for Will. It was a photocopy of a topographic map displaying our two peaks. The summits were highlighted with a swipe of my pink highlighter, my usual way to mark mountaintops. We sat in front of the 8.5- by 11-inch piece of paper, the black contour lines stacked one on top of the other until the final contour line of each summit made a complete circle, communicating to those who can read such maps that you can go no higher. I traced our proposed route with a sharp pencil.

The route was straightforward. We would park on the side of a road off Route 28 below nearby Casey Mountain, enter the woods, descend to a wide stream, cross it, climb a small hill, and then descend to another unnamed stream. With this stream located at the western base of Davis Mountain, it was uphill from there. Once on top of our first peak we would descend due south and then climb the north side of Ruby Mountain. With our two peaks in the bag, we'd descend the northwest ridge of Ruby Mountain, navigate around a series of wetlands, climb one last hill (which, being at the end of the day, would feel much bigger than it actually is), scoot down the backside of this hill and—boom—there's the car. I told Will it would take six hours.

Ruby Mountain held particular attraction for me. One, the place name is unique. There is no other Northeast hill named Ruby Mountain. However, there are no rubies on this mountain (if there were, I wouldn't tell you). The most precious stone to be found on this peak is garnet, which isn't very precious. Precious or not, garnet has the same dull, red glow of rubies, and that's how the peak probably got its name.

Two, Ruby Mountain has a connection with a hiking hero of mine who authors Guy and Laura Waterman called, in *Forest and Crag*, "a strange young man, tall, dark, but not handsome" and "almost completely humorless" with social interactions that ranged "from awkward and strained to overtly hostile." Verplanck Colvin was, if there is such a thing, a famous Adirondack surveyor. Colvin is my favorite Adirondack personality for two reasons. One, he was a mountain climber at heart. Two, he was strange. I sometimes wonder if I'm the reincarnation of this eccentric man of the woods.

Born in 1847 in Albany, New York, Colvin first studied law and geology and then topography. By the end of his studies he had no direction towards, or perhaps plans for, employment since he grew up in a wealthy household. With his family vacationing in the Adirondacks, by his early 20s Colvin was already climbing High Peaks on personal trips. By 1870 he had summited Mount Marcy, Seward Mountain, and Whiteface Mountain and explored Avalanche Lake, visiting this body of water a week after landslides poured into it from nearby Mount Colden. He called the devastation "a wild, savage scene." In between these adventures Colvin paddled the Cold River, explored Long Lake and a dozen other bodies of water, and completed his first bear hunt. He was hooked on the Adirondacks. Colvin traveled and worked in the Helderbergh Hills, southern Appalachians, and Rocky Mountains, too, but ran back to the Adirondack Mountains each time.

In 1872 Colvin gained appointment to the New York State Park Commission, leading topographic surveys throughout the Adirondack Mountains from that year until 1899. During his duties he explored thousands of miles of terrain by foot and boat, running survey lines, placing survey monuments, naming mountains, and fixing prior surveyors' mistakes. He made first ascents of four 4,000-foot mountains and ascended another eighteen that were climbed only a few times before his arrival. With guide Bill Nye, Colvin discovered and named the source of the Hudson River—Lake Tear of the Clouds—which he regarded as the "red letter point" of his surveying for that year.

Colvin took well to exploring, blossoming from an unemployed freeloader to a legitimate Adirondack woodsman and first-rate conservationist. If fault could be cited with Colvin though, it was his interpersonal skills. The biggest challenge during his formidable forays was not traveling day after day through uncharted terrain. It was finding men who could endure working with him. Colvin was the type of man who did not let a little freezing rain get in the way of his party's travel plans. The typical expedition with Colvin would begin by traveling into the interior via foot or boat and then bushwhacking up a remote summit while carrying fifty pounds of survey and camp equipment, cutting a path along the way. Once on top, Colvin would become absorbed in observations until dusk made it too dark for him to read the instruments. Then the party would bushwhack off the summit towards another destination.

Darkness would surround the men during their descent, and they would have to bivouac in the middle of nowhere on the side of a mountain. To keep from freezing they would build a bonfire, stomp their feet, and hide under piles of clothing and gear until dawn. In the morning the party would finish their descent, cross a valley, and head to their next mountain. By the end of the expedition, if the party had traveled into the interior via boat during fall, they found their lakes and rivers half frozen and sometimes impossible to navigate due to ice. It was tough, senseless work, but as Peter Preston rightfully asked in *Forest and Crag*, "If it had not been for a man like Colvin with his touches of compulsive madness who would have done the job?"

It should not be surprising to learn that many woodsmen walked off the job, choosing to find their way out of the wilderness on their own than follow Colvin. When Colvin summited Lyon Mountain in the northern Adirondacks during the last week of October 1883, the summit was "grisly with ice and snow." Upon establishing camp on the summit, "snow and storm, sleet and fierce winter gales" engulfed the men's campsite. Colvin remained on the summit until the 6th of November measuring what he called "absolutely necessary angles." Before these angles were measured though, Colvin found himself alone on his perch. "Deserted by my men, who refused no longer to endure the cold and exposure, I had remained in camp alone upon the summit . . ."

Beyond Colvin's unwillingness to plan safe, logical itineraries, the hunters, guides, and surveyors he employed could not temper their misadventures with a stiff drink. Colvin was a staunch teetotaler. So opposed to spirits, while petitioning to become superintendent of the Adirondack surveys, Colvin held a banquet for fifty influential politicians and served no alcohol. His hope was that through this social gathering he would gain their support for appointment. Socially inept, Colvin served no food. The only refreshment was an enormous bowl of ice water. The guests felt miffed and left early. As the Watermans reported, Colvin was oblivious to his social shortcomings: "Though the guests were outraged and left early, Colvin thought the party a grand success."

Colvin couldn't throw a party, but he shared his experiences in the Adirondack Mountains with perfection. The topographic reports he submitted to the State of New York were not like all the other dry bureaucratic reports others submitted. Quite the opposite, Colvin's reports read like adventure narratives where he made the ascent of a mountain sound like a dashing climb of the Matterhorn. His reports included intimate illustrations of mountains and camp life drawn by the surveyor himself.

Colvin's writing, which bordered on prose, pushed for protection of the Adirondack Mountains by suggesting formation of an "Adirondack Park or nature preserve." Unfortunately, as years grinded by Colvin felt he was not given due credit for helping create the Adirondack Park. He became bitter towards those who took credit for his idea of preserving the Adirondack Mountains, a range he described as "a region of mystery, over which none can gaze without a strange thrill of interest and of wonder at what may be hidden in that vast area of forest, covering all things with its deep repose." Disrespected, Colvin resigned as Chief Superintendent of the Adirondack Survey in 1900. He died twenty years later in a mental institution, a sad end for such an adventurous man. To honor him, we now have Colvin Brook in West Canada Lake Wilderness Area and Mount Colvin in Dix Mountain Wilderness Area. This mountain stands next to Blake Peak, named for one of the men who enjoyed working under Colvin: Mills Blake, assistant surveyor.

Colvin climbed Ruby Mountain during the late 1800s, perhaps 1896. He left his mark. At important surveying points Colvin and his men would sink a one-inch-diameter bolt into bedrock to mark the location. Bolt number 266, stamped with a date of 1896, was driven into the top of Ruby Mountain and remains today. It marks a triangulation station that helped the surveyor measure and map the Ruby Mountain area.

Colvin bolts are rare. I have found some of them on the tallest peaks in the state and one along a random stretch of the Cold River, this bolt being driven into an enormous boulder in the middle of the river. Knowing of no survey bolts on top of trailless peaks, I wanted to find the bolt and photograph it. It doesn't take much to make me happy. Just an old bolt in the woods will do. For Will's enjoyment, I reminded him that

Ruby Mountain was supposed to have a partially bald summit that offered an extensive view south.

To help Will decide what to bring and what not to bring on our day hike, I sent him a copy of my packing list, which I pointed out included "enough stuff to spend the night if I have to. You know—if I break my ankle or get us lost or something like that." I closed the list with, "If you're gonna bring anything else, you're probably not gonna use it." I gave him food ideas: peanut butter and jelly sandwiches, Pop-Tarts, cheddar cheese, chocolate, candy bars, cold pizza, fruit, or anything else calorie-dense, durable, and refreshing. I also let Will know what I was going to wear and added a warning. "Don't wear shorts."

When informing new hikers about what to expect, what to bring, and what to wear, you have to create a balance. Give them enough information so during the hike they won't say "I can't believe you didn't tell me about this," but do not overwhelm them with basic information so they don't say, while you're telling them this, "I'm not an idiot, you know."

I had to be especially careful with Will. On one hand, he had "humped" (infantry speak for "hiked") many miles and "bivouacked" (infantry speak for "camped") many nights while he was in the Army. On the other hand, the Army simply ruins hiking and camping, taking all the fun out of them and making them more confusing, miserable, and exhausting than they need be. Look at what the military did to intelligence and music. Shameful.

With a basic understanding of what to expect, bring, and wear, Will and I ended our workweek with a plan to meet the morning of Sunday, May 18, which happened to be the day after Armed Forces Day.

Sunday morning I poked my head outside my bathroom window and peered towards the west, where Upstate New York weather comes from. There was not a cloud in the sky. A faint breeze blew. No trace of humidity could be detected. Best of all, being mid-May, I presumed the biting bugs had yet to hatch from the thousands of acres of Adirondack standing water.

While finishing my bowl of raisin bran, I heard Will's car pull up in front of my home. Will got out and wore his pair of boots that he had worn in Iraq, his camouflage pants covering the tops of them. A standard issue Army brown t-shirt covered his torso. He looked as he did in the photo of his unit in Iraq, save for he wasn't holding an M4 carbine with a grenade launcher attached to the bottom, and he wasn't wearing a tactical vest full of ammo and grenades. Perhaps these were in his car.

I finished breakfast and grabbed my gear. Will gathered his gear (which to my relief did not include weapons) and tossed it in the trunk of my car. We drove west and then north on the highways, leaving civilization behind for the day. We enjoyed the thought of escape. As my car took us farther north we saw fewer signs of mankind. The elevation increased barely perceptibly yet noticeably consistently. The terrain rose into a jumble, from mounds, to hummocks, to hills, to, finally, legitimate mountains. We exited the interstate and took two-lane roads deeper into the park. We passed through Warrensburg, the last sign of amassed humans. I knew that during the remaining thirty miles of pavement we would pass no billboards, no chain stores, no fast food restaurants. We would pass under one stoplight, and chances were good it would be green.

We cruised alongside the Hudson River for much of the journey, watching the black and rust-colored water splash into neon shades of white when it spilled, churned, and poured over boulders from the last Ice Age. The water looked clean. You could certainly swim in it, and you would not become ill from drinking it. It looked like a completely different river from the same one that flows through the Capital Region by Will's home and my home. By the time the longest river in New York State reaches Albany the water is murky and dark, looking like a river of chocolate milk during storms. Rumors of fishermen reeling in evening meals from the Hudson River in Albany makes people scrunch their noses in disgust. People don't swim in this section of the Hudson. If you drink Albany river water though, you won't get sick from the pollution—no, you'll just drop dead.

Through The Glen, North Creek, and North River we went. A few clouds aimlessly wandered around the sky as if they had no plans for the day. At 10:00 we reached our pull-off on a side road off Route 28. Green springtime grass poked out of piles of sand from the plows sanding during winter, which ended six weeks earlier.

Efficient men, we popped the trunk, grabbed our packs, and shouldered them. Will wore his tan military day pack that he acquired while in the Army. I locked the car and hid the key in the woods. We each took out our topographic maps. Across Route 28, Casey Mountain arrested our attention, its 300-foot-tall cliff spilling nearly all the way down to the highway.

Will could already read a map well from his time in the Army, which made my life easier. Trying to teach someone how to read a topographic map—let alone ask that they then navigate up a trailless mountain—is not an easy task. Besides, years ago I had retired from being an outdoor educator. Nowadays I don't want to teach. I just want to hike.

With the leaves not out yet—only buds clung to the branches of May—we could see Davis Mountain in the distance. It looked far away to me. It must have looked very far away to Will. We spent a few minutes looking for a state land boundary, which would have been painted bright yellow by the Department of Environmental Conservation. The plan was to follow the boundary towards Davis Mountain. This would ensure we did not drift onto nearby private property, and if the boundary was well-marked we could follow this blazed course and not have to do much map and compass work.

As I had predicted, the line was not to be found. With literally thousands of boundary miles to mark, the Department of Environmental Conservation is like a hamster on a wheel, spinning and trying to keep up. Unlike a hamster running for no clear reason, this state agency tries to keep their boundaries marked to keep people on state land and off private land. As trees fall and bark peels and yellow paint fades, new boundaries are being marked only to fade and disappear like the rest of them.

We left the pavement, crossed the sandy shoulder and descended towards the bottom of our first hill, which led to an unnamed stream that flows out of Prier Pond to the southwest. We moved quickly and efficiently. Will stayed right behind me, not too close to crowd me or get smacked by branches but close enough to keep me within sight and follow the course—the easiest way through the woods—that I picked for us.

At the bottom of the descent I stopped to pee, adjust my pack, check my map, and check on Will, in that order. I asked how he was doing, and he replied he was doing fine. He looked around the woods and took it all in. Will was comfortable and confident for being flung into the Adirondack wilderness. A keen observer, Will pointed to a few trees, asking what species they were. I identified yellow birch, white ash, sugar maple, red spruce, and balsam fir, giving him tidbits of information on each one, like how yellow birch is made into toothpicks and how white ash is being attacked by the emerald ash borer beetle. For sugar maple I quickly explained the economics of maple syrup: why a gallon costs $60. Syrup production is labor intensive, it taking 42 gallons of sap to make one gallon of syrup. There wasn't much to say about red spruce except that it sucks to bushwhack through.

For balsam fir I took off my pack, found my ditty bag, and pulled a lighter from the bag. I found a thin, pointy stick, its end looking like a finely sharpened pencil. I poked the sharp end of my branch into one of the thousands of sap blisters on the side of our resident balsam fir. Clean, sticky, pungent sap oozed onto the end of the stick. I passed the end of the sap-smeared stick under the lit lighter, and the sap burst into flame and burned for nearly half a minute, the inflammable goo releasing thick, black smoke. "Great fire starter," I said. "Even works in the rain."

Will had one word to critique the experiment. "*Cool.*"

Our stream was high, as all Adirondack streams are during springtime. From what I could tell there was no snow left in the woods, even up high. It wasn't snow that was directly feeding the waterways draining the mountains—it was the woods being sopping wet, in our immediate area soaked from thousands of yards' worth of snow that disappeared three weeks earlier. Snowmelt takes an awfully long time to percolate down the sides of mountains and into the Hudson, Mohawk, Grass, Oswagatchie, and Black rivers, the major waterways penetrating the Adirondack Mountains. It would take another month for the woods to dry completely.

We patrolled up and down the stream looking for a spot to cross. Two boulders, one on either side of the stream, stood black and motionless, a four-foot gap separating them. Cold water poured forcefully between them. I handed Will my pack and leaped for everything I was worth—all five feet, six inches—barely making it to the other rock. After Will tossed me my pack, he stretched one of his long legs across, adding a little hop from his back heel to lift him across. Being six feet, five inches tall has its advantages in the woods.

Across our first checkpoint, we climbed a small hill in front of us, small at least compared to the two mountains we were bound for. We descended the backside, and encountered our second checkpoint, which was another unnamed stream, this one draining Gardner Pond and Grassy Ponds. Will would have to get a lot taller to cross this waterway. Beavers had been hard at work flooding the woods and turning our stream into a small lake. We bushwhacked along the shoreline heading downstream. Within a few minutes we found the beaver's dam and crossed on it.

Crossing a beaver dam, especially while wearing a backpack, is a delicate dance. With footing being a mix of mud and slippery, recently peeled branches coated in pond scum, it feels like you're walking on a greasy structure that's ready to give way at any moment, and into the drink you will go, falling upstream into a six-foot-deep beaver pond or downstream into a set of rapids. You're at least going to get your feet wet while crossing, fall or not.

In addition to the uncertain footing you have the slim chance of alerting the beaver who spent so much time doing such a fine job felling trees, lopping off branches, scouring the bottomlands for mud, and putting these components together to build one hell of a barrier. Whenever I cross a beaver dam I do it quickly. While crossing I imagine a pissed off beaver springing out of the water and lopping my foot off at the ankle. To a beaver a lower leg would be an oversized toothpick. I imagine my severed ankle and foot, still clad in my sock and hiking boot, shoved by the beaver into the small leak I had caused in his dam.

I crossed first and Will followed. When I reached the other side I had barely enough time to grab my camera and shoot Will crossing the dam. He got to my side. "Bet you never did that before," I inquired.

"Uh, no," he replied.

"Are your feet wet?"

With a smile, Will said, "Oh, they're totally soaked."

Since there were likely no more beaver dams to cross for the day, I gave Will the option of changing his socks. Like me, he knows there are few things more miserable than having soaking wet feet, which often lead to burly blisters and red raw spots. Will was unconcerned. "Nah, I'm good."

I knew exactly what Will was doing because I had done it myself twenty years ago. From serving in the infantry I had become so accustomed to being uncomfortable that I became programmed to not seek comfort at all. Suffering was just a way of life. Accepted. The mantra of the infantry is sometimes cited as "Complete the Mission." But there is a deeper meaning to what you read. What that saying really means is "Complete the mission no matter what. I don't care if your feet are wet, your pack is crushing your shoulders, you're sick, you haven't slept in a few days, you haven't eaten in a day, or you want to go home or stand there and die. Just complete the mission. Oh, and keep your mouth shut, too."

Another infantry saying is "High Speed, Low Drag," which communicates infantrymen are speedy and efficient. And there's "Drive On," which means don't stop for anything. The most recognizable combat arms anthem is one word: "Hooah!" (It's always yelled, hence the exclamation point.) Hooah! means "everything and anything but 'no.'"

There was no way I was going to defragment four years of U.S. Army programming inside Will's head. I had one word for him and his totally soaked feet, which I said with a sincere smile. "Okay." He'd eventually learn the civilian saying that accompanies hiking: "Smarter, not Stronger."

It was all uphill from there. A softwood forest crowded the shores of the beaver pond, the sun-loving species, mostly spruce, craving direct sunlight. We pushed through this dark forest and within a minute entered an open hardwood forest. The openness was comfortable. We breathed easier. I was thankful for the hardwoods' ability to grow in a world of well-drained soils and shade unlike the spruce thickets below us. An open 800-vertical-foot climb rose in front of us. The hiking was marvelous during my second favorite time of the year. Give me autumn first, spring second, and winter third. Summer finishes a distant fourth. If we had eight seasons, summer would likely come in eighth. How people love this season of heat, humidity, black flies, mosquitoes, no-see-ums, wasps, hornets, and poison ivy is simply baffling.

Slow and steady wins the race. I led the climb, methodically plopping one boot in front of the other, my upper body and arms relaxed whenever I wasn't grabbing hold of a tree to help haul my body up a steep section. Boulders occasionally poked their heads out of the soil. The ferns still lay matted to the floor, stomped flat by the heavy snowpack that buried them during the past five months. Only three wildflowers were out, the usual three I find first each year: trout lilies, red trilliums, and spring beauties.

The higher I climbed the farther Will slunk back down behind me. I slowed my pace to have him catch up and soon realized I would have to stop altogether. I peered down the side of the mountain at Will, his head down, his boots scraping across the flattened ferns. He looked tired. On the horizon behind him rose light blue peaks. The highest peaks in the state could be seen far to the north. Their tops held expansive snowfields.

I strolled uphill into an open area. Here the hardwoods were spaced far apart and short, plump greenery carpeted the floor of the woods. The green looked soft and inviting, a good place for a nap. I walked to the center of this area and sat down, leaning back on my pack while Will bore up the hill. Without a word he collapsed next to me, leaning back on his pack like I was leaning on mine. He caught his breath and kept commentary short: "*Dude.*"

"Dude," depending on the tone, can communicate many things, as all singular words can. Will's "Dude" carried an "I am so freaking tired" tone, a tone not to be confused with one that says, "Dude, I'm mad at you," or "Dude, watch out!" or "Dude, that's messed up."

Will always being a good sport, I chuckled. "Bushwhacking is not easy. You do this once a week for a few months, and you'll be a fucking Olympian."

"Wow. No shit. Fuck."

Another infantry bond came out of us: a love of curse words.

We caught our breaths, and I made attempts to motivate Will, but I've never been a good coach. "All right. Check it out. This is the biggest climb of the day. Once we get this out of the way, there's no climb that even comes close to this." That was a lie. Since much of my coaching centers on deceit, this is why I'm not a good coach. Though Will could read his topographic map, I doubt he had taken the time to calculate the climb up Ruby Mountain. That climb was a respectable 600 vertical feet.

With an unhealthy preoccupation with making sure my hiking partners are happy, I had to inquire with Will. "How's it going, Buddy? Are you having fun?"

"I *am* having fun." His tone communicated that he was surprised he was having fun despite being so tired. "I am just so out of fucking shape. I really need to get in shape."

The two up-and-coming Olympians got to their feet after ten minutes of lounging. Will looked refreshed. I felt great. I told Will we were halfway up our climb (that was true) and that the higher we went the easier it would get (that was a lie). With another thirty minutes of hiking we completed stage one of our mission. We reached the top of Davis Mountain. The summit was a tangle of briars, dead yet standing hardwood trees, and evergreens dotting the summit area in no discernible pattern. "Davis Mountain!" I reported.

Will was elated. I didn't think his elation stemmed from the climb ending and that he could sit down to eat and drink. I think Will was elated over earning the summit. There's an old saying in mountaineering: "If you have to ask why someone climbs mountains, you'll never understand the answer." True. But once you climb a mountain, especially a hard-earned one, you'll never have to ask again.

Most goals in our lives are intangible. An example I gave my outdoor education students is the grade of A. When you study hard and ace a test you receive a letter grade, perhaps an A. But that's all it is—a letter. It's the first letter of the alphabet, and it reports how you did. That's all. It's another creation of humankind that has no connection to something bigger. Your letter grade stands among the other letters that, at their very best, may form words that form sentences that form paragraphs that form books like this one. A letter gets lost in the shuffle and easily loses its identity.

A mountain, even though it may be lumped together with hundreds of other mountains within a range, retains a strong identity. As the author of *Adirondack Country* (written in 1954 and, in your author's opinion, still the best Adirondack book ever written), William Chapman White, wrote of Adirondack mountains and their identities: "Of the hundreds of hills and mountains in the Adirondack country, some are famous, others are little known, but each is as beloved in its own neighborhood as any famous peak." No one's ever said that about a letter, or most of humankind's temporary inventions. Mountains are forever.

The draw of climbing a mountain, being immersed in a world that is pure, is best summed by Paul Petzoldt, the man regarded as the founder of outdoor education. Petzoldt loved mountains because he could find a cycle of challenge and reward.

All my life, people have asked the question, directly or indirectly, "Why the hell do you climb mountains?" I can't explain this to other people. I love the physical exertion. I love the wind. I love the storms. I love the fresh air. I love the companionship in the outdoors. I love the reality. I love the change. I love the oneness with nature. I enjoy the hunger. I enjoy clear water. I enjoy being warm at night when it's cold outside. All those simple things are extremely enjoyable because, gosh, you're feeling them, you're living them, your senses are really feeling. I can't explain it.

I can't explain it either. On top of Davis Mountain that May day Will would have understood what White and Petzoldt were getting at. I looked over at Will. Facial expressions and body language, more than spoken words, reveal what a new hiker thinks of his new hobby in his new environment. Will gazed to the horizon and noticed the snow-capped peaks in the distance, their flanks pale blue. He "got it." Will looked down into the woods below us. He pointed out the Hudson River churning four miles away and 1,600 vertical feet below us. He examined the little world around our boots and packs. Like me, Will took in the trees, rocks, flowers, grasses, leaves, buds, and sticks and probably noticed they fit together well, better than a puzzle made by human hands.

I told him, "This is why I climb mountains. It's so different than what's down there," referencing the low country. "Up here it's just us. No one knows we're here. No one can find us. It's us and the mountain."

Will commented on how being disconnected from the manufactured world of email, smart phones, the Internet, phone calls, and the like was cool. Though not a misanthrope, the thing that Will enjoyed being rid of most were people and all their drama, needs, and opinions. All their stuff. Baggage. In the woods we were two men on a mission. Perhaps Will hadn't had such a feeling of purpose and camaraderie since 2004 when he was in Iraq. I didn't ask.

Before shoving off for our next peak, I found my journal. While I wrote Will swatted the blackflies swarming around him.

Haven't been to the mountains since March. But I've been running. First 5k trail race in two weeks. Black flies! Can't believe they are out. 5/18/14. Too early, especially with the late season snowpack. Snow long gone up here. Up with Will! Fun. Lilies, trilliums, spring beauties. Hardwood top. Moose poop the whole way up.

"You ready for Ruby Mountain?" I asked.

Will let out a sigh and said, "Yes, I am ready for Ruby Mountain. But I don't want to get up. The feeling's finally returned to my legs."

Packs back on, I took a bearing towards Ruby Mountain, which we could barely make out through the branches and buds. The descent was steep, and at times we had to slide down on our butts, the bottoms of our packs scraping the mud and leaves towards the col—the small, high valley—nestled near the bottom of Davis Mountain.

Just before reaching the col we were halted by a thirty-foot-high cliff. With no way to climb down it, we traversed right until the cliff was buried farther and farther, deeper into the Adirondack soil. We scooted down a ten-foot-tall crack in the cliff, hit the ground, and turned left back towards the top of the col.

The air was especially cool in the col, the ground being shaded nearly the entire year. Our thirty-foot-tall cliff rose on our left while a twenty-foot-tall cliff rose on our right. We picked our way through the narrow, dark canyon. Blocks of rock were stacked one over the other and bumped against each other, their sharp corners and well-defined lines making them look like cornerstones of massive buildings that crumbled. We exited the far end of our chasm, climbed a small hill, and made the final descent into the modest valley separating Davis Mountain from Ruby Mountain.

We took another break. Water tasted good and food tasted better. Will looked whupped. I proposed options.

1. We both climb Ruby Mountain.
2. I climb Ruby Mountain and Will rests in the valley.
3. We both not climb Ruby Mountain.

Will suggested plan four. I climb Ruby Mountain at my own pace while he slowly climbs behind me. But discussion eliminated this option from our already short list. I reasoned that with our luck I would reach the summit and then bushwhack down while he bushwhacked up, and we would not see each other during our respective descents and ascents. He'd get to the top, and I wouldn't be there. I'd get back to the valley, and he wouldn't be there. He saw my point.

We came up with plan five. We both climb Ruby Mountain, but Will would do it packless, leaving his backpack in the valley, me carrying my pack to the summit. We could both reach the top, have my gear for a safety measure, and Will would not drop dead getting to the summit. Then we'd come back down, grab his pack, and head out of the valley. I assured Will I would tell no one of his packless ascent. Mountaineers are a prideful bunch. To have been so tired that you had to leave your pack to complete the final climb is dishonorable. (Before the reader jumps to a conclusion, this promise to Will was actually not a lie since at that moment I had no intention of writing about our hike.) Will became convinced of plan five.

We left Will's pack, depositing it below a massive white ash that leaned hard through all the other trees. The ash made a proverbial X that marked the spot. Without his pack, Will became a man reborn. He was barely out of breath during our ascent. Refining my coaching skills by actually telling the truth, I reminded Will of the partially bald summit we were gunning towards, the view it was going to offer, and, of probably little interest to Will, bolt number 266 driven into solid rock by a surveyor who ended up dying in a mental institution. I told Will I was going to take my boots and socks off on top to dry them and then I was going to lie down and maybe even take a nap.

We climbed steadily at a respectable pace. The horizon in front of us got lower and lower while the altimeter on my digital watch blinked higher and higher. We hit the top of a rise where it was apparent we could go no higher. There was only a humble view; a filtered image of the surrounding hills. Where was all that open rock I promised? With trees standing tall all over our summit and grasses and briars guarding the ground in waist-high thickets, finding a copper bolt was going to be a hell of a task. Perhaps we were not on the summit.

I checked my altimeter, map, and compass, along with the time of day, knowing how long it should have taken us to get from Will's pack to the top. Surely we were on our summit. Then it occurred to me. In my hasty research of bolt number 266, I had failed to realize that the bolt was on the south summit still a half mile away. However, without exception, the destination of a mountaineer is the top of his mountain—the tippy-top of his mountain. With our north summit being 2,667 feet tall and the south summit being 2,648 feet tall, we had reached our mountaineering destination.

What about the partially bald summit with its stupendous view? More importantly, what about the 118-year-old bolt? I looked at Will and realized two things. One, by this point in our hike he probably didn't care about a view, let alone a piece of metal pounded into a rock. Two, he looked tired. I didn't have the immorality to drag Will to the southern peak, a one-mile roundtrip push through woods and briars. Besides, we had completed the mission of reaching Ruby Mountain's high point.

With the sun panning west and Will running out of gumption, we turned north to head back to the valley. The descent was easy. We nearly jogged down. Twenty minutes later we were at Will's pack. We ate and drank, and I wrote in my journal.

Bugs were bad, and Will was sucking wind on top, so I'm writing back down in the valley. No big view! Shucks. Must be over at the lower, southern peak. Oh well. This is the one that counts. Open woods. Very pretty. Easy. Trek out may be bumpy and wet. Can't believe the bugs are out. Fun.

"It is all downhill from here," I said to Will with a smile.

Noticing my pattern of deceitful coaching, Will asked, "Don't we have to go up the hill that we first climbed over this morning?"

"Um," I thought. "Yes. Yes, we do. But that's the only uphill we'll have."

Will looked at me with doubt, his eyebrows raised. "Are you sure?"

"You know, I forget."

Following a drainage into the valley, Davis Mountain on our right and Ruby Mountain on our left, the drainage soon filled with springtime water and turned into a strong-flowing stream, funneling all the percolating water towards Grassy Ponds, our lowland destination and next checkpoint. The stream ran in the shadows of beautiful cliffs on our right side, the bottom of Davis Mountain that ended with a bang. The vertical rock formed a dark wall of hard stone hundreds of feet long and up to thirty feet in height. Sharp blocks the size of couches were scattered at the bottom of the cliff, having been peeled off during centuries' worth of freeze and thaw cycles. We hung close to the cliff, inspecting its tiny caves and deep crevices. Our necks strained back to see the top of the wall where spruce and birch held on for their lives. Their branches and even their trunks reached out over the cliff to catch sunlight.

Will spotted a particularly deep crevice, one that was big enough for a few people to hunker in. "Right there, man," he said pointing to it. "When the shit hits the fan, and it's every man for himself, we'll regroup there. Forward Operating Base Davis." I promised to be there.

Past the cliffs the grade eased. Soon our stream barreled into a murky, shallow pond. We had reached Grassy Ponds, three ponds stacked one upon the other from south to north. As we neared the shoreline, we turned a hard right to avoid the speckled alders and red spruces that grew in tangles along the shoreline.

Walking through a majestic white pine forest above the wetlands, the forest floor composed of soft, orange-brown pine needles, one of the pines caught my eye. It was an old one, certainly more than a century old and probably closer to three. I guessed the height at over 100 feet. Using my outstretched arms as a makeshift measuring tape, I calculated the circumference to be 132 inches, an imposing 42 inches in diameter.

Grassy Ponds ended at the downstream end of pond number three. The stream continued, flowing out an abandoned beaver dam. We hopped back and forth across the stream, following the left shore when it was smoother, returning to the west shore when that side looked more inviting. Small marshes became frequent, reflecting a crowded beaver population. Soon the stream turned into a long series of wetlands where it was difficult to strike a balance in route selection. We desired to keep shorelines within sight so as not to stray off course, but we needed to keep far enough above the sluggish waterways to stay out of the alder and spruce thickets.

At one point a broad meadow opened up next to the stream. It seemed to be our ticket to fast travel downstream. I took us down through the pines and pushed through the thick shoreline forest until we hit the meadow. I looked back at Will. "Now this is the way to travel."

I led the way into the middle of the meadow and continued alongside the stream, the thickets of woods far off to our right and the stream to our left. The traveling was easy and smooth, akin to walking across a soccer field that had not been mowed in a decade. I confidently led us towards the middle of the meadow, but it turned out to not be a meadow at all. It was a wetland with only tall, dry grasses growing from it. The initial dampness of our route soon grew into pure, cold Adirondack water. While I stood in a few inches of water, shallow enough to not reach the tops of my waterproof boots, I turned to Will and reported my mess up, which was obvious enough that it didn't need to be reported. We could hike back to the wood line or just plod through the water in front of us. Will responded with little emotion. "Let's go straight through. My feet are soaked anyway." Four wet feet made it to the other side. I knew the end was near—perhaps another forty minutes of hiking—and didn't bother taking off my boots and wringing out my socks.

With fifteen minutes of hiking we hit a familiar feature: the beaver dam we had crossed five hours ago. Will was impressed with my spot-on navigation, especially since I had not glanced at my map or compass during the prior hour. I felt like a polished pearl. "Now *that's* how it's done. Boom! Back at the dam."

Our return across the dam went smooth though we were tired. We both knew what the dam would feel like under our feet, and I had little worry that a beaver would surface and bite off my foot. Our sopping wet feet helped too. Since they couldn't get any wetter, we didn't put much thought into where we stepped.

Over that last hill, which indeed seemed bigger than it did six hours earlier, and down the backside of that hill we went.

A little off course, we wandered out from deep within state land towards private land. We encountered the state land boundary we had searched for in the morning. I strolled past the boundary. Will's keen eyes, now sharp in the wilderness, spotted it. An old metal Department of Environmental Conservation sign was on the ground, ripped off years earlier when the tree it was nailed to fell during a storm. I asked Will if he wanted the sign as a souvenir. On the tree it was state property with a purpose. On the ground it was trash. I stuffed the sign into a large storage pocket on the outside of my pack, taking care not to cut my pack with the sharp corners.

An opening in the woods was uphill and ahead of us, but I didn't know what it was, thinking perhaps Route 28, perhaps our side road, perhaps a meadow. It was a power line that runs behind a private summer home. We met the line, got our bearings, turned left, and followed an ATV track that ran down the power line swath. After cresting a tiny hill under the power line, we saw it: my car. We strolled across the shoulder and onto the pavement. God, that pavement felt good. Flat. Smooth. We dropped our packs behind my car, and I pushed into the woods to find the car key. I popped the trunk and reached for what I had been looking forward to: my sandals. Will looked like he had been duped. "Sandals? Oh my God, those look so comfortable."

"Yeah, man, you gotta bring your sandals." I reached back into the trunk and pulled out a container of baby powder. "And you need the baby powder."

"Why didn't you tell me to bring sandals?"

"I thought you knew." Then I thought back to my days in the infantry. Sandals were never allowed in the field. Will was learning. "Bring 'em next time."

After drinking more water, eating more snacks, and me dumping my muddy, stinky, wet socks and boots in the trunk, it was time to head back to civilization. I would stretch our time away. We pulled out to Route 28 and coasted down the road, gaining speed down the enormous hill that drops from the cliffs of Casey Mountain to the Hudson River. When the road flattened next to the river I set the cruise at fifty miles per hour, which didn't feel slow after our six-and-a-half hours of hiking one or two miles per hour.

As I promised Will earlier in the day—a sort of bush-whacker's carrot on a stick—we stopped at my favorite ice cream stand in the Adirondack Region: Martha's Dandee Cream, just north of the Village of Lake George. Will had earned a cone. Actually, he had earned an ice cream cake. I knew he finished the final two or three miles of our hike on sheer guts.

Named for Martha Schoelermann, Martha's has been serving ice cream for seventy years as of this writing. The LaFontaine family, which purchased the business in 1982 and runs the stand today, has developed nothing short of a cult following. The 11,000 fans on Facebook will surely attest to this. Daily flavors often include birthday cake, peach, cotton candy, coffee, strawberry, cheesecake, marble cake, mocha, raspberry cream twist, black raspberry, coconut, apple pie, banana, pumpkin, mint chocolate twist, pineapple, strawberry, chocolate, chocolate and vanilla twist, and vanilla. At least a dozen other flavors are offered, each depending on which day of the week you stop by.

Will, looking like an American soldier turned refugee (he was covered in mud, spruce sap, and dried sweat and looked very tired), teetered in line next to me. I spoke to him words sweeter than anything he could have ordered. "Get whatever you want. It's my treat." He wisely chose a raspberry and chocolate twist cone. A man of few needs, a small vanilla cone had been on my mind since I started the car that morning.

We sat at a picnic table eating our hard-won ice cold calories. We were in heaven. Lick after lick our senses returned to us. Will's bushwhacking hindsight was being given a silver lining as each calorie melted in his mouth. He forgot about the mud holes, stream crossings, climbs, cliffs, descents, and the branches that smacked him in the face. He looked refreshed, perhaps not remembering how tired he was up on Davis and Ruby mountains. My own tiredness melted faster than my ice cream.

At sunset we pulled into my driveway. Will was spent. I think the only reason he did not fall asleep during the car ride home was because of pride, feeling self-conscious about dozing while I was awake. Back at my home we talked about the hike, especially our favorite parts and how good it felt to reach the top of Ruby Mountain. I remembered that Will still had his wet combat boots on. Like any good soldier, he gave no hint of how miserable those boots felt.

At 8:00 the following morning, Monday, Will and I were reunited. He came hobbling down the flight of stairs into our downstairs offices like a man who had the bottoms of his feet beaten with a switch. He gripped the handrail intensely. Hobbling is actually too soft of a word to describe Will's gait. He was limping. Staggering. I was at my desk when he entered my office. "My God, are you that sore?" I asked. "What did you do to yourself?"

"Dude, I am so sore. I think I'll have to go home early today. I've barely been able to walk since I got home. Since I live upstairs I was considering just sleeping on the ground in front of my front door last night."

He would have benefited from crutches. No, a stroller would have been better. Actually, a wheelchair. I offered him some Tylenol and asked if he'd like a cup of coffee. The coffee maker was twenty feet from his desk, and it must have seemed twenty kilometers away to Will. He passed on both. Maybe it was that pride of his, or he thought no amount of Tylenol could cure his pain and no serving of coffee could perk him up.

I thought I had run a combat infantryman into the ground in a matter of six or seven hours of hiking. I should have known better. By noon Will had not gone home. During lunch I spied him looking at online topographic maps of the Adirondack Mountains. By the end of the workday he asked when we were going bushwhacking again. I realized the only thing more durable than Will's pride was his toughness; his ability to complete the mission and be sent out on another with no complaints. It was his toughness that would bring him back to the Adirondack Mountains. Or maybe Will just plain fell in love with the woods.

Two Dark Days

Named for a pair of twin ponds, 115,000-acre Siamese Ponds Wilderness Area is resigned to be the younger, homely sister of bigger, "better" Adirondack wilderness areas. Siamese Ponds Wilderness Area actually has two big sisters' shadows to stand in: 172,000-acre West Canada Lake Wilderness Area and 193,000-acre High Peaks Wilderness Area.

West Canada Lake Wilderness Area hosts a thirty-mile-long ribbon of trail that cuts across the entire region, providing excellent access to the backcountry. Popular destinations include scenic Spruce Lake, Brooktrout Lake, West Lake, South Lake, and West Canada Creek; a dozen lean-tos, all of which are in good shape; and historic remnants like the former locations of Department of Environmental Conservation ranger cabins. Beyond these features is a jumble of peaks that stand above remote waterways. No trails penetrate this region. It is perhaps the biggest piece of feral land in the Northeast. West Canada Lake Wilderness Area even had its own hermit: French Louie.

Louis "French Louie" Seymour was the second most popular hermit of the Adirondacks, being outshined only by Noah John Rondeau discussed below. Born in Canada circa 1832, French Louie ran away to the United States when he was a kid, at first working in traveling circuses (back in the 1800s kids literally ran away and joined the circus). Later he became a mule driver on the Erie Canal and then became a logger, back then called a lumberjack. Gaining a taste for the Adirondack wilderness through being a logger, in 1873 French Louie moved deep into today's West Canada Lake Wilderness Area. He fell in love with a reclusive lifestyle because he, in the words of his biographer, Harvey Dunham, wanted to be "free as a hawk, and not be bothered by rules and repression of lumber camps and settlements . . . where no one would tell him to pick it up or lay it down."

High Peaks Wilderness Area is the most visited mountainous area in New York State. The tallest mountains in New York are contained in this wilderness area. Nearly all of our 4,000-foot and both of our 5,000-foot peaks stretch their necks towards the sky. Mount Marcy, New York State's high point, stands supreme. The next closest higher peak is in northern New Hampshire or southwestern Virginia, 150 and 800 miles away, respectively. Approximately 30,000 people climb Mount Marcy each year while a quarter-million enter the wilderness area. An impressive infrastructure is in place to host so many visitors: 300 signs, 100 outhouses, and 70 lean-tos, most of these shelters set on picturesque bluffs, lakeshores, and riverbanks. Seventy-eight different trails totaling 268 miles guide hikers to most nooks and crannies. High Peaks Wilderness Area had its own hermit, too: Noah John Rondeau.

Rondeau, the most famous Adirondack hermit, resided on a bluff overlooking the Cold River from 1928 to 1950. He was the self-elected Mayor of the Village of Cold River, population one. The settlement consisted of several wigwams and two small cabins. This lonesome resident had the Adirondack image nailed. Rondeau had a long, gray beard, stood barely five feet tall, and was usually outfitted in a handmade buckskin suit. He looked half human, half woods gnome. Biographers have recorded his life, scholars have deciphered his journals (they were written in code so as not to incriminate himself for illegally hunting), and his cabin is displayed in the Adirondack Museum. Anyone worth their weight in Adirondack black fly bites has heard of Noah John Rondeau.

Siamese Ponds Wilderness Area is not usually remembered for what it has. It is remembered for what it has not. While West Canada Lake Wilderness Area is home to sections of the Northville Placid Trail and Trans Adirondack Route, and High Peaks Wilderness Area has nearly 250 miles of footpaths, Siamese Ponds Wilderness Area has only eighty miles of trails, and about a third of those are unmaintained. It's nearly impossible to plan a day hike that makes a loop. The highest peak in this wilderness area is a bump compared to Mount Marcy: 3,451-foot Puffer Mountain, a trailless nondescript pile of trees. Siamese Ponds Wilderness Area hosts only a few lean-tos. Most of your camping options are limited to uneven patches of mud. The Department of Environmental Conservation has rated half the campsites in this wilderness area as "being in poor condition, primarily due to excessive amounts of debris and garbage."

The majority of day hikers who enter Siamese Ponds Wilderness Area contain themselves to Chimney Mountain, a peak named for its unique summit area, a narrow and tall jut of tan rock that looks like . . . well, you know. It's a nice mountain, as all mountains are, but while 30,000 people go for Mount Marcy each year, only 5,000 people want to see the top of a mountain that looks like a bloated chimney. The area doesn't even have a famous hermit. Pathetic.

Even after this trash talking about Siamese Ponds Wilderness Area, it does have something I'm particularly attracted to. It has lots of little peaks. While most hikers pursue the tallest mountains in the state, I prefer the little ones. The Siamese Ponds region contains twenty mountains between 2,500 and 3,000 feet in height, these modest hills looking like mounds of rich, green broccoli during summertime. During winter the woods are asleep, finding no sense being awake during such a cold time of year.

With these twenty mountains on my to-do list, I imagined a first-rate trip would involve tackling half of them in one go: ten individual mountains, each of them trailless. I'd make my way up Ruby Mountain and Davis Mountain as a day hike while on my way to the main Siamese Ponds Wilderness Area trailhead at Kings Flow and sleep somewhere in the woods.

On day two I'd begin a two-night trip into the backcountry. On this twenty-mile loop I'd thrash my way up Humphrey Mountain, Horseshoe Mountain, and two unnamed mountains near Siamese Ponds. My campsite at the end of day two would be near the ponds themselves. On day three I'd summit Hayden Mountain and Puffer Mountain's south peak. Then I'd camp a few miles from the trailhead. Once back at my car during the morning of day four, I'd trade in my overnight pack for a day pack to run up Chimney Mountain's west peak, Kunjamuk Mountain, and Crotched Pond Mountain. Ten for ten.

I packed my car on the last day of August 2013 and left early the following morning, ringing in my favorite month of the year with what looked like one hell of a trip. But during my two-hour drive towards this area where three counties—Essex, Hamilton, and Warren—meet, I changed my plan. Instead of hiking Ruby Mountain and Davis Mountain on day one, I'd save them for the fourth and final day. With the shining brightly during my drive towards the mountains, I figured I should take advantage of the weather and head straight into the backcountry.

I pulled into Kings Flow trailhead. A gravel parking lot with weeds popping up here and there provided room for forty vehicles. The trailhead was half full. Most hikers were on their way up Chimney Mountain to look at its funny head and explore the summit top caves that held ice through much of the summer. I was headed the opposite direction: south down Kings Flow East Trail. I shouldered my pack, which weighed barely ten pounds, not counting food and water.

I strolled down an old roadbed from the 1800s narrowed by softwood forests to accommodate one hiker at a time. I passed Kings Flow on my right, choosing not to take any photos of this body of water due to the humidity. The blue-green wooded horizon blended into the blue-green sky in a chalky haze. The distant woods, horizon, and sky looked pixilated, like a low-resolution image. The humid air stuck to my clothes and skin.

I climbed away from Kings Flow, gently heading up, up, and away from the wet country and into the high and dry hardwood forests. Strolling down a wide section of trail an hour from the trailhead, a great commotion burst out of a yellow birch sixty feet ahead of me on the left side of the trail. I stopped in my tracks to see a black bear climb a few feet up into the tree's canopy and then come screaming down the branchless trunk like a fireman zooming down a brass pole. The hacking and scratching of his claws barely checked his speed. The crash of leaves and his claws hanging on for what seemed to be dear life was startling. As I watched him descend at incredible speed, I anticipated him losing his powerful grip, losing control, and spilling to the floor like a boulder.

He held firmly, arms and legs ratcheting up and down like a well's pump arm madly yanked up and down. In such a hurry to get away from me, when his hind feet hit the ground they were already spitting up leaves and soil in a frantic search for traction. His front claws, still on the trunk, ripped down, leaving ten final gouges in the trunk, one from each pointy claw. The bear ran thirty feet into the woods, straight away from me. And then he stopped.

With a bit of room now between him and me, the pesky human, he relaxed, like none of what he had done had even happened. I was impressed that he was not panting from his mad descent. He looked like he had woken from a nap. We looked each other in the eye. His expression looked almost human. He slowly turned away, gave a last look over his shoulder, sauntered, and then ran. I tiptoed down the trail hoping to see furry black ears or his furry black tail, or even his big gleaming teeth, but he was long gone. He knew there were thousands of other acres to stroll around in. As long as he stayed off Chimney Mountain and away from me, he'd have his solitude. The show was over.

I went to hike on but stopped. Nearly under the shadow of my boot was an animal that my bear would have seen as an hors d'oeuvre: a tiny mouse. I slowly brought my boot back to view this custodian of the trail. I took a few steps back and slowly took off my pack. With the mouse still standing his ground, I dug out my camera. If I couldn't get a photo of that bear, at least I'd get a photo of this mouse. To be honest, I couldn't decide which one was cuter.

I got down on my hands and knees and inched towards him until I was a few feet away. I clicked my camera over and over, taking a series of photos. It was difficult to focus on him since my camera is designed for long-distance shots. I hoped at least one of them would come out well. He sat on his little, furry hind legs with his big—at least in proportion to his body—white feet neatly resting on the dry leaves. I turned off my camera and set it down. I found myself fully sprawled on the ground on my stomach, my muddy boots stretched about behind me with my hands supporting my chin. I looked at him, and he looked at me. I wondered what it would be like to be a mouse. I doubt he wondered what it would be like to be a human.

Some people are "dog people," "horse people," or "cat people." Me? I'm "mouse people." Mice love me. I'll admit it. I love them. I like their little ears and their little feet, their little squeaks and their beady, little eyes. I like their whiskers. They'll walk, then hop, walk, then hop, like walking isn't enough fun on its own. But I know when a mouse must die.

My first real outdoor job was in Maine. Working as an Appalachian Trail caretaker and ridgerunner among the wild high peaks of Western Maine, my schedule called for me to work ten days in the backcountry followed by four days off. During those ten days my Subaru wagon sat still at a grassy trailhead. It turned out that that trailhead was home to many, many mice. And they really liked my car.

I used my Subaru as a poor man's RV during days off, driving down the long, lonely dirt roads that penetrate paper company lands and car camping way the hell out in the middle of nowhere. Workdays I hiked and days off I hiked. Those are still the wildest months of my life. During my 150-day season, I slept inside a building five nights. When I wasn't sleeping in a tent during work I was sleeping in the back of my car during days off.

As my season progressed I started seeing mice inside my car. I'd open the door and one would dart under the seats. I'd pop the back hatch and one would scurry out of sight. While driving down the highway I'd look down and there was a mouse sitting on the shifter, looking up at me as if to ask, "Where are we going, Erik?" He darted into the dash through one of the vents. I knew they had established firm residency when I heard them chasing each other at night through the frame of my vehicle. They also ate most of my road maps and stole—elbow by elbow—a ten-pound bag of macaroni.

Something had to be done. I became a mouse-hunting mercenary, setting traps on the passenger side floor when I slept in the back storage area. In the middle of the night when I was deep in sleep or having a good dream, I'd hear the "snap" of my trap. The mouse would flail around for a few seconds, but most died instant deaths, which was all I wished for them. Once one was only crippled by the trap, and I had to pound on his little head with my enormous police flashlight. I felt terrible. By the end of my season I killed 27 mice inside my car, the tally written with permanent marker on a piece of duct tape stuck to the back storage area. Next to my record of confirmed kills I drew a skull and crossbones.

But my little friend in the middle of Kings Flow East Trail was not running through my car frame, gnawing the wires in my dash, or packing my dashboard vents with leaves. He bothered no one. I was in his home. He was not in mine. I slowly raised myself off the ground, put my camera away, hoisted my pack, and walked around him. I left my trail guardian with a request. "Don't let any riffraff down this trail, okay?"

My hiking break with the 200-pound bear and the one-ounce mouse was energizing. But it was still uncharacteristically humid for the first of September. The first day of autumn was less than three weeks away. Mosquitoes drafted behind me, occasionally diving in for a taste of the back of my neck. Deer flies dive-bombed the top of my baseball hat, emitting a soft "tit, tit, tit" as they bounced off, gained altitude, and then pitter-pattered back down like hail. It felt like July.

As I neared the base of my first peak, Humphrey Mountain, on a well-maintained trail, I had my topographic map and compass handy. I knew there was a key turn coming up on the trail: a faint and perhaps unmarked intersection where I needed to get on an abandoned path towards my mountain. Approximately two miles from the trailhead I encountered an unsigned junction. Unsure of how to proceed—left or right—I left my pack and jogged down the right-hand trail for a few minutes and encountered a large brook, which I presumed was Humphrey Brook. I jogged back, grabbed my pack, and crossed the brook, remaining on my trail.

I soon encountered another intersection, subtler yet just as important. It was the turn up the old Humphrey Mountain Trail. I turned left, leaving the maintained trail behind. My senses were alert, noting the undulations of the trail and which direction it was headed. I would then compare these observations with my detailed topographic map. With the terrain matching the map and vice versa, I was confident Humphrey Mountain was somewhere ahead of me through the dense forest and thick, stagnant air.

As the trail got steeper and climbed higher, I knew I was on the correct track. The trail pulled away from an unnamed brook coming down from the top of the mountain. I stopped, drank a quart of water, and refilled my bottle. The water was cold and refreshing. It felt good to stop and sit in the shade, though the killer wasn't the sunlight. It was the humidity.

I was particularly interested in climbing Humphrey Mountain because I had heard rumors of a mine near the summit. I was told it was a titanium operation from the early 1900s, this precious metal sought for use in the First World War. A broad region centering on my peak was mining country, something rare in the Adirondack Mountains. In 1878 Henry Barton started a garnet mine on Gore Mountain ten miles away, and in 1894 Frank Hooper started another garnet mine on Ruby Mountain, which was also ten miles from Humphrey Mountain. The mine on my peak operated from 1900 to 1918. The miners never sought titanium. They wanted garnet. Garnet is a silicate mineral used as an abrasive. When fine particles are mixed with high-pressure water, this slurry can cut through steel. Garnet is also a gemstone, its typical red-amber color and dull sheen being cut into beautiful arrangements (garnet can also be found in green, but this color is rare). You can't miss garnet since no other geological oddities in the Adirondack Mountains look like it. We have plenty of dull gray, black, and tan rocks, but bold shades of ruby red? Not so much.

With such standout colors, it was easy to tell I had found my mine perched in a small gap at 2,600 feet. Here the trail ended. Chunks of broken, black rock lay strewn about with bumps of garnet bonded to them, the black and burgundy complimenting each other. The mine had obviously been abandoned long ago. Ferns and grasses swallowed small mounds of crumbled rock while no traces of human meddling, save for the existence of the pit and a small section of wire screening I found, were present. I was expecting something more, perhaps like most us do when we hear the word "mine." An image of heavy timbers supporting a dark tunnel that bores into the side of a mountain is the vision I get.

I hiked over bands of crumbled and smashed rock, my boots crunching the remnants of the mine into even smaller pieces. I climbed a false summit, dropped into a small pass, and then made the final climb to the top of 2,982-foot Humphrey Mountain. The summit was a mix of well-weathered hardwoods and thick webs of briars. I smashed down a section of greenery with my boots so I'd have somewhere to sit and rest. One peak down, nine to go.

It was hotter than I would have liked. I had never experienced a September that scorching. As I peered down the steep east side of the mountain towards a valley 1,000 vertical feet below, deer flies, loving the heat, dived down onto my baseball hat, which was damp with salty sweat. There was little shade to be had, and the view wasn't that good. The humidity made it look like the mountains across the valley were underwater, languid and soggy. The deer flies were annoying, and the weather was getting to me, but they weren't the reason for the realization that I didn't want to be on that mountain. I didn't want to be in the woods at all. For a year leading up to my Humphrey Mountain hike I had been slipping deeper into depression.

Likely caused by a chemical imbalance in my brain, behavioral psychologists believe many cases of depression may be caused by a disproportion of serotonin. This imbalance is caused by low brain cell production of serotonin, a lack of receptors to receive serotonin, or a failure for serotonin to reach receptors. Hence my mental health team's prescription of choice, Citalopram, a selective serotonin reuptake inhibitor (SSRI). SSRIs keep neurotransmitters from reuptaking (taking back) serotonin that's bound for receptors. If enough serotonin is not received by receptors you may experience depression and the sister conditions that come with it such as hopelessness, frustration, panic, paranoia, and memory loss. Your world starts to unravel, one strand at a time, until all you're left with is absolutely nothing. A set of lyrics may put it best.

Ever feel like dying? Ever feel alone?
Ever feeling like crying? Lost child in a store.
Ever feel like pushing? Shoving you away.
Ever feel like breaking down? Funeral in the rain.
Feel like slipping away.

One can see where such feelings can take all the fun out of hiking. In therapy journals I've described entering depression as "falling into a deep, dark well where it's warm and safe and lonely and scary and deadly." When I land at the bottom I become "the human version of a dark, quiet cave." That's one of the unexpected components of depression: how opposites interact. Depression is scary but safe, familiar but terrifying. In journals I've written how I experience hyper vigilance, indecision, an inability to recognize how I feel, and an inability to trust anyone. I rarely listed powerlessness as a symptom because to be unhappy with powerlessness you need to want power. With depression it's easier to be resigned to the fact that "it is what it is." In severe cases there is no escape save for the all healing grave.

I didn't want to die on top of Humphrey Mountain, and I didn't feel intensely depressed. Emotions were subtle. I was unfulfilled, which was hard to accept since mountains usually bring me great joy. Between 1999 and 2011 I had been climbing mountains like a wild man because of all the good tidings they brought. My three bumper crop years of ascents were 2003 (181 mountains climbed), 2009 (175), and 2010 (200). By comparison, during 2013, the initial year of my depression, I summited 34 mountains—fewer than three a month.

I recorded my thoughts on top of Humphrey Mountain, making no mention of my discontent.

> *Haven't hiked in almost two months. But June, July, and August are hot. 75 degrees up here. Too hot. Bugs annoying but not terrible. Spooked a black bear up and then down a tall, straight yellow birch. Very cool. Then found a tiny mouse. Mixed woods with briars on top. Bring on October. Took 3.5 hours to get to the top. 2:40.*

I drank more water, ate some food, and stared into the distance. After writing in my journal my mind went blank. I enjoy the isolation on such remote mountains. I always have. I likely always will. But that day the "oomph" was gone from the wild man climbing of years ago. There is a chasm between being depressed and being discontented. On top of Humphrey Mountain I didn't feel depressed. I just wasn't invested in a journey through the wilderness. I wanted to do nothing.

I packed my things and decided to plot a course for the next mountain. 2,805-foot Horseshoe Mountain stood two miles to the southeast. The route looked straightforward. I would descend Humphrey Mountain's steep south ride, bottom out near the Kunjamuk River, avoid a series of beaver wetlands, cross an unnamed brook, and then tackle the climb to the top of Horseshoe Mountain.

I cautiously stepped down the south side of Humphrey Mountain, at times having to slide down on my butt, the grade being so steep. Briars grabbed at my sleeves and pant legs while the deer flies bombed down in little squadrons. Sometimes I would stop and smash a couple of them because it felt good, but with the sun tracking towards the western sky, I knew I should keep moving to make it to the top before dusk. I swooped around the beaver lands keeping my feet dry and started my second big climb of the day. At an unnamed stream I drank another quart of water and topped off the bottle again. With a plan to sleep on top of Horseshoe Mountain because it would be cooler up there (and, besides, it's just enjoyable to spend the night on top of a mountain), I made sure to squeeze every drop into that one bottle.

The climb went well. The grade steepened halfway up the mountain, but it was nothing like the burly up and down of Humphrey Mountain. As I neared the 2,700-foot-level the grade slacked. It would have been a stroll had it not been for the stunted American beech and red spruce forests that guarded the summit.

Like earlier in the day, a great crash came from in front of me. Another bear! She was plus-size and beautiful, her big head running down into a big neck, which blended into a big body that flowed all the way back to a big butt. She flew down the American beech as quickly as my first bear had flown down his yellow birch. Upon hitting the ground, bear number two wasted no time in making her escape. She crashed through the woods and dropped off the south side of the mountain. Out of sight and out of ear shot, the interaction lasted only a few seconds. My heart beat in my ears. She, too, had startled me.

I tiptoed to the top hoping to get a second glance at my mama bear. She was not to be seen. Truth be told, she was probably halfway down the other side of Horseshoe Mountain and on her way to the low country around South Pond. She knew the woods better than I ever would. She was likely on her way to another favorite American beech forest of hers. A valuable food source of the Northern Forest, American beeches release beechnuts, garlic clove-sized spiny pods that hide nuts in their middles. Black bears are known for their love of beechnuts, which provide valuable calories and fat to a bear that wants to get ever fatter. Look on the trunks of big, old beech trees, and you'll likely see scrapes and scars from bears climbing up and down to feast, then nap, feast, then nap.

I reached the top. Clouds had moved in. The humidity had not abated.

Two down, eight to go. Fewer bugs here. Saw another bear! Big one. Those big, fat, cute ears! Just fifty vertical feet below the summit. Up in an American beech. Off she goes. Won't camp on top since finding a good site would be a challenge. Down I go. Skinny summit ridge. 5:00.

The summit was a mess. Not only was the top merely the size of a small bedroom, but the spruce forests were so thick that not an open piece of ground could be found. Where there were not spruces there were firs, beeches, birches, and striped maples elbowing for room, each tree trying to shove the other away. Below this jungle were rocks popping their heads out of the damp soil. What a lousy campsite. I looked at the gray sky and reasoned that an August thunderstorm was on its way. The vision of hunkering on a high summit while a lightning storm plowed towards me was not a vision I enjoyed. Camping on top was out.

Camping anywhere didn't sound appealing. I wanted to go home. The humidity, deer flies, briars, and heat sapped my motivation. If this hike had taken place years earlier, back when I was a wild man, things would have been different. The culprit here was depression. Deep down inside I knew I still loved the mountains, the rivers that ran below them, the streams that ran down them, and the forests that grew all over them. Such a desire could likely never disappear. But I wasn't feeling "it," whatever it was. Passion? Affection? Intimacy? I was just a guy bumping around in the woods. There was no point to any of it.

Instead of dropping off the east side so I could visit Siamese Ponds, I headed northeast towards the headwaters of Humphrey Brook. I plodded down the ridge feeling like I had failed my mission. Could I have pushed myself to go up more and more mountains? Yes. Would it have been fulfilling? No. I would have wasted those mountains, feeling that I *had* to go up them instead of feeling that I *wanted* to go up them. We could wait to meet another day when I was feeling better.

After two hours of descent I hit the low country and found Humphrey Brook. It was a sluggish, dark waterway lined with black rocks. Sections of the brook widened into narrow but long wetlands marked with beaver activity. The clouds grew darker and darker until I thought it might rain. The rain held off.

I entered a beautiful hemlock forest nestled far below Horseshoe Mountain. With the evergreen canopies not letting any sunlight filter to the ground, there was no undergrowth. No ferns, no briars, no grasses. It was as if a battalion of gardeners had come in and plucked all the greenery, leaving a forest floor carpeted only in tiny hemlock needles and cones. I had found my campsite. I decided to camp next to an enormous boulder with a teenage hemlock growing on top of it. The young hemlock's root system clung to the sides of the boulder and stretched all the way to the ground where they disappeared into the Adirondack soil. The roots looked like grotesque, alien-like tendrils. I kept looking up at the top of the boulder and the tree.

I knew rain was on its way. I set up camp, changed clothes, and hung my hiking clothes and socks on nearby branches in an attempt to have them dry. The woods were so damp with humidity that I wondered if hanging my clothes would actually somehow make them wetter. The mosquitoes showed up, which was surprising. By the middle of August usually all biting bugs are dead, and mosquitoes, for whatever reason, usually do not like hemlock forests. These pests were not dead, and they didn't mind my hemlock forest at all. I went to the brook and yanked out a big, flat rock and plopped it down in my campsite. I searched the area for tinder and kindling to get a small fire started. I set some grasses and tiny twigs on fire and then let the flames die down. Once I had a modest collection of coals I laid more dry fuel on top and added damp greenery. Soon I had a smudge fire going.

The smudge fire has been around since two creatures crossed paths in the Adirondack Mountains: bugs and people. During the 1800s, the climax of Adirondack exploration by surveyors, land speculators, homesteaders, and loggers, smudge fires reached their peak of popularity. With the inventions of effective insect repellent and no-see-um bug netting decades away, Adirondack explorers had to go cave man on all them damn bugs. Smoke them out. The point of the smudge fire is not light or heat or ambiance like your traditional campfire. It's to produce the thickest choking cloud of smoke that can be had. As I like to say when I start a smudge fire, "Smudge it up!" Then I watch the bugs hightail it away from me, perhaps letting out inaudible coughs, their tiny eyes red and burning.

My hemlock forest was about four acres, 400 feet by 400 feet. Uphill, downhill, and to the left and right stood hardwood forests beyond my hemlock forest, the hardwoods' gray trunks standing out. To my left was Humphrey Brook meandering to Kings Flow three miles away. Forty feet upstream was a small, silent wetland an acre in size. Its waters were held back by a small beaver dam. With grasses growing on the dam, it was evident the resident beaver ceased construction operations long ago. He had moved onto the Happy Hunting Grounds.

It was a scenic but dreary scene. I found my journal and added a footnote to my Horseshoe Mountain entry: "Bugs, rain, humidity, wet. Went home." The eight other mountains would have to wait another month or another year to be reached. They would certainly have to wait, at the least, until another trip.

Dinnertime. I assembled my kitchen, which took less than a minute, the entire set up consisting of my beer can stove, cooking pot, pot stand, tin foil lid, and spoon. I poured a small amount of denatured alcohol into the stove, lit it, set my pot of water on the pot stand surrounding the stove, and watched the blue flame work water to a boil. I dumped in my usual dinner, one I had eaten hundreds of times in the backcountry, which was two packs of beef Ramen with a handful of textured vegetable protein and a liberal splash of Tabasco.

After dinner I was bored. It was probably the first time I had ever felt lonely in the woods. My depression was creeping in like dusk was through the woods. I did what most depressed people do. I went to bed. When the smudge fire died the mosquitoes found me again. They did not bite, and there were only a couple of them, but a couple is all you need to be annoyed by the high-pitched whining of their wings. I put on my bug head net. I dozed on and off, my legs thankful for the rest after carrying me up and down two mountains.

Around midnight the rain began to fall. Here a few sprinkles, there are few big drops that had built up on the hemlock branches and lost their grips. The sound lulled me into a deeper sleep where I was no longer part of the forest. It felt good to be dry while the rest of the world was wet. I remembered no dreams, only darkness and the sounds of raindrops splattering on my little tarp. I woke at dawn, looking forward to getting out of the woods. The desire to leave was unfamiliar. I had always found the woods to be my big, broad safe haven. I usually loved entering them and abhorred leaving them, and my change of attitude did not set well inside me.

I packed up within minutes. I searched around my campsite to make sure I hadn't left anything behind. I followed Humphrey Brook downhill while munching on a Pop-Tart. The rain ceased, but big dollops of rainwater fell from the wet branches overhead. Forcing my way through branches and forest floor greenery, cold water splashed against my legs and ran into my boots. At one point the going was too rough on the right-hand side of the brook. Looking for a place to cross the swollen waterway I found a gravel bar fifteen feet wide where the brook squeezed into a width of a few feet. I could jump over the condensed waterway. When I hit the gravel bar, which had no greenery growing on it and no branches hanging over it, it was a respite from sloshing through the wet forest. I needed a break.

My mood was dark. I seriously questioned ever coming back to the woods. What was the point? For what? See some trees, see some rocks, get wet, bash my shins, get a stick in the eye. The idea of hiking, whether on trails or otherwise, didn't seem dumb, or difficult, or annoying. It was only pointless. I stood in the streambed motionless.

Fate, destiny, chance, providence—whatever you want to call it—is a powerful force that knows exactly what a human needs at that particular spot, at that particular time, during their particular emotions. Munching on a handful of Cheezits, I noticed, out of the corner of my eye, something move. Up the middle of the gravel bar came a gorgeous animal. He bounced up the streambed without a sound, his padded feet not firm enough and his one-pound body not heavy enough to dislodge any rocks. Without throwing me a glance this beautiful mink bounded a few feet from me up the streambed, his brown fur silky, his little nose, ears, and eyes pointed forward to find the safest way up the streambed. Once past me he jumped into the air like a kitten and disappeared into a fat pile of tree trunks that had swept downstream during spring and grounded on the bank. He was gone.

I looked towards the sky. No way was the sun coming out this day. I looked down at my shirt, pants, boots, and, to the side, my backpack. All were covered in dirty rain water, mud, sand, and an assortment of needles and leaves from the hundreds of branches I bumped into since I had left camp. I couldn't help but smile. I remembered why I hike: to escape a world that is manufactured. I knew that when I left this brook crossing the mink would continue to hop up and down his stream in search of food, a mate, a better home, or a place to sun himself. He'd be safe. Chances were zero that a human would find him and do him harm. He was set to live out his days along the brook and likely never see another creature like me. I was happy for him.

Down Humphrey Brook, back to the trail, and back past Kings Flow, I reached the trailhead before noon. The parking lot was empty except for my car. It was a weekday. The day hikers from the day before were back at work after their jaunt up Chimney Mountain. The rain had stopped. I imagined fighting my way up the peaks I was supposed to be climbing at that time. I cringed at the thought. I was happy I was leaving the woods. The bear, mouse, and mink wouldn't see me for a long time to come. But I knew I'd be back. I knew I'd get better.

Across the Adirondacks

synergism (sin__r·jiz__m) n. "The joint action of different substances in producing an effect greater than the sum of the effects of all the substances acting separately."

I had a hypothesis. Long-distance hiking is fun, bushwhacking is fun, and combining these two forms of travel could synergize into something greater. Long-distance bushwhacking would be born, new to me and new to the Northeast backpacking community.

When snow and ice gave way to buds and sun during the spring of 2005 my long-distance pedigree was young yet respectable. I had thru-hiked the Metacomet-Monadnock Trail, Northville Placid Trail, Cohos Trail, Long Trail, and Florida National Scenic Trail. During a five-month season working for the Department of Environmental Conservation in the Catskill Mountains I had hiked more than 300 miles, though half of those were accumulated by day hiking. I had also completed two long-distance mountain bike trips. I rode 900 miles down Utah and Arizona and 2,300 miles along the United States-Mexico border. My trips shared a theme: The longer the better. By 2005 I also had enough bushwhacking experience to feel as at home off-trail as on. A year earlier I had finished climbing the Northeast's 770 mountains above 3,000 feet. 420 of them have no trails to their tops. You have to be proficient at, and just plan like, off-trail travel to do it more than 400 times.

The first trailless Adirondack mountain of consequence I ever climbed was 3,983-foot MacNaughton Mountain. It was September 1994. I was participating on a Wilderness Education Association (WEA) field course at North Country Community College, course completion being necessary to earn an Associates of Science degree in Wilderness Leadership, which I was working towards. This 33-day course, held entirely in the woods, was designed to mold students into hardened outdoor leaders. The WEA's eighteen-point curriculum covered all aspects of outdoor leader expertise.

WEA, teamed with North Country Community College, took me to the Adirondack Mountains for my field course. Recalling a specific instance, during the 23rd day of that 33-day field course my two instructors, Eric and Matt, and one of my classmates, Judy, bushwhacked to the top of MacNaughton Mountain. During the scramble up this first high trailless mountain of mine, I noticed that bushwhackers are a curious bunch. By the end of that day I had become one of them.

MacNaughton Mountain raises its head towards the sky, its summit ridge clad in murky spruce and fir. Looking like a massive rectangular block, especially when viewed from the north or south, MacNaughton Mountain is the middle school kid who keeps lying about his height. First measured in 1904 by the United States Geological Survey, this peak, named for a local mining entrepreneur, was recorded as 3,976 feet in height. In 1953, it rose to an even 4,000 feet, promoting it to the varsity list of Adirondack summits. By joining the 4,000-footer club that year, MacNaughton Mountain started rubbing shoulders with the ranks of great peaks like Giant Mountain, Dix Mountain, and Mount Marcy. MacNaughton Mountain must have been beaming, perhaps even smug. However, in 1978, more precise measurements sent Mac-Naughton Mountain tumbling down to 3,983 feet. Receiving a dishonorable discharge, its sword broken, its stripes shorn from its sleeves, MacNaughton Mountain was deemed a High Peak imposter. Back to junior varsity it went and remains, a mere seventeen feet making the difference between topographical fame and anonymity. It retains one unique though second-rate claim to fame: highest trailless peak in the Northeast.

With long-distance hiking under my belt and bushwhacking in my heart, I reasoned that traveling 200 miles off-trail across the entire Adirondack Park—a synergistic melding of long-distance travel and off-trail travel—would be the trip to surpass all trips. It was a most appropriate adventure for two reasons. One, during the first decade of the twenty-first century I was a sponsored athlete. Sponsors maintain relationships with athletes who do what other athletes are not doing. If you approach a potential sponsor and tell them how you're going to thru-hike the Appalachian Trail, climb the 4,000-foot peaks of New Hampshire, or bike the Blue Ridge Parkway from end-to-end, they will respond with a yawn. "Been there, done that, kid." I knew no one had bushwhacked across the Adirondack Park. If I was successful, my accomplishment would be newsworthy (sponsors love newsworthy athletes). It would be, in adventure parlance, a "first."

Two, I'm drawn to routes that fully run from one end of a political or topographical feature to the other. By 2005 my favorite adventure had been the Long Trail since it runs clean from Massachusetts to Canada along the length of Vermont. On the other hand, the Metacomet-Monadnock Trail begins on the Massachusetts-Connecticut line and ends in a random spot in New Hampshire. The Cohos Trail begins on the U.S.-Canada border and ends at an obscure trailhead. The Florida Trail begins on the extreme western edge of the Panhandle and ends a hundred miles north of the Keys. The Northville Placid Trail traverses little more than half the Adirondack Park. These long-distance hikes felt incomplete. Adirondack Park border to Adirondack Park border—Blue Line to Blue Line—is as complete of an Adirondack adventure as possible.

I planned my long-distance bushwhack. I dubbed it the Great Adirondack Traverse. I would begin my hike at the extreme southwest extent of the Blue Line on Route 10 one mile south of the settlement of Rockwood. Three to four weeks later I'd end at the extreme northeast extent of the Blue Line on Alder Bend Road two miles south of the settlement of Irona. Along the way I would try to not set foot on any roads or trails for the estimated 220 miles.

Like the Long Trail, the Great Adirondack Traverse would climb mountains: eighteen peaks above 3,000 feet. The high-point of the route was 4,091-foot Seymour Mountain, 33rd highest in the state. The course climbed a plump 43,000 vertical feet end-to-end, the equivalent of climbing Mount Marcy a dozen times. When not on these evergreen-clad summits, I'd hop from lake to pond, lake to pond, touching 35 bodies of water. Six New York State Wild, Scenic, and Recreational Rivers would be met: West Branch of the Sacandaga River, West Canada Creek, Otter Brook, South Branch of the Moose River, Cold River, and Saranac River. Significant cultural and topographical features included the Northville Placid Trail, Northern Forest Canoe Trail, T Lake Falls, former locations of four Department of Environmental Conservation ranger cabins, a rock slide on Mount Emmons, and Ouluska Pass. All these features are on state land, contained within eight wild forests, six wilderness areas, and one recreation area. Since there was not a perfect connection of state land across the entire park, I would have to walk on roads for twenty miles, a mere nine percent of the route.

I planned the Great Adirondack Traverse on twenty topographic maps, marking resupply points and hasty campsites and tracing my course from Blue Line to Blue Line. Then, I anxiously waited for the first of August 2005, the proposed start date, to arrive. If I was successful on this trip, the Great Adirondack Traverse would be the burliest bushwhack ever completed.

In my *Blue Line to Blue Line: The Official Guide to the Trans Adirondack Route* I wrote that "I [didn't] recall why the Great Adirondack Traverse never happened." I merely offered a guess: "I would guess it had something to do with a realization that traveling cross-country for 220 miles, which would have taken at least three weeks, eventually didn't sound fun. At all." Well, folks, that was no guess. It was fact. As you can tell from my writing, I love off-trail travel as much as the next man does. But bushwhacking 220 miles straight? No thank you.

When it came time to take on the Great Adirondack Traverse, I hung my head in shame and put away all the maps portraying this off-trail route. Thank goodness I told only a few people about my proposed long-distance bushwhack. By cancelling my trip yet not letting many know I was even going to do this trip, I didn't have to lose much face for cancelling.

I redeemed myself, regained a sense of masculinity, and made my sponsors happy by replacing the Great Adirondack Traverse with a solo mountain bike ride from Canada to Mexico. My sponsors found this expedition newsworthy, and to this day that 52-day ride, on a course of my own design, is the most memorable trip I've completed.

After the summer of 2005 I took on additional long-distance journeys. I hiked the Long Path, Tahoe Rim Trail, Baker Trail,

Foothills Trail, Northville-Placid Trail again, a traverse of the Catskill High Peaks, a circumambulation of High Peaks Wilderness Area, and crossings of Great Smoky Mountains National Park and Allegheny National Forest. In the Catskill Park I managed to traverse the park's 320-mile trail system. I also rekindled my love of peakbagging by climbing the 200 highest peaks of the Catskill Mountains during winter.

All of these journeys stood on their own. They weren't training hikes for the Adirondack Mountains just like they weren't judged better or not better than the Adirondack Mountains. They were long-distance journeys and peakbagging quests entirely of their own personality. However, I can't help but admit that during many of these hikes I thought about what it would be like to traverse the Adirondack Park by foot. The Great Adirondack Traverse was unfinished business. Like any other conscientious man, I would not let unfinished business stand.

Five years after cancelling that bushwhack across the Adirondack Park, I dug out those Great Adirondack Traverse maps. The route was of course still highlighted from one Blue Line to the other, my hasty campsites and resupply points identified. After scanning the route for a half-hour and completing a little additional planning, I came to a conclusion. Bushwhacking 220 miles did not look appealing still. It likely never would.

As I was about to pack these maps away to have them resurface only God knew when, I stopped and thought. With the maps in my hand I asked a few good questions that had me recognize where I was and where I was headed: "What is this all about? What do I want? What's more important: *Bushwhacking* across the Adirondack Park or *crossing* the Adirondack Park?" Questioning my motives and goals had me realize there was immense difference between bushwhacking and crossing. From 2005 to 2010 the ethos was "Bushwhack across the entire Adirondack Park, or don't go at all." It had never occurred to me that there could be a less painful way to get from

Blue Line to Blue Line. I realized the goal of crossing the park by foot superseded the actual course of travel.

After spending the rest of the day poring over the original Great Adirondack Traverse maps in addition to United States Geological Survey, National Geographic, and Adirondack Mountain Club topographic maps, as well as snowmobile trail and property maps of the park, I saw a possibility. I could piece together dozens of different trails to get from one end of the park to the other. There would still be off-trail travel to join trails that didn't connect directly with others, but the amount of bushwhacking, a measly ten miles, was acceptable. After all, it was about 200 fewer miles of bushwhacking than I had first intended to do.

My updated proposed expedition, which carried no name, stretched 235 miles and climbed 24,000 vertical feet—fifteen miles longer than the Great Adirondack Traverse but climbing was cut in half. I would use maintained hiking and snowmobile trails for approximately 145 miles, dirt and paved roads for about 65 miles, abandoned pathways for nearly 15 miles, and there would be those ten miles of bushwhacking. I'd cross eight wild forests and five wilderness areas, top out on the fifth highest peak in New York, visit fifty bodies of water, and pass through three tiny settlements.

I was happy as a pig in slop when new life was breathed into traversing the park I fell in love with decades ago. This was the trip I had always wanted: to be in the North Country for a two-week journey that was absolute. Only one question needed to be answered: How would I get to the beginning of this hike and then back home afterwards?

The simplest arrangement was to drop my car at the end of my route and then get a ride to the beginning of it. I planned on hiking south to north. However, hiking northbound was not to be. There is no public parking close to the northern terminus, downtown Ellenburg Center. The closest public parking is at a fishing access site along the Chateaugay River seven miles west of my intended end point. Additionally, upon contacting the local forest ranger he reported that parking at this fisherman's lot was ill-advised. He said he would be surprised if my car was not vandalized during its two week sleep next to the river. A call to the State Police of northern New York squashed my idea of parking on the shoulder of a road near Ellenburg Center. A trooper made it clear that a car parked along a road for more than two days would be regarded as abandoned and thus dutifully impounded.

I contacted the forest ranger who patrols the southern Blue Line and received much better news regarding parking. There was the East Road trailhead smack dab on my proposed route, one mile north of the southern Blue Line. This forest ranger, Ted Carbine, was cautious as well, admitting he would not leave his car there for two weeks. Stories of broken glass and flattened tires were not unheard of at this remote trailhead.

When you get an "in" with an Adirondack person of influence, such as New York State forest ranger Ted Carbine, you reap the benefits of his relationships. In Carbine's case, he knows nearly everyone of consequence in the southern Adirondacks. He knows who poaches deer, who lets black bears eat out of their bird feeders, who owns a float plane, who owns the backwoods cabins, who usually has extra cord wood to give away, and who will drill a well for cheap. Advantageous to my situation, ranger Carbine knows who owns land close to the end point of my trans-Adirondack journey.

My in was gained through a ten-minute phone conversation with ranger Carbine. We established a fine rapport quickly, talking about our common explorations of areas such as the old roads into the Kunjamuk outside Speculator, the former fire tower site on Hamilton Mountain, the swim holes and waterfalls on Cold Brook above Piseco. He thought my idea of traversing the entire park by foot was downright cool. Carbine knew I loved wilderness for wildness's sake, and he knew I was authentic in my goal to traverse the park while doing it no harm. Letting it slip, too, that I had worked for the Department of Environmental Conservation for three seasons helped gain his trust, too. His colleagues were my former bosses who trusted me to oversee state land and put a good face on a besieged bureaucracy. I had my in.

Ranger Carbine put me in touch with Jared Wells, a name not of little consequence in the Adirondack Mountains. By the time I learned who Jared Wells was and what he had done for the Adirondack and Catskill parks, I was surprised I had never heard of him. A great lead from ranger Carbine, Mr. Wells lived right on my route, towards the end of East Road, a half-mile inside the southern Blue Line. Perhaps Wells could assist me in finding a place to park.

Wells is a retired Department of Environmental Conservation forester. "Retired" doesn't do the man's career justice though. He worked for the Department of Environmental Conservation for 54 years, the longest I have ever heard of a person working, let alone working for the same employer. As a forester, Wells oversaw development plans for Belleayre Ski Center in the Catskill Park and Whiteface Mountain Ski Center and Gore Mountain Ski Center in the Adirondack Park. He had chimed in on, and often oversaw, every major decision regarding state land in these two parks for a half-century. He had critiqued everything from what dirt roads get gated, to which ranger cabins get burned to the ground, to where float planes may land, to where wilderness boundaries creep, to if a boulder in a streambed can be moved to build a footbridge. Wells knows the ins and outs of Forest Preserve creation and maintenance better than anyone living or otherwise. I find two aspects of his knowledge most fascinating.

First, he thinks—no, *knows*—that the famous "Forever Wild clause" of the state constitution, which is often cited as the singular term most responsible for creation and maintenance of the Adirondack (and Catskill) Park's legally-binding wild character, has been selfishly interpreted to serve personal needs. During later conversations Wells pointed out that there is no "forever wild" terminology anywhere in the state constitution. New York State's preservation language actually reads, in Article XIV from 1894, "shall be forever kept as wild forest lands." Reconstructing this maxim is to take words out of context to make new meanings to serve personal interests, in this case the needs of environmentalists who think the Adirondacks were set aside as wilderness. Actually, the Adirondacks were set aside for multiple use. Not a fan of environmentalists, just like your author is not, Wells feels this population has misinterpreted the intent of park creation and purpose.

Second, Wells said that the idea of enormous pieces of land being set aside exclusively for foot travel is not accurate. He assures anyone who will listen, which unfortunately isn't many, that nearly all gates that block dirt roads or hiking trails within the borders of both parks are illegal. While serving as the Department of Environmental Conservation's lead forester for decades, Wells forbade forest rangers under his authority to close, let alone lock, gates. Gates discriminate against certain users and defy management intent. "It would take way too long to explain," Wells told me, "but none of those gates are legal. Look at the wording in the constitution. It's a shame. The woods are being locked up, and no one's aware of this supposed preservation being illegal. Want to change it? Change the constitution. Change the laws. Don't break them."

Wells, a devoted lover of the woods and a genuine protector of resources, made clear he isn't trying to open the woods to destructive activities nor is he in opposition to wilderness. He sees himself as the messenger; one man who follows his state's highest proclamations. Wells's impressive insight and one-of-a-kind knowledge of environmental law and park history goes unappreciated and supports an old saying: "The truth has never set anyone free. The truth has only pissed people off." But I didn't piss forester Wells off. Like when I spoke with ranger Carbine, Wells and I established a sincere rapport, despite our age gap of fifty years. I let it slip again that I had worked for the Department of Environmental Conservation, like he did, albeit 51 years fewer.

Wells likes men who do not beat around the bush. I asked him if I could park my car on his property and leave it there for two weeks. During that time I'd be hiking 235 miles towards it. Owning an expansive tree farm, Wells told me he had plenty of room for one measly Toyota Camry. I asked if he would like to be compensated for this service. He refused. All he asked was that I put the key somewhere on the car in case he had to move it.

As arranged, on the last afternoon of July 2010 my mother and stepfather met me at Jared Wells's property. I left my car and the key and said goodbye to this vehicle that had been through so many mountain journeys with me: White Mountains of New Hampshire, Green Mountains of Vermont, Southern Appalachians, and all over the Adirondacks and Catskills. I scribbled a note on a piece of paper and left in on the dash: "Thanks, Jared!"

We drove to my mother and stepfather's home in Glens Falls. I slept fitfully that night, filled with anticipation to begin a journey I had dreamed about. The next morning I awoke. We drove north. The two-and-a-half-hour drive reminded us how big our state is and how far north the Adirondack Mountains extend. We pulled into downtown Ellenburg Center, population 800, during afternoon. It was sunny with a few puffy clouds skirting the Canadian border nine miles to the north. It felt and looked like fall. The only remaining wildflowers were white wood asters and goldenrod, the last pollen and nectar sources for North Country honeybees. I wore shorts and an old, ratty short sleeve polyester dress shirt. My little running socks extended an inch above my little running shoes. I was chilly. Since 235 miles is a hell of a walk in the woods, I made sure to go light. Not counting food and water my pack weighed eleven pounds.

They dropped me off in front of the Ellenburg Center post office and asked if I had everything. I assured them I did. If I didn't it was too late anyway. My mother wasn't concerned about leaving me in the middle of nowhere to fend for myself.

She had given up worrying about me long ago. It was easier to trust in my talent and realize the odds of me perishing in the wilderness were slim. They drove away, heading south. It was awfully quiet, and I felt out of place standing in the tiny settlement with a backpack on. The nearest hiking trail was twenty miles away.

I entered the community's Riverside Cemetery and walked to the northernmost back corner of the property where the northern border of the park is. I left the headstones and manicured grass behind and entered the woods near an old ATV track. Looking at an enlarged photocopied map of the area, I consulted it and searched for some sign of the park's northern boundary such as a cairn, old stone wall, paint blazes, posted signs, state signs, fence, anything. I found nothing but woods, the trees stunted and prickly from the cold North Country winds. I put my detailed map away, pulled out a New York State snowmobile trail map, and started my 235-mile walk.

The long days of summer were over, and the sun dipped surprisingly low towards the western horizon. It was barely 4:00 P.M. I strolled back past the post office and took Bradley Pond Road due south. The road climbed and provided a surprising panorama. To the north, outside the park, stood wind towers. Their long blades circulated round and round lazily in the light breeze. Off to the east the land rose gently through cornfields that had been worked over and left barren a week or two earlier. To the south Lyon Mountain, highest peak in Clinton County, dominated the skyline. To the west was the bright, white sun descending. Not a cow mooed and not a crow cawed. No cars passed by.

I turned right on Patnode Road to connect with a snowmobile trail. A long-abandoned farm house marked the end of Patnode Road and the beginning of my snowmobile trail. Everyone seemed to have left town. A rugged dirt road during summer, the trail tracked west while woods hemmed in the right side and a late season cornfield grew on the left. I crossed the upper reaches of the North Branch of the Great

Chazy River on a stout snowmobile bridge and then turned south towards Steam Mill Road, still on my trail.

Past an old sandpit and across an overgrown field I wandered. The shadows grew longer, and I knew I had to move quickly to get the next off-road section out of the way before sundown. I planned on camping next to Bradley Pond Road after hooking back up with it around dinnertime. It was the only camping option I could think of in this land of private lands.

Down the meadow I dropped, and the footing became wetter and wetter. Soon I was hiking down a pathway that supported seven-foot-tall cattails, plant life more often found in marshes than meadows. I found myself in a swamp, which was a concern I had about traveling on snowmobile trails. Snowmobile trails often travel through swamps and even across lakes because such surfaces are frozen during the coldest months of the year. But during August, not even an ATV can force its way through the roughest, wettest sections of snowmobile trails. And I was no ATV. I plopped my sneakers through ankle-deep mud and water and hoped the trail would climb to higher, drier ground or at least reach the next section of pavement soon.

I T-boned Steam Mill Road after traversing an elegant upland plateau of goldenrod and milkweed. My intention of crossing Steam Mill Road and continuing off-pavement was stomped out like an ember. I looked behind me. Posted signs marked where I had come from (there were no posted signs where I first got on this snowmobile trail). Even more posted signs marked where I wanted to go. I thought, "Weren't snowmobile trails conservation easements open to public travel?" After all, these snowmobile trails are portrayed on official New York State maps. The amount of signs that read "Private Property," "Posted and Patrolled," and "Keep Out—This Means You!" in front of me had me consider that I was mistaken in my understanding of conservation easement use. I assessed my hiking options carefully for nothing puts a hitch in a two-week backpacking trip like spending the first night in the Clinton County Sherriff's holding cell.

I turned right on Steam Mill Road and left on Sears Road, intending to follow Sears Road all the way to the end to connect with an abandoned dirt road that led back to Bradley Pond Road. I found the old, overgrown, nasty roadway—another snowmobile trail—plunging off the side of Sears Road near its end. It was a mess of briars, blowdown, more cattails, and hummocks of grass and ferns. Pits in the pathetic pathway snuck under my footsteps and sucked in my ankles to wrench them from side to side. Dusk descended into the forest. It was time to stop, lest I break an ankle or get a stick in the eye in the fading light. I stealth camped next to the road-turned-trail, unable to reach the pavement.

My newsworthy expedition did not start with a bang. It started with a sigh and a grunt and a confused expression. My lower legs were bleeding from the sharp blades of cattails, my arms pockmarked with pinholes from briars. My socks and sneakers were filled with cold North Country swamp water, I was perhaps camping illegally, and I barely knew where I was. The remaining 227 miles seemed a mighty obstacle to overcome.

I cooked a pot of Ramen noodles, ate a Snickers Bar for dessert, downed a quart of water, and slept in the open, not bothering to set up my tarp. With no experience hiking snowmobile trails prior to this trip, I learned two things quick. One, according to the posted signs, locals do not take kindly to tree-hugging hikers crossing their property during the warmer months of the year. Two, snowmobile trails are not worth traveling between March and December. I had a lot of road walking ahead of me.

Knowing day two could not disappoint more than day one, I got up at dawn and removed myself from the maze of snowmobile trails and the sections of private property they ran across. I popped out on Bradley Pond Road barely ten miles into my route. The morning was chilly. Long spruce shadows stretched across the pavement, keeping it cool, almost cold, under my wet feet. Looking down at my scratched and sliced legs and mud-caked running shoes, it looked like I had covered fifty miles.

Day two and three were uneventful, just the way I like my hiking. When a snowmobile trail popped out of the woods I peered down it, but it would invariably have a gate, a posted sign, or both. One of the signs communicated the owner's love of guns and possibly shooting them at trespassers: "This Property Patrolled with Firearms Three Days of the Week. Do you Think this is one of Those Three Days?" Avoiding games of chance, I stuck to the tarmac out of respect and my aversion to being shot and killed.

I passed through downtown Lyon Mountain, population 450, hiked around the mountain that is named for this town, and left the Town of Ellenburg behind. Clicking off townships one by one, I traversed the Town of Dannemora and entered the Town of Black Brook. When I reached Taylor Pond I had covered fifty miles of the route, and just about all of it had been on pavement. My legs felt strong and tight, my feet were hardened by the pavement. Though I was on roads for nearly the entire time, this part of the park—a part new to me at the time—felt remote. It represents what the Adirondack Park is, which is a mix of private and public land, a situation nearly unique to parklands. While traversing this region, save for my first night camped in a patch of cattails, my pristine campsites on islands of Forest Preserve were rugged but cozy. Best of all, by hiking southbound I had gotten nearly all the road walking out of the way. At Taylor Pond I could move into the woods and follow a series of snowmobile trails and hiking trails on state land.

Less than a quarter of the way to the southern Blue Line I strolled above the shores of Taylor Pond on a high and dry snowmobile trail. As the clouds darkened and threatened rain towards the end of the day, I increased my pace, hoping to reach the northernmost shelter on my route, the Taylor Pond lean-to, before the heavens opened up. As I reached the shelter, it began to sprinkle. I took off all my clothes and waded out on a natural sand beach and took a French bath. Without soap I scrubbed my body with a bandana soaked in chilly Taylor Pond water. I held my running shorts in my teeth. If a hiker stumbled down the trail I could quickly put my shorts on before they saw a man, buck naked, scrubbing himself with a rag.

The rain fell. I retreated to my little shelter, dried off with a pack towel, cooked dinner, aired out my gear, and recorded my visit in the shelter's log book. "Hiking across the entire Adirondack Park—235 miles from Ellenburg Center to Scotchbush. First lean-to of the trip, and it is welcome in this rainstorm. Happy trails to all!" I slept well that night, the rain pitter-pattering on the shingled roof and Taylor Pond lapping at the shoreline. No cattails, no briars. The hard lean-to floor felt good, straightening my spine and supporting me without pause.

Fog drifted across Taylor Pond early next morning. It was dead quiet. I ate a Pop-Tart and drank a quart of water, packed within five minutes, and set a course for the first peak on my route, 3,168-foot Catamount Mountain. The mountain not having a trail on its north side, I bushwhacked to the top and then took the trail down the south side to Forestdale Road. From there it was up and across the Stephenson Range, my crossing point on a shoulder of the range. Like on Catamount Mountain, a trail led down the south side.

One more climb would finish the day, and it was the principal climb of the route: a mean 3,200 vertical feet up Whiteface Mountain, the highpoint of the route. By the time I finished the knee-popping descent down the south side of this 4,865-foot mountain I was officially whupped. The day's distance of fifteen miles wasn't that far, but the climbing was a showstopper at nearly 7,000 vertical feet. When I later wrote about this hike, I called it a "double ouch" day. I reached the Whiteface lean-to. Like at the Taylor Pond lean-to, as I finished my French bath, this time in Whiteface Brook, the heavens opened up, and the rain poured down. My timing of arriving at shelters, cleaning up, and then taking refuge was perfect.

My legs felt like they were made of stone when I woke up next to Whiteface Brook seventy miles into the route. Five miles' worth of gentle trail walking and road walking loosened up my legs. The blood circulated to muscles deep inside my thighs that got shredded the day before. I took my morning break next to the lazy Ausable River next to River Road. The water was rust-orange like it always has been, the river's amber sands shooting dark sunlight back towards the surface. I took three Advil, ate a bagel, cheese, and pepperoni sandwich, and downed a rust-orange quart of Ausable River water.

With all major road walking in my past I left River Road and crossed the Sentinel Range via a cross-country ski trail from the 1932 Olympics and a bushwhack through forests that have been growing for the past 10,000 years. After the Sentinel Range I completed a short road walk and then stomped up the third and final peak of the route, Mount Van Hoevenberg. The summit provided a stunning view across High Peaks Wilderness Area, the largest wilderness area within a 1,000-mile radius. I camped on the southern flanks of this peak. The weather held, a little hot but not unbearable.

The night was cool and clear. The stars slowly circled my open camp, the Big Dipper arcing around the Little Dipper and the star that hinges the entire night sky, Polaris. An arm of the Milky Way Galaxy streaked across the sky. I thought back to my first outdoor job as camp counselor at North Country School three miles from where I slept. The camper kids from the cities were speechless when they looked up and saw thousands of stars looking down on them. These urban residents thought there were only four or five stars in the night sky, the glaring light pollution in their neighborhoods giving them a distorted view of how big and beautiful the nighttime universe is.

I entered High Peaks Wilderness Area. It looks more like the wilds of Montana or Idaho than something you can find five hours from New York City. Foot trails wind below dramatic peaks, run next to small lakes, and cross the headwaters of powerful rivers. Some of the peaks wear gray granite caps, so tall that trees can't grow on their tops due to thin soil, whipping winds, and brutal cold. The High Peaks are stunning, but by the time I passed through them during this trip, I had seen them too often. Their beauty faded over the years.

I climbed my first High Peak, Big Slide Mountain, during the winter of 1994/1995. After that introductory hike I ended up climbing the rest of the High Peaks, totaling somewhere between 41 and 46 peaks, depending on what rules you use to call a mountain a mountain. I returned to the High Peaks to climb them all in winter and lead a series of backpacking leadership courses. Eventually my drive to climb the high ones became paler. The towering peaks took on a watery gray complexion where they all looked the same. The hikers who swarmed these peaks looked the same, too, with their zip-off hiking pants, trekking poles, expensive backpacks, and new hiking boots. I haven't been in the High Peaks since 2010. Usually wearing old work pants and an old polyester dress shirt with the front pocket ripped off, I now wander the unnamed, unsung hills that make the Adirondack Mountains what they are.

The High Peaks have their chasms (Mount Colden), alpine areas (Algonquin Peak), rock slides (Dix Peak), and gorges (Haystack Mountain), and these dramatic features have their place, rightfully so, in the Adirondack landscape. For all their theatrics, there is something to be said—more to be said, in my mind—about the rolling hills and sleepy forests of lower summits. When I'm on a junior peak, it's just me and that mountain, with no hikers on their cell phones on the summit. I never see their brightly-colored tents clustered next to each other to form mini Mount Everest base camps. When it comes to mountains, like many things in life, nothing is lost in subtlety. The little peaks are introverts, the massive peaks extroverts. Extroverts eventually lose their charm. Introverts endure.

I exited the Eastern Zone of High Peaks Wilderness Area at the 100-mile mark and drifted into the Western Zone of this wilderness area. I entered my old stomping grounds. When I passed Duck Hole, Mountain Pond, Moose Creek, Rondeau's old hermitage next to the Cold River, and Long Lake I felt like I had returned to work as a backcountry ranger. There's no place like home.

Since reaching Duck Hole I had been hiking south on the Northville Placid Trail. Some call this 133-mile footpath "a trunk line trail," but despite hiking this trail four times and working on it for two seasons, I still have no idea what that means. I've been more interested in other aspects of this attractive trail, like the way it meanders from pond to pond, how it is not popular, and how it dates back to the early 1900s.

Since the Northville Placid Trail was opened to the public in 1924 it has been a stage for impressively speedy performances. In 1973, Richard Denker completed a fully-supported traverse of the trail in 1 day, 16 hours. Thirty-two years later, in 2005, Tim Seaver scorched the trail in 1 day, 13 hours (both Denker and Seaver covered "only" 122 of the 133 miles since both ends of this trail are on pavement and usually not covered by backpackers). The most recent record involved ground-breaking woman Sheryl Wheeler. She bested Seaver's time by two hours, following his rules of support and distance. During 2008 yours truly completed an unsupported thru-hike of the full 133 miles in 3 days, 8 hours. A former student of mine, Drew Hass, knew he could leave my time in the dust (or, actually, the mud) and did so. One year after my hike Drew completed an unsupported run of the full length in 2 days, 13 hours. I was having so much fun on this trip that I couldn't imagine running to the end. I wanted it to last.

At the halfway point of my trip I detoured into the Village of Long Lake to resupply, my initial six days' worth of food nearly gone. I reached Northern Borne, a seasonal grocery store in downtown Long Lake, just as it opened. It was another beautiful day. I went inside and felt spoiled. During the past six days I had lived out of a small stuff sac full of durable, predictable foods. Standing in the narrow aisles of Northern

Borne, I looked at all the options and had to pick carefully. All of it—vanilla icing, coffee cake, red peppers, bananas, brown sugar, ice cream sandwiches, pork chops, hot dogs, loaves of bread, and more—looked good. I could indulge in a few perishables this day, mostly fruit, but my shopping basket would have to be filled with more durable, predictable food. I looked for foods that packed at least 100 calories per ounce, packing a wallop of energy for their respective weights and sizes. After this resupply my pack was weighed down by another six days—10.5 pounds—of food. Like any good long-distance hiker, I had brought enough hot sauce to last the entire trip.

I left town eating a granny Smith apple. I returned to the hiking trails and finished my apple, chucking the core into the woods. Despite completing Leave No Trace's Master Educator Course (which an outdoor educator colleague, with disdain in his voice, calls "a $700 course that teaches you how to take a shit in the woods six different ways"), I'm still realistic enough to know that Leave No Trace techniques are guidelines to be used in a way one deems fit. I see no harm in hucking a measly apple core off a hiking trail. Others do not stand for this. It's a matter of style. I can assure readers, however, that I'm likely more sensitive to my influence on wilderness than most users are. But most others probably say that, so who are we to believe?

I crossed the highest point of the Northville-Placid Trail, a 3,000-foot unnamed pass. I wouldn't exceed this elevation for the remainder of my hike. Into the "big wilderness" I went, penetrating the second-biggest wilderness area in the Northeast, West Canada Lake Wilderness Area, through its northern border. I remained in familiar country since I stayed on the Northville Placid Trail for the most part. I passed features whose names eulogize the men who were first to enter this land of lakes and woods: Josiah Prentiss Brown, Verplanck Colvin, Ebenezer Jessup, William Payne, Louis Dwight Pilsbury, William Wakeley, Anson Wilson. I thought about the authors who took me on historical journeys through this wilderness area: Ted

Aber, Stella King, Barbara McMartin. I even thought about my own name and how it could one day fit into this vast wilderness area's culture. I quickly deduced my name deserved no mention in any story of this region. I was just a backpacker. The men and women above were so much more.

The last person I saw on my route was at Spruce Lake. This long body of water held the final lean-to on my route, Spruce Lake No. 1. I passed the shelter, opting to camp pristinely. I was having too much fun and feeling too isolated, in a good way, to run the chance of a conversation or observation that bothered me. Once I left the Northville Placid Trail in Piseco, letting this popular trail finish its thirty miles to Northville without me, I followed snowmobile trails, joining them with short road walks and bushwhacks.

I entered the largest wild forest in the state, 147,000-acre Ferris Lake Wild Forest, on the next-to-last day of the trip. Having never set foot in this piece of land before, I enjoyed its modest beauty. A few humble mountains dot this wild forest, their reflections found in the bodies of water this region is known for. I encountered Kennels Pond, avoided private land around it, connected with a hiking trail, and reconnected with a series of snowmobile trails. I settled in for the last night of the trip near Good Luck Lake.

I woke early the final morning. I had slept like the dead. I hiked by Third Lake and Fourth Lake after rounding the northern flank of West Lake Mountain. I dumped out on a dirt road above Pleasant Lake. The seven-mile segment from Good Luck Lake to Pleasant Lake became one of my favorite parts of the journey because it was entirely new ground for me and because I had it all to myself. Something about this stretch drew me into it (I've hiked it two more times since). Along the final forty miles of my hike I saw no one else in the woods.

At Pleasant Lake I left my snowmobile trail behind for a short road walk and reentered the woods and Ferris Lake Wild Forest on the south side of Route 29A. I headed due south towards Stewart's Landing, a dam site at the far eastern edge of

Canada Lake. The snowmobile trail ran straight south, obviously an old road. A half-mile south of Route 29A I crossed the unnamed outlet of Pleasant Lake. The crossing was a quiet, pretty spot, the brook spanned by a weathered bridge, the decking bleached a harsh light gray by the sun. It being the last day of my trip, I tried to stretch the day for all it was worth.

I took off my pack and took off my sneakers and socks to dry them. Though it wasn't lunchtime, there is no inappropriate time to eat in the woods. I munched on the last of my raisins and M and M's, dumping both of them in my mouth to crunch down on a gooey slurry of sugar, carbohydrates, and fat. I dipped my water bottle in the stream and drank. The water tasted like sand, but it was cold and wet. I sat peering around my little world, checking out the speckled alders that grew along the languid waterway. I looked for birds hidden in the trees. Sitting so still, I was soon surrounded by a small flock of delicate white admiral butterflies, and some of them landed on me to rest.

All good things must come to an end. I bid my little fluttering friends goodbye and continued south. In less than a half-hour I encountered an unsigned split in the trail. I became most confused. The vague snowmobile trail map I had didn't show a split, and my topographic map dating back to 1997, with field data checked well before that date, showed no snowmobile trails at all. Branches of this mystery split went towards where I wanted to go, which was south. I stood at the intersection for a while, scratching my head.

Guessing which way to go, I took the right branch, which headed southwest. Within a half mile this branch turned west and even a little northwest, which was surely not the way I wanted to go. I was on the wrong trail. I trudged back to the intersection and took the left branch. This branch headed southeast, running on the level through a pretty forest. Things were looking good. But then, within a half mile this branch turned east, then northeast. This was surely not the way I wanted to go either. I backtracked to the intersection for a second time. It was time to observe and plan.

I took off my pack, lounged against a sugar maple, and took out a snack (I had eaten thirty minutes earlier, but, again, there is no inappropriate time to eat in the woods). I munched on some crackers. Staring at my snowmobile trail map, I realized how lame my map was. I had absolutely no idea which way to go. I wasn't lost. I had kept track of my course from Route 29A, but I'd be damned if I knew which way to proceed.

I decided to try the left branch again. Who knows? Maybe this trail turned back south. Perhaps I didn't hike down it far enough. Back on the left branch I hiked again, this time for more than a mile. By the one-mile mark I was heading due north straight back towards Pleasant Lake! I was surly. I arrived back at the intersection for the fourth time after wasting two hours of a perfectly sunny afternoon. I cursed the Department of Environmental Conservation for not signing the intersection, and I cursed the cartographer who didn't include this intersection on my lame snowmobile trail map. I cursed myself for relying on such a lame map in the first place. As my last effort I decided to try the right branch again. If this trail headed west I would leave the trail altogether and bushwhack until I hit Stewart's Landing, which lay due south through a mile of swampland. I was so frustrated at the ambiguity of the map, the trails, and myself that I knew I could have bushwhacked through a swamp and not been put in any worse of a mood.

Down the right branch I went for the second time. As I knew would happen, the trail bent west and northwest. I was close to leaving the trail behind to begin the bushwhack towards Stewart's Landing, but then, for whatever reason, I decided to follow the trail a little farther. The trail turned a hard left—south—and headed straight towards Stewart's Landing. Thank The Lord! Now I was in a fine mood, and things began to make sense. I saw that the right branch turned east and then northeast to merely wrap around a flooded area to the south. On a dry trail headed straight south, life was good again.

I rounded a bend and surprised a bear that was standing fifty feet in front me. He bounded off the trail and sprinted towards a nearby wetland. He was absolutely as black as black can be. I stood in the middle of the trail silent and motionless. He crashed headlong into the wetland 300 feet in front of me. Then, all was silent.

He was hiding in his little fortress, likely looking at me or at least smelling me. I peered through the conifers and alders of the swamp he was in, but I could see nothing of him. It was humbling to realize a 250-pound bear, an animal that can run 35 miles per hour and crush my bones with his jaws, knew where I was, yet I had no clue where he was. It was a thrilling experience. My usual place at the top of the food chain was yanked out from under me. To be deep in the woods and realize, "Hey, I'm not in charge" is improbably comforting. During times like this I feel I'm giving power back to the critters.

As the bear and I played our game of cat and mouse—me being the mouse—I thought back to the confusing intersection behind me. I realized that wasting two hours of a perfectly sunny afternoon trying to determine the correct trail was the best thing that had happened to me during my trip. Without that time wasted, the bear and I would have likely not crossed paths. I felt blessed to have not initially known which branch to take.

I left the bear behind. The trail still headed south, which kept a smile on my face. My pathway ran straight as an arrow, south through a conifer swamp just below the 1,600-foot-level. The trail pushed through the middle of the swamp, the surprisingly clear water seeping through the sides of my sneakers and then just pouring into their tops. I got to the other side of this 300-foot-long flooded section, wrung out my socks, hung them on the outside of my pack to dry, and put on my spare dry pair. For the rest of the trip my feet would stay dry.

I hit a dirt road above Stewart's Landing. The roadside campsites were overflowing with cigarette butts, beer cans, and assorted other trash. The final eight miles beyond the dam site were peaceful. I passed silent Tamarack Vly, climbed a hill, descended, and then saw a cabin ahead, just off to the side of the snowmobile trail I was on. With the building not identified on my maps and thinking there was not a stitch of private land between Stewart's Landing and my car at forester Wells's property, the building took me by surprise.

This red cabin with white trim stood on the left side of the trail. Being so remote and apparently abandoned a long time ago, I had to check it out. Besides, not a soul was around. Finding the door unlocked, I crept inside and was surprised to find a furnished bungalow. Inside was a fifty-gallon drum that had been converted into a woodstove. A table for dining, a propane stove, and accoutrements of cabin life such as a drain board for dishes, a broom, some hand tools, a couple old pots and pans, and spare mouse traps filled the nooks and crannies. There were three unopened Coors Lights on the kitchen counter. If they had been cold the next person to enter the cabin would have found one Coors Light on the counter. Crude stairs led to the upper level where there were mattresses strewn about, most of them well-gnawed by mice. The cabin had no running water or power and was dingy and dusty. It would have been good enough for me to live in for a year or two as a free man, far from the confines of the techno-industrial system. I could find no hint of who owned this cabin. I took a photo of the interior and then went to leave. On my way out I noticed a piece of scrap wood on a table near the door. A penciled message on the block of wood read, "Leave it better than you found it. Thanks. Nate." Nate sounds like my kind of man.

I passed the final large body of water of the route, Hilla-brandt Vly, and then crossed Glasgow Creek, the last water-way of the route. My final climb topped out across a broad, flat, unnamed hill. A maze of ATV trails broke off from the main snowmobile trail and faint paths entered the trail from the left and right. I stayed on the path most traveled, which was also the path that tracked straightest. I spotted Royal Hill to my left, which confirmed the end was near. The backside of this hill hosts a downhill ski center that's barely within the Blue Line.

I left the Town of Stratford and entered the last township of the route, Ephratah. The name is of Biblical origin, appearing twice in the good book: as a woman, the second wife of Caleb; and as a location, the town near Bethel where Jacob buried his wife Rachel. The Ephratah region was settled circa 1720. It had an eccentric founder, Anthony Beck, a man who assured people he could see into the future. When locomotives and other steam powered machinery were invented, Beck insisted he had seen all of this before. Beck is known for having a great vision of a large, wealthy, active city forming in the current location of this township, this vision being seen from the top of a nearby hill. Many moons later the location Beck spied would become the settlement of Ephratah. But the village of Ephratah isn't large, wealthy, or active. Beck has some explaining to do. Or perhaps Ephratah's glory days just haven't arrived yet.

Past the final trail intersection and to the last trailhead I hiked with purpose. I hit the trailhead that ranger Carbine had warned me not to leave my car at for two weeks. Here state land ended and private land began. I would not set foot on Forest Preserve for the remaining two miles.

The trailhead was empty. Ancient stone walls ran away from both sides of this north end of dirt East Road. I imagined old farmers and their sons plucking these rocks from their fields and heaving them into wagons drawn by oxen or horses. Each year more and more rocks poked out of the dark soil like so many gigantic potatoes only to be piled for hundreds of feet, or sometimes entire miles, to mark property lines and keep the cows near the barn. Bright yellow paint blazes stuck to the hardwood trees above the stone walls and ran away into the woods, marking the state land boundary. An old metal sign facing where I had come from read: "State Land. State of New York Department of Environmental Conservation. Forest Preserve."

Where the maples, ashes, pines, and oaks now grow around the trailhead there were once farms. During the first decade of the 1900s at least four buildings stood where this trailhead now is. These were part of a series of modest farms established on East Road during the mid and late 1800s. The pioneering farmers eventually found the winters too cold, the soil too rocky, and the wilderness too lonely. No farms remain though at least nine cellar holes can be found nearby.

East Road dipped and leveled. One mile to go. The road curved and then ran straight through two clearings. I passed two evergreen plantations on my right side. My car was parked in one of them. The tires held air and all the glass was intact. No one was bold enough to mess with a vehicle on Jared Wells's property. I could have ditched my pack at the car, but ethical long-distance hikers—"purists" in long-distance hiker parlance—rarely cheat. My pack had been with me for 234 miles. One more mile wouldn't hurt.

I passed Wells's house. No one was home. Civilization was coming at me. I passed four houses, two on each side of East Road. It was a pleasant walk down a well-maintained lane. It wasn't sunny, but there was no chance of rain. High gray clouds held in an Adirondack sky, not letting it drift away. Exactly one-half mile south of Wells's home I reached it: the southern terminus of my route, the southern border of the Adirondack Park. Like the northern border, the southern border was not marked in any way. I found its location by examining a detailed map. The trip was over.

I walked the mile back to my car. I gave thanks for my success and then threw my pack in the trunk, put on my sandals, Gold Bond powdered my feet, and changed into a clean pair of pants and t-shirt. I started my car, at the time having a proud 340,000 miles (it died a few years later with 377,018 miles). I drove to Wells's house to drop off a gift I had for him. I was surprised and pleased to see him in his driveway. He was on a trip into Northville when I had walked down and then back up East Road. He was happy to see me and to be assured I was okay. After all, even Wells had never heard of a person walking across the entire Adirondack Park. He found the journey to be very long, longer than he'd ever want to do.

We shook hands. His hands were tough, strong, and leathery. Wells had a woodsman grip. They were the hands of a man who swung an axe, pulled on strands of barbed wire, and carried firewood. Despite being in his mid 80s, Wells was still splitting his own cord wood, puttering around on his ATV, and managing a 100-acre woodlot. I figured that if I worked a day in the woods with Wells, something I would have loved to do, I would have slept well that night.

Surprisingly, Wells had few questions about my hike. He mainly wanted to know what course I took to get from Ellenburg Center to the Town of Ephratah. No matter what section of my route I mentioned, he recognized where I had been. At one point I narrated, "I approached Taylor Pond near the Silver Lake Mountains trailhead and bushwhacked down Bear Brook to hit Taylor Pond. From there I got on a snowmobile trail, passed through the campground and stayed at the lean-to on the north shore of the pond." Wells cleverly commented that that was the northernmost lean-to on my route. I spoke of Third and Fourth lakes, Hillabrandt Vly, Preston Ponds, Clockmill Corners, Lake Colden, Esther Mountain, and other features. Wells had heard of them all and possessed genuine knowledge regarding their surroundings. He had visited most features I mentioned. The forester—a sort of *professor emeritus* of the woods—had an especially good feel for what parts of the Adirondacks were settled first and by whom. I could have talked to Wells until the porch light came on.

I bid Wells goodbye while standing with him in his living room. I thanked him again for letting me keep my car on his property. Then I remembered—his gift! "I have a surprise for you," I said with a smile. I asked Wells to hold on while I ran to my car.

I carried the case of long-neck Budweisers up his front steps and into the living room. His eyes lit up. I told him I knew he asked me not to pay him for his assistance, but beer wasn't money, and so I had gotten around his rule of no payments accepted. He looked down at the case of beer. I didn't know if he drank beer, let alone liked domestic beer, or that brand. After thinking for a few seconds, Wells looked up at me. He smiled. "Oh. This is very nice. Very nice, Erik. I just knew it was a good idea to let you park here." He opened the case and drew out a bottle. Peering over his glasses down at the label he promised, "This will certainly go to good use." We said goodbye again, and I drove away.

Surprisingly, after hiking 235 miles my Adirondack journey had just begun. After returning home, washing clothes, cleaning gear, reviewing photos, and eating the good things in life that pack calories, like pizza and ice cream, I had a thought. Would someone else like to hike across the Adirondack Park? I slept on the question, as I do with all important questions. I woke up with the answer.

The decision to share my route was not easy to make. When I took that first step south in that far corner of Riverside Cemetery, I had no intention of sharing my route with others. The route didn't even have a name. I wasn't sure I'd make it to the other end of the park. If I was successful, newspaper articles would be written and some magazine articles would be produced. Likely an interview or two would take place. Beyond the media exposure that keeps sponsors happy, the idea of sharing information so detailed that others could follow my footsteps felt foreign. My trips, particularly a special one that spans the Adirondack Mountains, are personal. Colleagues have consistently suggested I maintain a blog about my adventures in the Adirondack Mountains and beyond. I have little interest in sharing the bulk of my personal time in the woods. Even this book was a hurdle. I enjoy the writing. Few things in life bring me such reliable joy; but sometimes I find sharing invasive to my character. Within this book I share a mere ten adventures while hundreds of other adventures remain close to my heart, chronicled in my journals, portrayed in my photos. Part of me is here with you, and most of me is not.

What convinced me to share my route across the Adirondacks, now known as the Trans Adirondack Route, was a view to other men who love good adventures, especially ones that take place in their own special neck of the woods. Steve Roper could have wandered the Sierra Nevada Mountains the rest of his life, keeping all the alpine tarns and rocky spires to himself. Instead he shared his 195-mile Sierra High Route and wrote *The Sierra High Route.* Kim Robert Nilsen enjoys a special relationship with New Hampshire's far north. Selflessly he created the 165-mile Cohos Trail and shares it in his *The Cohos Trail.* Tim Ernst loves the woods of Arkansas and Oklahoma like no one else. He says so himself: "I'm a genuine trail nut . . . Not your ordinary peanut variety of nut, but rather more like a cashew or macadamia. Pretty much everything that I do relates in one way or another to trails, to the outdoors, or to something similar." Ernst created the 225-mile Ouachita (pronounced "wah-she-tah") Trail and 220-mile Ozark Highlands Trail, guiding backpackers along these paths with his *Ouachita Trail Guide* and *Ozark Highlands Trail Guide*, two outstanding guidebooks, the best ones I've ever read.

I followed these fine authors in their footsteps through the wilderness and by their fingers on the keyboards. Like their respective trails and publications, the authors reinforced my view that my hike across the Adirondacks was the finest hike I had completed. What's best is that it took place in a range I love. It is a range I started exploring when I was 8 years old, back when my parents rented a cabin each summer in the Town of Wells.

Who knew that the easiest part of this project would be hiking across the largest park and forest preserve in the Lower Forty-Eight? The numbers speak for themselves. Hike 235 miles: twelve days. Write *Blue Line to Blue Line: The Official Guide to the Trans Adirondack Route*, the hinge point of sharing: three years. When one long journey ended, a longer one began.

The Trans Adirondack Route has taken on a life of its own now, which I enjoy. I regard the route as an offspring of mine. I built the nest, kept the egg warm, and nurtured it. When the shell cracked at just the right time, and a little head poked out, I fed it. There was only one thing to do once its feathers came in and its eyes looked down upon our world. I let it spread its wings and fly where it chooses.

Erik Schlimmer is a man of few needs. Give him a burrito, a good nonfiction book, and the Adirondack Mountains, and he'll be "as happy as a carp in a septic tank."

During the thirty years he's been exploring the Adirondack Mountains, Erik has nurtured a relationship with the woods, valleys, and mountaintops like few others have. Highlights of his Adirondack explorations include climbing more than 500 mountains, visiting every named feature in Pharaoh Lake Wilderness Area, creating the Trans Adirondack Route, and working as a backcountry ranger and trip leader.

Erik is the author of three other books: *Thru Hiker's Guide to America*, *Blue Line to Blue Line*, and *History Inside the Blue Line*. He lives in the Capital Region of Upstate New York.